TITANIC

Destination Disaster

The legends and the reality

John P. Eaton & Charles A. Haas

REVISED AND EXPANDED THIRD EDITION

Haynes Publishing

In loving memory of Beatrice Virginia Haas

First published by Patrick Stephens Limited in 1987
Reprinted in 1992, 1993 and 1994
Second edition published by Haynes Publishing in 1996
Reprinted in March 1997 and February 1998
Third edition published by Haynes Publishing in October 2011

A catalogue record for this book is available from the British Library

ISBN 978 0 85733 025 3

Library of Congress catalogue card no 2011927867

Published by Haynes Publishing, Sparkford, Yeovil, Somerset BA22 7JJ, UK
Tel: 01963 442030 Fax: 01963 440001
Int. tel: +44 1963 442030 Int. fax: +44 1963 440001
E-mail: sales@haynes.co.uk
Website: www.haynes.co.uk

Haynes North America Inc.,
861 Lawrence Drive, Newbury Park, California 91320, USA

Printed in the USA by Odcombe Press LP,
1299 Bridgestone Parkway, La Vergne, TN 37086.

Cover illustration
Front: A distress rocket explodes high above *Titanic*'s bow as the crew of the doomed liner try unsuccessfully to attract the attention of another vessel which came into view sometime after 1.00 am on 15 April 1912.
'Sinking of *Titanic*,' reproduced by kind permission of the artist, E.D. Walker. Prints of this and many other Titanic paintings may be obtained through the artist's website at http://www.edwalkermarine.com.

Contents

Introduction		7
Chapter One	'Iceberg, Right Ahead!'	9
Chapter Two	Lights that Pass in the Night	37
Chapter Three	A Burst of Cheering	53
Chapter Four	From the Four Corners of the Compass	67
Chapter Five	Park Lane and Scotland Road	75
Chapter Six	Westwards to Destiny	85
Chapter Seven	City of Sorrow	97
Chapter Eight	Questions and Answers … and Questions	106
Chapter Nine	With Time's Passing	124
Colour Section		129–136
Chapter Ten	Dateline: North Atlantic	140
Chapter Eleven	Explorations and Exhibitions	157
Chapter Twelve	Into the Second Century	178
Appendix One	Comparison of ship dimensions	209
Appendix Two	*Titanic*'s life measured in hours	210
Appendix Three	Memorial statues, plaques and buildings	212
Appendix Four	Search co-ordinates	218
Index		219

Introduction

TITANIC

The very name conjures up thoughts of disaster and doom, of inevitable fate, of man's fallibility.

TITANIC...

The world's newest and most beautiful passenger liner, whose maiden voyage from the Old World to the New was cut short by collision with an iceberg, resulting in a loss of 1,512 lives.

Titanic. If the ship had not been lost in one of maritime history's most memorable disasters, her name would probably still have lived today, but for rather different reasons. The luxury and comfort of her passenger accommodation exceeded those of any vessel of her day. Her size was greater than any other ship. Her equipment and engines, the integrity of her construction, were the best that money could buy.

If *Titanic* had been allowed to live out her normal, expected life span, she would have taken her rightful place in the pantheon of great liners: *Mauretania*, *Aquitania*, *Europa*, *Queen Mary*, *Normandie*, *United States* ... Ships of luxury and comfort, ships of beauty.

In her brief life *Titanic* was a ship of pride and bright honour to her owners and builders, and to the countries which claimed her as their own.

During her single, interrupted voyage one element of misjudgement was added to another in a deadly chain. Warnings went unheeded. Errors in safety standards and navigation were combined and compounded to generate the inevitable tragic conclusion.

And from the ashes of her loss arose new rules for safety, for navigation, for judging ships themselves, and the men who sailed in them.

Titanic ... As she lived, myth and legend had already begun to form around her. Her passengers and her crew for the voyage were the stuff of which legends are made. Even the facts of her loss assumed an air of fantasy. And when the fertile imaginations of contemporary journalists and writers began to stir the mixture of fantasy and fact, myth and legend into a single swirling tale of tragedy, an aura was created which, today, makes it difficult to separate fiction from fact; indeed it makes it difficult to discover and authenticate fact itself.

When considering *Titanic*'s facts, myth and fantasy must also be given due regard. Seldom has there been an ocean liner about which so many facts are known. Never has there been a ship whose history is clouded by so many fallacies, whose very legend seems to endure because of these fabled traditions.

Titanic's life begins on 31 March 1909 when her keel was laid down. It continues through her launch on 31 May 1911 and her triumphant 10 April 1912 departure on her maiden voyage. It ends in the early hours of 15 April 1912 when her stern plates vanished beneath the chill, starlit North Atlantic waters.

But her name lives on in the imagination, captured by the elusive blend of romance and realism.

Titanic's life, her loss, her legend weave a fabric of wonder and disbelief. From beginning to end they tell of a beautiful liner's incredible voyage through history's pages, and of her ultimate fate, her…

Destination Disaster.

Authors' Introduction to the Third Edition

Titanic's story continues to add new chapters. In the 15 years since *Titanic: Destination Disaster* was last revised, James Cameron's 1997 blockbuster film *Titanic* introduced the liner's basic story, albeit slightly fictionalised, to a new generation. A Broadway musical offered a new way of telling *Titanic*'s story.

A series of expeditions using increasingly advanced scientific equipment recovered poignant new artefacts that enthralled millions in worldwide exhibitions, and added new knowledge as scientists and historians worked together to interpret photographs and experimental data. Management changes at the company declared *Titanic*'s 'salvor in possession', a reported attempt to loot artefacts from the ocean floor, and legislative efforts to protect the wreck, have helped keep *Titanic* in the headlines.

Interest in *Titanic*'s story shows no signs of abating. Record prices obtained for *Titanic* memorabilia at auction houses, thriving memberships in *Titanic* societies around the world, active Internet discussion groups – all suggest a fascination that will extend far beyond the ship's 2012 centennial.

The Internet has enabled the latest research to be shared more readily, and made available a myriad of sources from *Titanic*'s era, offering new understanding of the ship, her short life and her people.

Finally, the thoughtful questions and helpful suggestions from our readers, fellow researchers, friends and others have encouraged us to produce this revised and expanded third edition.

We express our deepest gratitude to them, and to all who have generously shared their knowledge, their photographs and their support with us.

John P. Eaton, Cold Spring, New York
Charles A. Haas, Randolph, New Jersey
Autumn 2011

CHAPTER ONE

'Iceberg, Right Ahead!'

Aboard *Titanic*. At sea. Westbound.

Sunday, 14 April, 1912.

Ashore it was another day of rest, at sea a day of routine activity. There were meals to be prepared and served, brightwork to be polished, decks to be scraped and sanded, passengers to be tended to. On this maiden voyage there was equipment to be checked, performances to be monitored and recorded. And far below there were boilers to be fired, coal passed and trimmed, steam pressure to be maintained, all to speed the ship westwards.

In the saloons and smoking rooms there were rumours of a record crossing. Many passengers, and indeed some crew, believed the company wished to display its new liner in a most favourable light by bringing her across to New York with a new speed record. The rumours had some basis. Each day at sea, from noon to noon, had seen an increasing number of miles logged. There was talk that the White Star Line's managing director J. Bruce Ismay had called chief engineer Joseph Bell to his cabin while *Titanic* was stopped at Queenstown. There the two men purportedly had discussed the feasibility of setting a speed record during the crossing.

Indeed, there had been a discussion between them. But it was concerned mainly with the amount of coal in the bunkers (a logical point, in view of the recent British coal strike), and of *not* driving the ship too fast lest she arrive at New York late on Tuesday night (instead of on Wednesday morning, as planned) and be unable to enter the harbour and dock safely.

Ismay later testified at the British inquiry that he had talked with Bell about the possibility of driving the vessel at full speed for several hours on Monday if the weather were suitable. *Titanic* never had been truly tested at full draught, top-speed conditions, and such an all-out but brief run would give builders' representatives and the ship's own engineering staff a chance to collect additional data.

Sunday saw 24 of *Titanic*'s 29 boilers in service. During the day preparations were made to light the remaining boilers to make ready for the next day's speed test. But though the boilers were lit they were not brought on line. Even with approximately 84% of her boilers operating, *Titanic*'s engines drove the propellers at 75 revolutions per minute, giving a speed of 21½ knots, almost 24¾ land miles per hour. Top speed was estimated to be over 22 knots, perhaps as high as 24. Whatever the figure, it would surely be nowhere near the *Mauretania*'s 26-knot record. Monday's high-speed run might tell…

Sunday saw two breaks in shipboard routine. There was no daily inspection of the vessel. And that morning, passengers convened in the first and second class dining saloons for Divine Services. The former was led by Captain Edward John Smith using the company's own prayer book. In second class, second purser Reginald Barker used the Church of England's Book of Common Prayer. Pianists drawn from the ship's musicians provided accompaniment to hymns sung at both services. Priests traveling in second class offered spoken masses daily in second and third class.

Even as he led Divine Service Captain Smith was aware that a potential danger loomed – quite literally – over the horizon. At 9 am, ship's time, *Titanic* had received a wireless message from *Caronia*, eastbound from New York to Liverpool via Queenstown.

> Captain, *Titanic* – West-bound steamers report bergs, growlers and field ice in 42 degrees North from 49 degrees to 51 degrees West, April 12. Compliments, Barr.

The message was delivered to Captain Smith on the bridge. After noting it he posted it for his officers to read.

Sunday, 14 April. The day was bright and clear. During the afternoon it became noticeably cool. First class passengers deserted the decks and sought comfort and warmth in the spacious lounge or the comfortable smoking room. The murmur of conversation was punctuated by an occasional genteel laugh, the rattle of teacups, the clink of glasses. The veranda café's outer doors were slid closed. But seated in the red and brown cushioned wicker furniture there, young merrymakers could still watch the sea speed past through the bronze-framed windows nearly seven feet tall.

In the first class reading and writing room – its floor carpeted in old rose, its windows hung with pink draperies – passengers leisurely read books and the latest magazines placed there by the *Times* of London's book club.

The library's quiet contrasted with the convivial atmosphere of the smoking room where whist, bridge and poker games were in full swing. Here there was no sea view: light entered through painted glass windows depicting landscapes, ancient ships and historic and mythological figures. Over the marble fireplace hung a large oil painting, 'Plymouth Harbour', by the well-known British painter Norman Wilkinson. (Wilkinson had also painted the picture that hung above *Olympic*'s fireplace, 'Approach to the New World', which depicted a New York Harbor view.)

In the reception room, outside the lounge, a trio from the ship's orchestra played the day's popular songs: music from operetta, the musical stage, or the new sensation, ragtime; salon pieces, reminiscent of a smart continental café; selections from 'The Quaker Girl', 'The Chocolate Soldier', and 'The Merry Widow'. Gems from Gilbert and Sullivan operettas 'Mikado', 'Pirates of Penzance', 'Iolanthe'; waltzes by Strauss and Waldteufel; the popular waltz 'Songe d'Automne' by the British composer Joyce; 'Oh, You Beautiful Doll', 'Alexander's Ragtime Band', 'The Navajo Rag'...

The second class smoking room aft on B deck, and the second class library, directly below on C deck, were no less thronged with conversing passengers, while others, such as

Mrs Esther Hart, rested in their cabins. But most strolled the corridors. Children played in the enclosed promenades flanking the library. The brown linoleum floor and mahogany, tapestry-covered furniture in the second class library were well set off by the green silk draperies, creating a comfort and intimacy usually found on other liners only in first class accommodation. It was a splendid apartment in which to spend a cold, bright April afternoon at sea.

The falling temperatures also drove indoors the men, women and children of third class. Unlike most Atlantic liners, *Titanic* contained comfortable public rooms for them as well, plain though light-filled and clean. This Sunday afternoon, with the after and forward well deck promenades now feeling chill, the public rooms' warmth and companionship were especially welcome.

For the men there was the smoking room and two bars – one forward in the open space on D deck and another adjacent to the smoking room at C deck's after end. Women and children had the general room, to starboard of the smoking room. And it may be assumed that, with or without stewards' approval, children used the lower decks' stairs and corridors for their games.

There were no games, no relaxation for the ship's two wireless operators: John George Phillips, senior Marconi operator, age 24, wage £4 5s (£4.25 or $21) a month; Harold Sidney Bride, junior Marconi operator, age 22, wage £2 2s 6d (£2.12½p or $11) a month. Though signed on with the crew (their official title, 'telegraphist') the two men were actually employees of the Marconi International Marine Communication Company, Ltd.

Under its agreement with the Marconi Company, the White Star Line was provided with free wireless messages between the ship, its owners or other ships regarding navigation, safety, or ship's business, provided the messages did not exceed a 30-words-per-day average. Excess wordage was charged to the ship's owners at half the current tariff rate. In return, White Star was to provide the Marconi operators with their meals and lodging.

On this Sunday, 14 April, Bride and Phillips had been busy receiving, logging and transmitting passenger messages. Wireless transmitting and receiving ranges increased markedly at night, and night signals from the powerful British land station at Poldhu (call letters MPD) relayed by intermediate ships, had included news, stock reports and some personal messages.

The news bulletins were typed by the purser and posted in the first class smoking room. (It was not for another six weeks – commencing 1 June 1912 – that these 'bulletins' were formalised into a printed sheet, the *Ocean Times,* for distribution among White Star passengers.)

There also had been the day traffic: personal messages to and from *Titanic*'s passengers. The ship's 1½-kilowatt wireless apparatus, among the most powerful afloat, had a 400-mile daytime transmitting range. This trebled at night, but during the day, particularly now in mid-Atlantic, its function was limited to 'conversations' with other ships.

Signals were transmitted and received on closely-adjacent standard frequencies, with two, three or even more signals being sent or received at the same time. Much of the operator's skill involved being able to discriminate and select the particular message addressed to his station. To assist operators, each station had its particular identifying call letters. With few exceptions, call letters for British ships generally began with 'M', while those of German ships started with 'D' and United States naval vessels with 'N'. *Titanic*'s were MGY, while her sister *Olympic* had MKC.

The hours were long, the work was tedious and pressured. At least Bride and Phillips were fortunate to be working together, so they might set shifts and 'spell' one another at the key. In 1912 laws did not require two operators or 24-hour manning of ships' wireless. Among those ships equipped with wireless, many passenger liners and all freighters had single operators whose long, tiring hours were unrelieved except for brief naps.

Operators were supposed to intercept for their own captain's attention all messages relating to navigation and safety of his vessel. Thus on this Sunday, 14 April, *Titanic*'s operators received several messages regarding ice conditions in an area for which *Titanic* was now headed directly. At 9 am a message from *Caronia* was taken immediately to the bridge, where it was posted for the officers' attention. *Titanic*'s position at this time was 43.35 N 43.50 W, and her course S 62° W. Her position had changed to 42.34 N, 45.50 W by 1.42 pm, when a message was received from *Athinai* via *Baltic*:

> Capt Smith, *Titanic*:
> ... Greek steamer *Athinai* reports passing icebergs and large quantities of field ice today in latitude 41.51 N, longitude 49.52 W.

This message placed icebergs within a few miles of *Titanic*'s track. It, too, was taken immediately to the bridge and very shortly thereafter to Captain Smith, who was lunching with J. Bruce Ismay. The captain handed the message to Ismay with the remark that the ship soon might be encountering ice. Ismay put the message in his pocket and later showed it to several passengers, repeating Smith's statement. The message was not posted on the bridge or entered in the scrap log until 7.15 pm when Captain Smith requested its return from Ismay.

At 5.50 pm, slightly ahead of schedule, *Titanic* reached the 'Corner', the position along the 42nd degree of north latitude at which, according to sailing orders, the ship was to cross the 47th degree of west longitude. At this point the course was changed from S 62° W to S 86° W.

As the bright day turned to dusk and then to dark, the cool air began to turn cold. As passengers prepared for and ate dinner in the dining saloons' warm comfort, the outside temperature was dropping. At 7 pm it was 43 degrees (6°C). Because of the day's wireless messages, an iceberg watch was ordered. At 7.15 pm the officer of the watch, first officer William Murdoch, ordered lamp trimmer Samuel Hemming to secure the forward fo'c's'le hatch to prevent glow from interfering with the crow's nest watch.

By 7.30 pm, a mere half-hour later, the temperature had dropped to 39 degrees (3.9°C). At this time, as fourth officer Joseph Boxhall, responsible for navigation, took a star sighting, a message from the freighter *Californian* to the eastbound freighter *Antillian* was overheard by *Titanic*'s wireless operator. Harold Bride delivered the message to the bridge and handed it to an officer. (Later, Bride could not recall who.) The message reported ice at 42.3 N 49.9 W about 19 miles north of *Titanic*'s track. This message was not taken to Captain Smith personally, as he was in the *à la carte* restaurant attending a party given by Mr and Mrs George D. Widener. Other guests included the Carters, the Thayers, and President Taft's military aide, Major Archibald Butt.

The ship sped on, the time passed: 8 pm… 8.30 pm… At 8.40 pm second officer Charles Lightoller, now officer of the watch, ordered ship's carpenter John Maxwell to watch the fresh water supply as it might freeze. 9 pm… The air temperature had fallen to 33 degrees (0.6°C).

At about 8.50 pm Captain Smith bade his dinner companions 'good night' and made his way to the bridge. Upon his arrival Lightoller briefed him about weather conditions and the ice precautions that had already been taken. Remarking that the night was quite clear, the captain left the bridge at about 9.30, telling Lightoller that if visibility or weather conditions 'become at all doubtful, let me know at once. I will be just inside.' He then went to his cabin on the starboard side behind the bridge.

9.40 pm… In the wireless 'shack' Bride had turned in for a nap before working the busy late night traffic. Phillips was manning the apparatus alone when a message was received from the westbound *Mesaba*:

> To *Titanic* and eastbound ships:
> Ice report in latitude 42 N, to 41.25 N, longitude 49 W, to 50.30 W. Saw much heavy pack ice and great number large icebergs. Also field ice. Weather good, clear.

The land station at Cape Race, Newfoundland (call letters MCE), was in range now, and Phillips was very busy transmitting messages which had accumulated during the day. Unable or unwilling to leave his set unattended, he 'spiked' the *Mesaba*'s ice message. (Later, perhaps,

During the two hours and forty minutes of Titanic's *sinking, the wireless station at Cape Race (MCE) relayed disaster news to ships at sea and, over land telephone lines, to Montreal, Quebec, for distribution to the rest of North America.* (Canadian Marconi Company)

when relieved by Bride, he might have a chance to take it down the corridor to the bridge… Later, perhaps…) The message, which described ice directly ahead of *Titanic*, never did get to the bridge.

10 pm… Four bells… First officer Murdoch relieved second officer Lightoller on the bridge. Look-outs Reginald Lee and Frederick Fleet climbed the iron ladder inside the forward mast to the look-out's cage, where they relieved Archie Jewell and George Symons. Before they departed, Symons passed the word received earlier from Lightoller to keep a careful look-out for bergs and growlers.

Lights gleaming, *Titanic* sped on through the night at 21½ knots. The sea was calm, perfectly flat. There was no moon, though the stars shone brilliantly. There was indeed a chill in the air. Between 7 pm and 10 pm the air temperature had dropped from 43 to 32 degrees (6° to 0°C).

Earlier, during Sunday forenoon, *Titanic* crossed a cold front whose overcast skies and brisk northerly winds had lain to the west during Saturday–Sunday night. This caused the rapid drop in temperature during Sunday afternoon and evening. Now, the cold front behind, *Titanic* was entering the influence of a large Arctic high, situated off Sable Island and moving south-eastward toward the liner's course. Skies cleared. The north wind diminished, then became calm.

Titanic steamed on, speed undiminished. The minutes passed.

In the wireless quarters, Phillips was still busily engaged in the Cape Race traffic and in sending and receiving messages to and from other ships. A few minutes before 11 pm his concentration was abruptly interrupted by a signal from a nearby ship, a signal so loud that it probably deafened him momentarily. It was from the freighter *Californian*, about 19 miles away to the north: 'We are stopped and surrounded by ice.' Still smarting from the loud intrusion, his own signals jammed, Phillips interrupted: 'Shut up. I am busy, I am working Cape Race.'

Californian's wireless operator, Cyril Furmstone Evans, tired from his long, lonely day with

The Leyland Line steamer Californian. (Harper's)

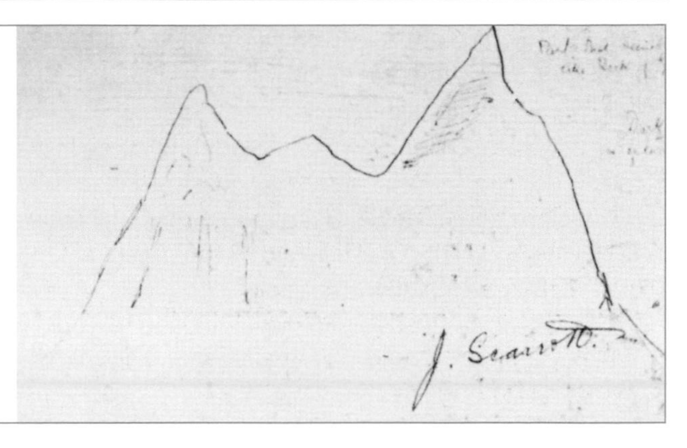

A sketch of the iceberg was prepared later under the direction of Joseph Scarrott, Titanic *seaman.* (Daily Graphic)

the wireless apparatus and now rebuffed, listened for several more minutes to *Titanic*'s Cape Race traffic. Then, around 11.30 pm, he turned off his equipment, took off his earphones and turned in. In his fatigued state he didn't bother to rewind his mechanically powered detector. It had been a long day ... the rewinding could wait until morning.

11.30 pm ... Seven bells ... Less than five miles ahead *Titanic*'s destiny awaited ...

Fred Fleet and Reginald Lee swung their arms and tried to keep warm in the frigid blasts caused by the ship's rapid forward motion. In the look-out cage's narrow confines 50 feet above the fo'c's'le deck this was not easy to do. The air was cold and they still had more than 20 minutes before their midnight relief. Their eyes strained to pierce the darkness ahead and around them. Moments before, what seemed to be a slight mist or haze had appeared on the horizon and a moist, clammy smell filled the air. The men wished they had something to aid their vision. (When *Titanic* left Belfast there had been binoculars in the look-out's cage. But very shortly after departure from Southampton, before the ship reached Queenstown, it was discovered that the binoculars had been removed. None of the officers seemed to know why or by whose orders. But their absence mattered little, since binoculars were used only to get a closer look once unaided eyes spotted an obstruction.)

Suddenly, without a word to Lee, Fleet hunched forward and peered intently ahead. His hand reached for the lanyard of the 16-inch brass bell which hung several feet above the crow's nest. Still staring forward Fleet gave the cord three sharp pulls. The bell's brittle sound fractured the night's stillness. Fleet then reached across to the telephone in its compartment on the starboard side and urgently rang its bell.

After a short interval – it must have seemed long minutes to Fleet – sixth officer James P. Moody answered on the bridge. Fleet's message was brief, Moody's response even more so:

'Iceberg right ahead.'

'Thank you.'

Fleet and Lee gripped the crow's nest rail. They could see the huge berg's irregular, pinnacled shape, a black hulk against the darkness, blotting out increasing numbers of stars as it came nearer and nearer to the speeding liner's starboard bow.

On the bridge first officer Murdoch acted almost immediately on Moody's repeat of the message. He ordered 'hard-a-starboard,' which, under the system of 'indirect helm orders' then in use, meant turning the wheel to port. Simultaneously he telegraphed to the engine room 'Stop. Full speed astern.' In almost the same movement he pulled the lever that electrically closed the 15 watertight doors in the engine and boiler room bulkheads.

The telemotor wheel spun by quartermaster Robert Hichens inside the enclosed wheelhouse did its job well. *Titanic* had turned two points (22½ degrees) to port before the collision occurred. (Later experiments with *Titanic*'s almost-identical sister *Olympic* showed that at 21½ knots it would take about 37 seconds to produce a course change of two points once the wheel was hard over. In this time the ship would travel about 466 yards.)

At the start of her port turn, *Titanic*'s bow began to swing away from the approaching berg. To Fleet and Lee it seemed as though a collision might have been avoided. The berg's dark mass was level with *Titanic*'s bow, then slipped past along the starboard side, its top more than 25 feet above the crow's nest platform.

Though there was no apparent collision with the berg, large ice chunks fell from it, cascading on to the forward well deck as though dislodged by some vibration deep within the berg.

The berg glided along the ship's length, scraping and bumping against the first 300 feet of the hull, deep below the waterline. As *Titanic* was still moving at about 21½ knots she would have passed through 300 feet in less than ten seconds. The ice passed amidships and Murdoch ordered the helm hard to port so that the stern would clear. As the berg receded beyond the stern, the look-outs for the first time saw a tip of white at the iceberg's very crest, which appeared to be emitting an almost-luminous haze.

Bobbing slightly from the impact, the berg disappeared from view, astern.

Many passengers and crew were only slightly disturbed by the collision. Some who slept were not even awakened. To able-bodied seaman Walter Brice, on watch outside the seamen's mess, it felt like a heavy vibration, not a violent shock or bad jar. It was a rumbling noise that continued for about ten seconds. Other crew members thought the ship had lost a propeller or that the engines had suddenly been placed full astern. Several described it as a scraping or grinding sound on the ship's bottom, as though the anchor had suddenly been let go and its chain was dragging along the side.

Passengers' descriptions were more vivid. Preparing for bed in cabin A20, Lady Lucile Duff-Gordon described it 'as though someone had drawn a giant finger all along the side of the boat'. Mrs J. Stuart White, in cabin C32, said, 'It did not seem to me there was any great impact at all. It was as though we went over about a thousand marbles.'

Second class passenger Lawrence Beesley in cabin D56 recalled, 'There was nothing more than what seemed to be an extra heave of the engines and a more than usually obvious dancing of the mattress on which I sat. Nothing more than that – no sound of a crash or of anything else; no sense of shock, no jar that felt like one heavy body meeting another.'

Look-out Reginald Lee, who had observed the actual collision, noted, 'She heeled slightly to port as she struck along the starboard side. There was the sound of rending metal right away; it seemed to be running right along the starboard side.'

Deep inside the ship, in number six boiler room, on the starboard side, forward, leading

First class passenger Archibald Gracie knew there was something amiss when, following the collision, the ship stopped and began to blow off steam. (The Truth About the Titanic)

Science teacher Lawrence Beesley felt the shock of the berg's impact in his second class cabin, D56. He said it was 'a more than usually obvious dancing of the mattress on which I sat.' (Illustrated London News)

stoker Frederick Barrett heard the impact's crunching and then a sound like thunder rolling forward towards him. Before his startled eyes suddenly appeared a line of water pouring through a thin gash in the ship's side about two feet above the stokehold floor. Barrett barely escaped up the boiler room's emergency ladder. The watertight doors slid closed amid the raucous shrilling of the alarm bells activated by Murdoch on the bridge.

Roused from his rest by the collision, Captain Smith rushed on to the bridge. 'What have we struck, Mr Murdoch?'

'An iceberg sir. I hard-a-starboarded and reversed the engines and I was going to hard-a-port around it, but she was too close. I could not do any more.'

'Have you closed the watertight doors?' demanded the master.

'They are already closed, sir.'

Smith and Murdoch hurried to the starboard bridge wing and peered aft into the darkness looking for the berg.

Returning inside, the commander ordered fourth officer Boxhall, who had just arrived on the bridge, to inspect the forward area below and report back to him as quickly as possible.

The other officers, alerted by Boxhall, hurriedly presented themselves on the bridge. Boxhall returned about 15 minutes later to report that while he had seen no damage above F deck, a postal clerk had told him water was entering the sorting room on G deck and the mail was being moved.

A rock-hard protrusion from the iceberg had struck *Titanic*'s hull about 15 feet above the keel and had then sliced along the steel plates, stabbing a series of narrow slits which penetrated the forepeak tank, numbers 1, 2 and 3 holds, and the forward boiler room (number 6). It was later determined by naval architect Edward Wilding that the total area opened to the sea by the impact did not exceed 12 square feet. Rivet heads sheered off, allowing additional water to enter through seams between *Titanic*'s hull plates.

But the '12 square feet' of punctures and the compromised plate seams extended over 300 feet of the ship's length and allowed five compartments to flood. *Titanic* could float with any two of her watertight compartments flooded. She could float with even the first four compartments breached. But she could not float with water filling the first five compartments.

Only number one bulkhead, the first one forward, extended to the uppermost continuous deck, C. Bulkheads two and eleven to fifteen extended to the second continuous deck, D, while bulkheads three to nine extended only to the third continuous deck, E. The forward bulkheads would have contained water in the first four compartments so it would not have risen above D deck. But flooding of the fifth compartment – boiler room number six – caused water to rise above E deck, thus spilling over into the sixth compartment and causing the bow to be pulled further under. This in turn permitted water to flow into successive compartments, each pulling the bow still further down until the ship foundered.

From the moment that thin jet of water spurted through the plating in front of Barrett's startled eyes, *Titanic* was doomed.

One legend said *Titanic* had been doomed from the start, when hull number 3 9 0 9 0 4 supposedly had been assigned by her builders – a number, legend said, that some shipyard workers read in mirror images as 'N O P O P E'. But Harland & Wolff did not issue 'hull numbers', merely yard numbers, and *Titanic*'s was 401.

If this were not enough to cause fear and doubt in the minds of the superstitious, a horoscope cast for a 31 May 1911 birth (*Titanic*'s launch date) at 12.15 pm on latitude 54°36' N, longitude 5°56' W (the co-ordinates of Belfast), predicted, among other things, danger on or near water, accidents in travel and sorrow and loss through relatives.

Superstitions notwithstanding, many factors contributed to *Titanic*'s loss. Some of them – design and outfitting flaws – were correctable; some – faulty navigation, failure to deliver warning messages – were the result of human errors. Some – collision and near-collision, weather conditions – were unpredictable. Yet all occurred in their proper sequence, in their proper place and time, and combined to provide an unalterable schedule for disaster.

If the design of the *Titanic* herself had called for watertight bulkheads to be carried one deck higher there would have been no overflow, no spillage from forward to after compartments, pulling the ship's head lower in the water and causing further overflow. If the Board of Trade's lifeboat capacity requirements had been more up to date (the last major rules revision was in 1894 when few ships exceeded 10,000 tons) and had demanded boat capacity for all persons on board, there would not have been so many crew and passengers lost.

One of *Titanic*'s chief designers, Alexander Carlisle, had indeed provided a plan for additional lifeboats. A copy of a deck plan indicating these boats was entered in evidence at the limitation of liability hearings held at New York. It showed accommodation for 32 boats, potentially more than *900* additional seats. In the event, however, there was insufficient time to launch even the boats *Titanic* had.

By 18 September 1911 *Titanic*'s maiden voyage date had been set: 20 March 1912. What if *Olympic* had not collided with the cruiser *Hawke* at Southampton on 20 September? Following this accident, *Olympic* had to return to Belfast for repairs, usurping the large dry-dock, equipment and workers which might otherwise have been used for *Titanic*'s construction. *Olympic*'s presence at Belfast delayed *Titanic*'s completion and caused her owners to set 10 April as the date for the new liner's first departure. Would *Titanic*'s accident have occurred if there had not been the three-week postponement?

On sailing day... What if *Titanic* had actually collided with *New York* while departing from her pier? What if the pilot's and the commander's skills had not been sufficient to avoid an accident? A collision, no matter how slight, would have delayed the voyage for how long? Hours? Days?

What of the time *Titanic*'s departure was delayed by the near-collision in Southampton? What of the hour or more that was never actually made up?

For almost her entire voyage *Titanic* had been advised repeatedly of ice conditions at or near the position her sailing orders required her to occupy. Throughout the day of 14 April, as she approached this location, her wireless operators received at least six messages which described field ice and ice bergs on her course and directly ahead.

One message (from *Athinai* via *Baltic*) was not posted on the bridge until more than five hours after it had been received. Another message (at 7.30 pm, *Californian* to *Antillian*) was not shown to the captain, since to do so would have interrupted his dinner. Yet another message (from *Mesaba*) was never taken to the bridge as the wireless operator was working alone and could not leave his equipment. The receipt of a final, perhaps crucial message (from *Californian*) was interrupted and never completed when *Titanic*'s operator impatiently cut it off so that he might continue his own commercial traffic.

The air was clear, the sea calm. There were no waves and there was no breeze. Either would have created a wash of water against the berg's base, giving it a low white 'collar' which would have stood out starkly against the dark water. The sky was moonless. On such a clear night, the light from even a quarter moon would have made the berg visible.

Recently – probably only an hour or two earlier – the iceberg had turned over in the sea. With its water-filled portion now above the surface, it thus presented a dark face, making it practically invisible against the night sky. An hour or two later the berg's face would have been lighter, perhaps even white as the water drained away, and visible...

The impact... Would it have been different if the look-out had spotted the berg sooner? (Perhaps the ship might have had time to dodge the ice?) Later? (Fewer watertight compartments would have been breached had the ship struck head-on. Ignobly down at the head but still afloat she might have been able to reach Halifax, 750 miles to the north-west.)

Titanic's lifespan can be measured in hours, her maiden voyage in minutes. A slight shift of time – several minutes more, or several minutes less – would have changed the ship's position and put her ahead of or behind the precise spot where the berg was struck.

But once the flow of time began, there could be no modification. The inevitable was already set in motion. *Titanic* had but one destination: the disaster which was her doom.

After returning from his inspection trip Boxhall was ordered by Captain Smith to calculate *Titanic*'s position. Using the ship's course (since 5.50 pm South 86 West true), the 7.30 pm stellar observation he had taken, and his own *estimate* of the ship's speed as being 22 knots, Boxhall worked out a position based on dead reckoning.

(If he did not take into account the one-knot southerly current through which *Titanic* was passing, an error of as much as four miles in latitude could have entered his calculations. During the eight-to-midnight watch the ship's clocks were set back 23 minutes to compensate for westward progress. Did he remember this time change in gauging the distance travelled? And the ship's speed was 21½ knots, not the 22 he estimated. These elements, combined into a very rough estimate, might approximate an actual position four miles south and six miles east of the calculated position.)

Boxhall scribbled his calculation on a scrap of paper and promptly handed it to Captain Smith. The commander hastily strode to the wireless room, gave the paper to wireless operator Phillips and ordered a call for assistance.

'CQD … CQD … (It was the call to alert all stations within range; 'Come Quick, Danger,' some called it.) This was indeed a call for help, a plea for the safety of more than 2,200 lives. By 12.15 am the message was crackling through a cable piercing the Marconi room's roof on its way to the huge antenna that stretched between the masts, and sent hurtling through the night. 'CQD … CQD …' followed by *Titanic*'s position.

The signals were heard almost simultaneously by *La Provence*, *Mount Temple* and the land station at Cape Race. Interference from distance or other transmissions caused *Mount Temple* to hear the position as '41°46' N, 50°24' W', while Cape Race heard '41°44' N, 50°24' W'. At 12.18 am the ship *Ypiranga* also recorded the latter position in her wireless log.

But by 12.25 am the position was corrected to that which Boxhall had worked out:

> Come at once. We have struck a berg. It's a CQD, OM [old man]. Position 41°46' N, 50°14' W.

The ship to which this message was addressed … *Carpathia*.

Carpathia's sole wireless operator, 21-year-old Harold Thomas Cottam, had been on duty since 7 am Sunday 14 April. He was tired and wished to go to bed. There was, however, one last message he waited to receive, a confirmation of an earlier transmission he'd sent to the Allan liner *Parisian*. Except for this he would have shut down his station half an hour earlier and turned in.

Still there was no message. Half undressed, Cottam idly switched his receiver to the frequency used for ships nearby, hoping to kill a few moments in communication with *Titanic*. About an hour earlier, while waiting for *Parisian*'s message, he had been listening to the land station at Cape Cod. This station had many messages for *Titanic* but could not interrupt the White Star ship's exchanges with Cape Race.

Finding *Titanic*'s frequency and hearing a momentary lull, Cottam broke in with:

> 'I say, old man, do you know there is a batch of messages coming through for you from MCC [Cape Cod]?'

Scarcely waiting for completion of Cottam's message, Phillips responded with the distress transmission. Cottam could not believe his ears. 'Shall I tell my captain? Do you require assistance?'

From MGY [*Titanic*]: 'Yes. Come quick!'

Cottam tore off his headphones and ran forward to the bridge. He burst in and blurted out the distress message to the officer of the watch, first officer Horace J. Dean, who did not wait for a repetition. With Cottam propelled in front, the two men quickly descended the steep steps to the captain's cabin.

Captain Arthur Rostron had just gone to bed. Dean and Cottam pushed their way into his cabin without knocking and, rightfully, the master was irritated. Upon hearing the message he paused only to confirm it with Cottam. Then, hurriedly pulling on his uniform, he ascended to the bridge and consulted the navigation chart.

Rostron soon established that the Mediterranean-bound *Carpathia* was about 58 miles south-east of *Titanic*'s distress position, and that the most direct course to her was North 52 degrees West. *Carpathia* wheeled around to head north-west on her new course. Alerted by the bridge, the engine room officers and crew began building pressure in *Carpathia*'s ten-year-old boilers. The off-duty watches of the 'black gang' were called to add their efforts in the stokeholds. Before the night was over, the ship would comfortably exceed her registered 14½-knot top speed, achieving over 17 knots.

As *Carpathia* surged forward, Rostron assembled his officers and issued a series of orders to prepare the ship and her crew for receiving survivors. One of the many heroic acts performed that night, Rostron's commands were textbook examples of preparation and foresight. Issued under the great pressure of the moment, they demonstrated superbly the master's knowledge and skill. Cabins and public rooms were to be readied to accommodate survivors. Hot coffee and food were to be prepared, nets and portable lights strung along the ship's sides, gangways to be readied, slings rigged, canvas bags put in place to haul up the children, oil to be poured down the forward lavatories to make the surface of the sea outside as smooth as possible.

But for *Titanic*, the object of *Carpathia*'s mission, the drama had already taken an unlikely, unpredictable turn ...

After the collision but before completely stopping, *Titanic* briefly moved ahead at half speed under Captain Smith's orders. Evidence from a crewman on the fo'c's'le indicates that the ship's wheel must have been ordered hard-a-port immediately after impact, to prevent *Titanic*'s stern from striking the iceberg. Therefore, as she slowed to a halt in the calm water *Titanic* described a great arc to starboard. Once stopped, she drifted in the one-knot southerly current.

In the 20 minutes following the collision Captain Smith received damage reports. He consulted with the ship's designer, Thomas Andrews, and was advised that his command – the newest, largest, safest ship afloat – had but little more than two hours to live.

At midnight it became 15 April. Even with the ship stopped, most crew routines proceeded normally. The engine room relief watch, though not yet ordered below to their posts, stood by. In the crow's nest Lee and Fleet were relieved by George Hogg and Alfred Evans. (It is unlikely that the order to 'Keep a sharp watch for ice' was passed along.) Stewards put finishing touches to breakfast table settings in the dining rooms.

But on deck – amid the roar and hiss of now unnecessary steam exhausting overhead – the new day's first order was an unusual one: 'Muster the crew. Stand by to uncover boats.'

Titanic's deck crew had never acted as one to man and lower the ship's boats. A departure-day test-lowering for the Board of Trade inspector at Southampton had involved just two boats and their respective crews. Now, untrained and untried (perhaps some actually unfamiliar with the relatively new Welin davits), the deck crew turned out and hastened to the boat deck.

Chief officer Henry Tingle Wilde assigned second officer Lightoller to see to the stripping of the boats' covers. Running forward to boat 4 on the port side, Lightoller began pulling off the cover himself. As two or three men arrived, they were put to work at the task and Lightoller then directed the deck hands coming on deck to other boats on port and starboard sides. He used hand signals; the din of escaping steam made verbal commands impossible.

After making a complete circuit of the boat deck, parcelling out crewmen as he went, Lightoller asked Wilde if the boats should be swung out. Lightoller later said he believed Wilde had said 'No', or 'Wait'. Moments later, Captain Smith did give the order from the bridge to swing out the boats.

The tale of port side lifeboat number 4 is one of high drama. Assembled by their cabin stewards and directed by the ship's officers, a small group of influential passengers gathered at around 12.30 am on A deck's forward port side, beneath boat 4's davits but behind the glassed-in deck enclosure.

Thayers, Wideners, Ryersons, Astors… Husbands, wives and families, some with maids and valets: men and women accustomed to giving orders, not taking them. Now, however, they waited patiently, almost humbly, for the lifeboat to be lowered from the deck above. The lifejackets and light clothing they had hurriedly donned gave scant protection from the chill air. As the minutes passed some of the ladies sent their maids back for warmer clothing: fur coats for the women, warm sweaters or jackets for the men. And still they waited.

After swinging out number 4, Lightoller ordered it lowered to A deck, intending to load passengers through the deck screen's windows. But no one from the deck crew could be diverted to open them. After about half an hour, shortly after 1 am, second steward George Dodd directed the group to climb the steep stairway forward (its small brass plaque bearing the admonition 'These stairs for use of crew only') to the boat deck.

Since other boats were loaded from the boat deck, the crew might have thought that boat 4 would be hoisted back up and loaded in the same way. Again the passengers waited, now with the sound of the unseen ship's orchestra coming to them fitfully whenever the nearby door to the first class main entrance opened, with the hiss, flare and booming explosions of the distress rockets proclaiming the urgency of their situation. Around them they could see people boarding other boats which were then lowered. But still they waited beside the davits whose falls held number 4 captive against the side of A deck, below.

Finding that passengers could be loaded and lowered conveniently from the boat deck, Lightoller finally realised that passengers for boat 4 were still awaiting loading. Once again the Thayers, Wideners, Astors, Ryersons and their entourages were herded back down to A deck. By now the windows had been cranked open, but another problem became evident. *Titanic*'s port list created a gap between the ship's side and the dangling boat. This condition was remedied by pulling the boat inwards with boat-hooks and temporarily securing it with a wire hawser normally used for coaling.

A makeshift step-ladder was rigged up. The women mounted the narrow treads and awkwardly climbed through the windows, from the lighted deck to the outside darkness. Thirteen-year-old Jack Ryerson at first was prevented from accompanying his mother, but his father's appeal overruled the loading officer's objection.

Legend reports that John Jacob Astor, standing nearby, placed a woman's hat on young Ryerson's head, saying, 'There, now you're a girl and you can go.' But the story was not repeated in Mrs Ryerson's later affidavit. (Another legend attributed to Astor tells how, standing at the bar after the collision, he said, 'I asked for ice, but this is ridiculous.' This story is quite unlikely since Astor never was famous for his humour.)

Astor did assist his five-months pregnant wife into the lifeboat, then asked the officer in charge if he might accompany her. After being refused, Astor joined the other gentlemen on deck in assisting ladies into the boat. They assured their wives they would soon follow in other boats, that nearby liners were on the way, that the women were to obey the ship's crewmen and not to worry. Astor stood on deck smiling, waving gently as finally, at 1.55 am, boat 4 was lowered to the sea. Astor's final heroic act was to descend quickly to the dog kennels on F deck, next to the third class galley. (One wonders if he might have heard the roar of the onrushing water as it filled the nearest watertight compartment.) There, he liberated his Airedale dog, Kitty, as well as the other dogs caged there. Madeleine Astor later reported that as she looked back, trying to glimpse her husband, she saw Kitty running about the deck as *Titanic* settled, bow down, lower and lower…

Including hands there were 32 persons aboard boat 4 as it descended. It had taken so long to load that its downward journey was a mere 25 feet rather than the 70 feet it normally

Lifeboat number 4 was lowered to the promenade deck just before 1 am. But more than an hour's wait ensued until seamen could be spared to crank open the glass windows allowing access. John Jacob Astor assisted his 19-year-old wife of seven months into the boat, which was two-thirds full. Refused a seat himself, Astor stepped back, casually lit a cigarette and bravely waved goodbye to Madeleine as the boat was lowered away. A legend was born. (Authors' collection)

would have travelled from A deck. Past the lighted portholes the boat was lowered, past portholes through which water flowed in. On reaching the water only a single seaman had been found aboard (the other crew being storekeepers and firemen); quartermaster Walter Perkis slid down the fall and into the boat where he took charge.

It was now after 2 am. *Titanic*'s bow buried itself deeper with every minute. Boat 4, the last to leave, was just a ship's length away when, following the sinking, it picked up eight crew members from the sea. Two of these later died in the boat. After sighting *Carpathia* about fives miles away, boat 4 reached the rescue ship's side at about 7.30 am.

While lifeboat 4's story unfolded, tales from other boats were no less dramatic…

Generally on the port side only women and children were allowed in boats, while on the starboard side men could board if no women were present. Between 12.45 am, when the first boat – starboard number 7 – was lowered, and 2.20 am, when collapsible boats A and B floated off the sinking liner, 706 survivors managed to board boats and safely leave the ship. (Following the sinking 14 people, mostly crew but including one woman passenger, Rhoda Abbott, were pulled from the water; of these, only seven survived.)

Titanic had been planned to accommodate 2,435 passengers and 860 crew, a total of 3,295. On her maiden voyage she carried just 2,225. Yet the antiquated Board of Trade regulations, based on cubic footage, required a lifeboat capacity for only 980 people. *Titanic*'s lifeboat capacity was 1,176. The extra seating for 196 provided by her four collapsible boats was more than 10% beyond statutory requirements.

Titanic carried 14 lifeboats, with a capacity of 65 each, giving 910 seats in total; two emergency cutters, each for 35 persons, or 70 in all; and the four collapsibles, each capable of carrying 49, providing 196 additional seats.

Yet only four *Titanic* boats were lowered carrying anywhere near their full capacities; of the remaining 16 only three had more than 50 people aboard. Not including collapsibles A and B, which floated off, the average number aboard the remaining 18 boats was a startling 44.

But even loaded to total capacity, with every available seat occupied, 1,049 people would still have lost their lives even under the most ideal circumstances.

As the boats were filled and carefully lowered the great drama ran its inevitable course. The first boats were less than half-filled, their occupants boarding reluctantly, perhaps a bit ashamed of demonstrating so little faith in the liner's safety. But as minutes passed the danger began to dawn upon passengers and crew alike. More and more people crowded to the edge of the boat deck, the pushing becoming stronger until near-panic ensued.

Under Captain Smith's orders, fourth officer Boxhall fired the first distress rocket at about 12.45 am as the first lifeboat (number 7) was lowered. Far aft, walking his lonely watch at the stern, quartermaster George Rowe saw the boat slip past. Unaware of the evacuation, Rowe rang the bridge. He and quartermaster Arthur Bright were ordered to gather additional percussive rockets and report to the navigating bridge. Once there, they assisted Boxhall in firing rockets until 1.25 (Rowe may have been a bit off in his reckoning: Boxhall later stated that he kept 'sending the rockets up right to the very last minute I was sent away in the boat', number 2, which left at 1.45 am.)

Shortly before 1 am Bruce Ismay tried to assist fifth officer Lowe in putting boat 5 into the water. 'Lower away, lower away!' he called as he waved his arm in circles. Lowe could not stand the interference. 'If you will get to hell out of that I shall be able to do something,' he shouted. 'Do you want me to lower away quickly? You will have me drown the whole lot of them.' Abashed, Ismay turned and without a word quickly walked forward to boat 3.

Port boat 6 was also being lowered at about this time. Mrs James Joseph Brown (known today as 'Molly', though she preferred 'Margaret' or 'Maggie') was walking away from it to see what was being done elsewhere, having persuaded several of her more timid friends to board. Suddenly she was roughly seized by two acquaintances, Edward Calderhead and James McGough, and dumped over the side, falling four feet into the already-descending boat. There were just two seamen, Fleet and Hichens, in the boat and as they reached the water Molly made good use of her loud voice to demand another sailor. Major Arthur Godfrey Peuchen, a yachtsman, volunteered and was permitted by second officer Lightoller to join the boat. Swinging more than six feet out to the falls and then rapidly descending hand-over-hand more than 60 feet, Peuchen was soon aboard.

The boat now in the water, Hichens refused to row. Peuchen and Fleet were not strong enough together to row the heavily loaded boat. Doffing her lifejacket, Molly Brown seized an oar and, through her example, soon had some of the 24 other women 'manning' the boat. Later, when they were able to take another man aboard – a stoker from boat 16 – Mrs Brown wrapped the thinly clad man in her own fur coat and very likely saved his life. Throughout the ordeal her cheerfulness and strength of character did much to prevent panic.

Even though first officer Murdoch permitted men to enter starboard boat number 3, there were several gentlemen who, after assisting ladies into the boat, stood away and went elsewhere, to be lost: Messrs Case, Hays, Davidson and Roebling were men who had much to live for, men who saw their duty and did it unselfishly and superbly.

As portside boat 8 was loading, Isidor and Ida Straus, together with Mrs Straus's maid Ellen

During the lowering of the lifeboats, Ida Straus, wife of New York millionaire Isidor Straus, was urged to enter the boat. But she refused to do so without her husband who, in turn, would not board until all women had been embarked. The two were last seen as they left the deck to meet their fate together. (Authors' collection)

Bird, approached the boat. Miss Bird got in, but Mr Straus refused to board until all women and children were safe. Mrs Straus would not leave without her husband. When last seen the two elderly people were re-entering the ship, perhaps to go below to meet their fate together.

At about the same time that the Strauses were, so unselfishly, leaving space in their boat for others, starboard boat number 1, one of the two emergency cutters, was being readied for launch. First officer Murdoch ordered several firemen to enter the boat.

First class passengers Sir Cosmo and Lady Lucile Duff-Gordon, with the latter's secretary Miss Laura Francatelli, appeared and asked if they might enter the boat. Seeing no others – men or women – around, Murdoch helped the group into the boat, along with two American gentlemen who had just arrived. There were still no others – men, women or crew – in sight as Murdoch gave the order to lower away. And boat 1, capacity 35, reached the water with five passengers and seven crew aboard.

Later, following the sinking, while the cries of the freezing and the drowning rang in their ears, the boat's occupants refused to return to the disaster site for fear they would be swamped. Look-out George Symons, nominally in charge, kept his mouth shut. And no one objected when Lady Duff-Gordon suggested they should not return. The boat reached *Carpathia* with its 12-member party comfortably intact. Subsequently, Sir Cosmo provided each crew member with a five-pound cheque, ostensibly to replace their lost kits ...

Now as the situation's urgency became apparent, port boat 10 left with 55 aboard. There were 56 aboard starboard boat 9 as it, too, left at 1.20 am. As port boat 12 was lowered away, famed novelist and mystery writer Jacques Futrelle stood back and waved good-bye to his wife, May. Less than six days earlier, on the evening of 9 April, the two had celebrated Jacques' 37th birthday at a fashionable London restaurant ...

Boats 11 and 13 were lowered to A deck and loaded at almost the same time. Stewards formed a human chain and hurriedly passed women and children across the deck and into the boats. For one woman, an ordeal began that ultimately would be resolved by *Carpathia*'s Captain Arthur Rostron. As she awaited her turn to board, third class passenger Mrs Leah Aks was astonished to have her ten-month-old son Frank torn from her protective grasp.

Struggling to regain hold of her baby, Mrs Aks was pushed aside by the stewards, who believed she was 'rushing the boat'.

Frank Phillip Aks, or as he was nicknamed, Filly, was dropped into the now-descending boat. He was caught – much like a football – by Elizabeth Nye, who clutched the wailing baby in her lap, later wrapping him in a brown plaid steamer blanket to protect him from the cold.

In Frank Aks' own words, 'My mother was in a state of shock, having lost her baby. She was pushed into lifeboat number 13 next to Mrs Selena Rogers Cook. She was a warm, compassionate woman, comforting and watching over my mother throughout the night and during the transfer to and aboard the *Carpathia*.

> 'My mother and Mrs Rogers were sitting on the *Carpathia*'s deck when a woman passed by with a baby in her arms; that baby was me! When I saw my mother I immediately stretched out my arms toward her. [But] Elizabeth Nye claimed me as her own. Mrs Rogers went to Captain Rostron of the *Carpathia* with my mother and told him the story.
>
> 'He took the two ladies and me to his quarters. Proof of identification was made through a strawberry birthmark under my left breast. I was returned to my mother.'

At 1.25 am starboard boats 11 and 13 were lowered almost simultaneously – 11 with 70 aboard, 13 with 64. Also among those in boat 11 were eight-year-old Marshall Drew and his Aunt Lulu. He vividly recalled the evacuation not long before his passing in 1986:

> 'At 11.40 pm April 14th when the *Titanic* struck the iceberg, I was in bed. However, for whatever reason I was awake and remember the jolt and cessation of motion.
>
> 'A steward knocked on the stateroom door and directed us to get dressed, put on life preservers and go to the boat deck, which we did.
>
> 'There was a watertight compartment door next to our stateroom. As we left it was closed.
>
> 'I remember the steward as we passed was trying to arouse passengers who had locked themselves in for the night.
>
> 'Elevators were not running. We walked up to the boat deck. All was calm and orderly. An officer was in charge. "Women and children first," [he said] as he directed lifeboat number 11 to be filled. There were many tearful farewells. We and Uncle Jim said "Good bye".
>
> 'Waiting on deck before this I could hear the ship's orchestra playing somewhere off toward first class.
>
> 'Lifeboat number 11 was near the stern. I will never forget that as I looked over my right shoulder, [the] steerage [promenade area] was blacked out. It made an impression I never forgot.
>
> 'Now I know from reading that lifeboat number 11 was the only lifeboat filled to capacity. The lowering of the lifeboat 70 feet to the sea was perilous. Davits, ropes, nothing worked properly so that first one end of the lifeboat was tilted up and then far down. I think it was the only time I was scared.

> 'Lifeboats pulled some distance away from the sinking *Titanic*, afraid of what suction might do. I am always annoyed at artists' depictions of the sinking *Titanic*. I've never seen one that came anywhere near the truth. There might have been the slightest ocean swell but it was dead calm. Stars there may have been, but the blackness of the night was so intense one could not see anything like a horizon ...'

As it neared the water, boat 13 was almost swamped by a large stream of water being discharged from *Titanic*'s side by the labouring pumps deep within the hull.

Boat 13's safety was threatened further when it reached the water. It drifted astern before its falls could be cut and was nearly crushed under boat 15, lowered moments after 13 with 70 aboard (almost all third class women and children). Boat 13's falls were cut using

Lifeboat 13, with 54 of her 64 occupants women, was lowered at 1.25 am. Less than a minute later, the adjacent boat 15 was lowered. Boat 13 reached the water, but before her falls could be severed, she was washed beneath the descending boat 15. Disaster seemed imminent, but the falls were cut and boat 13 drifted clear just in time. (Daily Graphic)

Around 1.30 am when the ship's foundering seemed inevitable, Benjamin Guggenheim and his valet Victor Giglio appeared on deck in full evening dress. They had shed the heavy sweaters and lifejackets worn earlier. In Mr Guggenheim's words, 'We've dressed in our best and are prepared to go down like gentlemen.' Another legend was generated. (New York Times)

third class passenger Margaret Devaney's proffered penknife, barely in time to prevent a vertical collision.

Port boat 14 with 60 aboard was lowered at 1.30. As fifth officer Lowe assisted the more than 50 women aboard he flourished his gun to keep back the surrounding men who threatened to rush the boat. Lowe himself got in as the boat was lowered, not so much to take command as to keep an eye out for it as well as boats 12 and 14 which were lowered almost simultaneously. Once afloat, Lowe mustered boats 10, 12, collapsible D and 4 near his own number 14. Tying them together, Lowe oversaw transfer of crew and passengers between boats to balance their loads. He later rigged a mast and sail aboard number 14, to propel the flotilla towards the approaching *Carpathia*.

In the forward davits used to launch boat 1 now hung collapsible C, loading under first officer Murdoch's direction. The boat was already almost two-thirds full when a large group of men appeared ready to rush the boat. Chief purser Hugh McElroy, assisting Murdoch, fired his pistol twice and the sound so startled the incipient mob that the men fell back, leaving a wide space around the boat.

Travelling with his two sons, second class passenger 'Mr Hoffman' was actually Michel Navratil, who kidnapped the children in an effort to rescue a failing marriage. Shortly before 2 am he handed his two sons to second officer Lightoller through the ring of crewmen formed to protect the last boat, Collapsible D, from being swamped by the more than 1,500 still aboard. (Harper's)

Seeing no women nearby, Wilde ordered the boat to be lowered. It began to move below deck level, and seeing no one else in its vicinity, J. Bruce Ismay stepped quietly and quickly forward, boarding the boat as it descended. This act, while scarcely a cowardly one under the immediate circumstances, was later to cause him many agonised hours of intense regret.

As the bow dipped ever lower in the icy Atlantic water, there were those who stood fast and performed their duty as they saw it, those whose courage and bravery shine as bright stars against disaster's dark fabric ...

Chief steward Andrew Latimer, who gave his lifejacket to a lady passenger, then abandoned all hope of rescue and assisted to the end in loading and lowering the boats.

The 34 engineering officers – engineers, electricians, plumbers, boiler room personnel – who maintained electricity and lighting until almost the final moment. Of these brave men who laboured amid heat, sound, hot metal and shifting coal not one deserted his post, not one was saved.

In his fitting tribute to these courageous men, Lord Beresford wrote, 'Had it not been for their steadfast dedication to duty, many more lives would have been lost.' Legend subsequently said His Majesty King George V agreed, and decreed that henceforth British marine engineers would wear rank insignia against a royal purple background as a remembrance of their *Titanic* colleagues. But the practice actually had begun in the Royal Navy in 1863, and had begun applying to the merchant navy even before *Titanic*.

One must not forget the gallant postal clerks, five men, neither White Star employees nor *Titanic* crew members, men entrusted by their governments with the safety of the mails. Two British, three American citizens whose department forward on G deck's starboard side was among the first areas to be flooded. Within five minutes the water had sloshed around their knees as they dragged 200 sacks of registered mail from the storage room on the orlop deck to the dryer G deck sorting room. Their efforts were in vain. Even before the last sack arrived, water had already risen to that level. Continuing to struggle with the heavy sacks, weighing 100 pounds and more, sometimes enlisting help from available stewards, the clerks then pulled their precious bags of registered mail up the steep inside stairways to the starboard side corridor of D deck's forward cabins. They hoped to off-load the mail through the first class entrance, just aft of that area. It was a forlorn hope.

In the words of the Brooklyn (New York) *Daily Eagle*,

> 'The Brooklyn mail clerk [William Logan Gwinn] was then with the other four clerks, Oscar S. Woody of Washington, DC, John Starr March of Newark, NJ, John Richard Jago Smith and James Bertram Williamson of England. They were still working over their mail bags, cool and self-contained, until the explosion came and the darkness and the ocean swallowed them up. Not once did they waver or blanch from their duty. Not one can say that they attempted to get into the lifeboats or thought of themselves for a single instant. They stuck to that which their governments had entrusted to their care, and with it they died.'

It is estimated that 3,364 bags of mail and between 700 and 800 parcels were lost in *Titanic*'s sinking. But the tradition of trust and responsibility for the safety of the mails never saw a prouder hour.

The bandsmen... Much has been spoken and written concerning these valiant men's actions and behaviour. To recount in detail their last night almost would be superfluous. Memorials (more than for any other segment of the ship's company) have sustained the gallant eight's memory through the years. As long as music is performed, as long as hymns are sung, their heroism will endure: Brailey, Bricoux, Clarke, Hume, Krins, Taylor, Woodward – and their leader, Wallace Hartley.

Shortly after midnight the orchestra (tradition would have the group called a 'band') assembled in the forward first class entrance, where passengers began gathering before going to the boats. The band's music established a quick bright tempo which kept the passengers' feet moving to its beat. Suspicion, even panic, was quickly averted by the musicians' presence. ('Why, if they're playing here, things can't be *that* bad.')

Later, when passengers had stepped out on to the promenade and boat decks, the band reassembled outside the gymnasium near the first class entrance's starboard side. Around 12.45 am, as the first lifeboat, number 7, was lowered, they began playing a brave counterpoint to the sound of shuffling feet and the increasing murmur of confused passengers. The music helped bring order to the proceedings.

Their repertoire of marches, quicksteps and occasional waltz tunes was performed with cold-stiffened fingers through the next hour and 20 minutes. As the decks' pitch grew steeper there was no effort to leave. Even those without instruments, pianists Taylor and Brailey, remained with their comrades.

When, at around 2.10 am, the end was very near, bandmaster Hartley advised his men that they had done their duty and could save themselves if they wished. Not one man moved. They stood together on the slanting deck and, struggling to maintain footing, played a hymn, a solemn, soaring requiem to a great ship and its doomed people ...

Through the years there has been considerable speculation regarding the last music *Titanic*'s bandsmen played. Recollections have ranged from 'Londonderry Air' through the two best-known tunes for the hymn 'Nearer, My God, to Thee', a sentimental waltz 'Songe d'Automne', and yet another hymn (with its roots in a 1551 setting for a Psalm), 'Autumn'.

Some iconoclasts bravely suggest that no music was played or sung as the ship sank. They may be correct: the decks' steep incline at this point would preclude sure footing. And the sound of their music, if indeed they could have played, would have been drowned out by the roar of equipment and furnishings plunging towards the bow. Most references are made to music played immediately before the ship tilted, broke in two and sank.

For many years there have been strong supporters of the hymn 'Autumn', which surviving telegraphist Harold Bride reported hearing while he struggled in the ocean to save himself, indeed while trapped for some time beneath overturned collapsible B, his ears filled with water. Bride's supporters claim he was a trained technician, alert to his environment, better able than most to observe and remember. His story, which he wrote for a New York newspaper, received wide coverage. In the emotions generated by the momentous event, the music could be accepted as representing the occasion's nobility and dignity.

Some doubt can be cast when one vainly searches for any other person – passenger or crew – who recalls 'Autumn' as the final music. Credibility is strained further when one examines the hymn's tune. Its progressions and intervals do not lend themselves to *ad libitum* performance. ('Autumn' is not listed in the White Star Line's musicians' songbook for 1912.)

The sentiments expressed in the verses are noble ones: 'God of mercy and compassion, look with pity on my pain ...' and 'Hold me up in mighty waters, keep mine eyes on things above'. But there is good cause to doubt the tradition. The words do fulfil requirements of Victorian/Edwardian sentiment and resigned acceptance of calamity. Yet neither the hymn's tune nor its full lyrics lend themselves to singing, playing or recitation during stressful moments save, perhaps, by professional choirmasters. If there were just a single additional witness to Harold Bride's recollection there might be grounds for reconsideration. But there is none…

A far better candidate for the 'last music' is the hymn 'Nearer, My God, to Thee', although some doubt exists as to which *tune* was played. Was it 'Bethany' or 'Horbury'? (For those who have seen the three major *Titanic* films, 'Bethany' is used in the 1953 and 1997 American films, each named *Titanic*, while 'Horbury' was sung in the 1958 British film *A Night to Remember*.) Or was it any of the four other tunes to which 'Nearer, My God, to Thee' had been set?

Dr G. Edward Stubbs, in *The New Music Review*, August 1912, suggests that Arthur Sullivan's 'Proprior Deo' was likely the hymn tune used by Hartley. (It was this setting that was played at Hartley's funeral at Colne, Lancashire.)

A more recent (1995) suggestion from composer Gavin Bryars is that Harold Bride, who favoured 'Autumn', was misquoted by the press, and that he really said 'Aughton', whose lyrics contain the lines 'When at last life's journey's done, When at last the victory's won…'

Regardless of the tune, the hymn itself was more than likely the 'last music'. It was known to have been Hartley's favourite hymn. Indeed, when queried by one of his colleagues earlier, while both were playing in *Mauretania*'s band, Hartley stated that if he were aboard a sinking ship he would assemble his men and play either 'O God Our Help in Ages Past' or 'Nearer, My God, to Thee', as both were his favourites. The hymn had also been a great favourite of the late King Edward VII. And it was the hymn played at the graveside of all departed brothers of the Amalgamated Musicians' Union.

Perhaps the most telling quality is its ease of performance and harmonising in an *ad lib* playing of the simple, almost chorale-like melody, a style for which the intricacies of 'Autumn' emphatically were not suited.

It was the American survivors who recalled the hymn and its tune. Their cumulative recollections remained unchallenged at the time by the press on both sides of the Atlantic, but for Bride's lone exception.

In the absence of proven fact (in this case, direct testimony by an orchestra member), and in view of the many conflicting statements, one cannot state with certainty the tune, or even the title, of the last music. The speculation itself represents one of *Titanic*'s many fascinating unproven and unprovable facts.

One irrefutable fact, however, remains: the musicians stayed until all hope of rescue was gone. Who can say how many lives their efforts saved? The final moments of how many were cheered or ennobled by their music? 'Songe d'Automne' or 'Autumn'. Horbury' or 'Bethany' or 'Proprior Deo'. What difference? The memory of the bandsmen and their courageous music will never die.

Senior wireless operator John G. Phillips (left) and junior operator Harold S. Bride (right) heroically stood at their post until moments before Titanic *finally sank, bravely transmitting signals.* (Marconi Marine)

2.10 am – The water had done its work. Flowing over the watertight bulkheads, filling one compartment after another, the water's weight had pulled *Titanic*'s bow completely under. As the seconds passed the huge liner's immense bulk started a catastrophic arc into the black diamond-point sky.

As energy from the emergency dynamo faltered, the last wireless signal spluttered to a halt; a faint sound, received by the *Virginian*: '– – –' and then no more.

Marshall Drew recalled *Titanic*'s end:

> 'As row by row of the porthole lights of the *Titanic* sank into the sea this was about all one could see. When the *Titanic* upended to sink, all was blacked out until the tons of machinery crashed to the bow. This sounded like an explosion, which of course it was not.
>
> 'As this happened the hundreds and hundreds of people were thrown into the sea. It isn't likely I shall ever forget the screams of these people as they perished in water said to be 28 degrees.'

2.15 am – *Titanic*'s stern rose higher and higher. Inside the ship all furnishings and fittings, tableware, glasses, dishes, everything movable began to slide towards the bow. In a cacophonous blur of thunder every unattached chair, bed, lamp, every table and sofa followed.

By 2.18 the lights assured by the engineers' brave sacrifice finally glowed red, flickered once, twice, then went out, leaving *Titanic*'s curved hull blacker against the night's blackness, her three great propellers dripping streams of water once clear of their accustomed element.

The stern's upward movement reached its full extent, achieving an angle of about 20 degrees.

2.20 am – With the bow well under water, the remaining hull slipped downwards with a heavy gurgling sound. As they reached the water the funnels broke off one by one, sending clouds of soot and steam gushing into the air. The four funnels themselves, crushed and broken, planed off in as many directions.

Not yet fully under the surface, the tortured hull broke with a mighty roar near the after expansion joint and an engine room airshaft. The forward section, three-fifths of the ship, was now fully submerged, connected to the stern only by the keel. Portions of the ship's double bottom broke away and sank quickly. As the bow section plunged, its tenuous keel connection pulled the stern into a nearly vertical position before breaking under the strain. The stern section, containing the immense triple-expansion engines and the heavy turbine, together weighing more than 1,000 tons, remained afloat a few seconds more, then lost its buoyancy and plummeted straight to the bottom. A burst of trapped compressed air rose explosively to the surface in a single huge bubble, so close to the vortex as to appear part of it.

The stern followed the direction taken by the bow, pirouetting slowly as it sank further...

On the surface the black water was marbled with white-bubbled spume rising from the broken hulk. Debris torn from the hull's fractures bobbed to the surface. Soon there was a trail of it marking the sinking liner's direction.

Twenty boats, one overturned, another awash, floated in the glass-like sea. A mile or more away floated a great iceberg which resembled the Rock of Gibraltar, a smear of red paint running along its base...

Over the sea's surface the cries for help sounded loudly at first, then more faintly, until there was nothing... nothing but 'twenty boats and a quiet sea', and silence.

As the sounds ebbed, childhood fascination with what was occurring around him gave way to ennui. Marshall Drew recalled:

> 'The reader will have to understand that at this point in my life I was being brought up as a typical British kid. You were not allowed to cry. You were a "little man". So! As a cool kid I lay down in the bottom of the lifeboat and went to sleep.
>
> 'When I awoke it was broad daylight as we approached the *Carpathia*. Looking around over the gunwale it seemed to me like the Arctic. Icebergs of huge size ringed the horizon for 360 degrees.'

Nowhere is *Titanic*'s sinking so vividly described as by those who experienced the frightful disaster. And nowhere is the picture so graphically represented as when seen through a child's eyes.

Another youngster on board was 12-year-old Ruth Becker. Written in her mature years (now as Mrs Ruth Blanchard), this account recalls the hours of cold and uncertainty spent in *Titanic*'s boats. It is published here by Mrs Blanchard's kind permission:

> 'As our lifeboat number 13 pulled out from the side of the *Titanic* we could see the water rushing into the ship. Rowing away, looking at the *Titanic*, it was a beautiful sight outlined against the starry sky, every port hole and saloon blazing with light. It was impossible to think anything could be wrong with such an enormous ship, were it not for the tilt downward towards the bow... Finally as the *Titanic* sank faster, the

lights in the cabins and saloons died out. At the same time the machinery roared down through the vessel with a rattle and a groaning that could be heard for miles – the weirdest sound, surely, that could be heard in the middle of the ocean, a thousand miles from land.

'To our amazement the *Titanic* seemed to break in half, the prow slipping down quietly under the waters, and the stern remaining in an upright position for a couple of minutes, seeming to say, "Good bye – so sorry!"

'Then with a quiet slanting dive it disappeared beneath the waters, and our eyes looked for the last time on the gigantic vessel we had set out on from Southampton last Wednesday.

'Such a tragedy! Over 2,000 people on board, plenty of time to get off, but 1,500 persons went down with the ship because there were only 20 lifeboats available, definitely not enough to accommodate every man, woman and child.

'Lifeboat number 13 that I was in had about 65 people in it so it was filled to standing room with men and women in every conceivable condition of dress and undress. It was bitter cold – a curious, deadening, bitter cold. And then with all of this, there fell on the ear the most terrible noises that human beings ever listened to – the cries of hundreds of people struggling in the icy cold water, crying for help with a cry that we knew could not be answered. We wanted to pick up some of those swimming, but this would have meant swamping our boat and further loss of the lives of all of us.

'It was not until then that I realized that I was still holding on to the blankets I had brought up from our cabin. In the rush I had forgotten to give them to my mother to wrap around my brother, two years old, and sister, four years old. [They had left *Titanic* in another lifeboat.] The men who were rowing our boat were stokers. They had been working near the bottom of the ship near the boilers when the *Titanic* struck. Therefore, when the ship was ripped open, the water rushed in and soaked all of them. They escaped with nothing on except sleeveless shirts and shorts. So you can imagine how cold they were out in that freezing weather. The officer in charge asked me to give up my blankets to wrap around these men, which I gladly did. Also, the finger on one of the men was almost cut off. I happened to find a large handkerchief – my father's – in my coat pocket. So we tore that in strips and wrapped them around his finger.

'Standing on one side of me was a little German lady. She was crying [and] I asked her why. She told me – through an interpreter standing near – that her little six-weeks-old baby had been taken away from her on the *Titanic* and put into another boat. The baby was wrapped so heavily in blankets that she was afraid it would be taken for baggage and thrown in the ocean. All excess baggage was thrown overboard.

'All lifeboats were supposed to be equipped with oars, a compass, a light, and food (crackers). Our lifeboat had only oars. The other boats seemed to be in the same predicament because we were all scattered. But we were very lucky. The captain of the boat said he had been at sea for 26 years and had never yet seen such a calm night on the Atlantic.

'We all, of course, were watching for the light of a rescue ship. Finally about 4 o'clock in the morning we did see a light which came closer and closer. Rockets were being sent up and the foghorn kept blowing and blowing.

'You can imagine our joy because we knew it must be a rescue ship. All of us shouted and yelled. We were really happy because the sea was getting choppy and that was the first time I was a little concerned. Our tiny boat bounced around like a cork. The *Carpathia*, our rescue ship, stopped. We rowed to it, and our boatload was rescued.'

CHAPTER TWO

Lights that Pass in the Night

After checking on the damage forward, *Titanic*'s fourth officer Boxhall had reported his findings to Captain Smith on the bridge. Then, at about midnight, he roused officers Lightoller and Pitman, still in their respective cabins awaiting orders.

Boxhall next went along the port side seeing to the unlacing of boat covers. As he reached the bridge again he was intercepted by the captain and ordered to work out *Titanic*'s position. Entering the chart room he quickly established a position, and took his conclusions to Captain Smith, who, he later said, told him to take the position to the Marconi room. (In his American inquiry testimony, telegraphist Harold Bride stated specifically that Captain Smith had brought in the position report.)

It was as he returned to the bridge from the Marconi room, Boxhall told the Board of Trade inquiry, that he first saw the light of a ship near *Titanic*. He stated that with binoculars he distinctly could make out the ship's two masthead lights.

At about 12.45 am Boxhall fired off the first distress rocket. As he continued to do so at about five-minute intervals with quartermasters Arthur Bright's and George Rowe's assistance, he observed the ship approaching. Soon he was able to discern her red port sidelight and her green starboard lamp without binoculars.

The lights were observed by others on the bridge, including the captain. They first appeared about half a point (about 5½°) on *Titanic*'s port bow. Presently the approaching vessel's red port light, alone, could be seen. Captain Smith ordered Boxhall and Rowe to try contacting the vessel with the Morse lamp, and they did so in between firing rockets. Rowe later judged that the ship was four or five miles away, while Boxhall thought the distance five or six miles. There was no response from the other vessel to either the overwhelming din of the distress rockets or to the powerful Morse signal lamp. She seemed to be turning slowly; just before Boxhall departed from *Titanic*'s bridge at about 1.40 am (to join number 2 boat, lowered at 1.45 am), he observed only the vessel's stern light, now two points (about 23°) off *Titanic*'s bow. It seemed to Boxhall that, in spite of frantic Morse lamp and rocket signals, the other vessel was sailing off.

(It should be noted that *Titanic* was stationary in the water. She was drifting with the southerly current, but not turning. What Boxhall emphatically and realistically describes, augmented by quartermaster Rowe's observations, is a vessel that approached, passed about two points off *Titanic*'s bow at a distance of five miles, then turned and sailed away – *a moving ship*.)

About 19 miles from the sinking Titanic, *the* Californian *had been stopped by ice since 7.30 pm. Hours later, her crew saw the lights of a vessel less than eight miles distant. While* Californian's *Captain Stanley Lord (1) dozed in the chart room and her radio operator Cyril Evans (2) was off duty, donkeyman Ernest Gill (3) thought he saw the nearby vessel throwing rockets. Third officer Charles V Groves (4) tried unsuccessfully to signal the ship which he later described as a small tramp steamer five to eight miles away.* (Washington Evening Star; New York American; Boston Journal; Daily Sketch)

At about 12.45, while loading boat number 6 which left at 12.55, second officer Lightoller also had observed a light about two points off *Titanic*'s port bow. The light did not move. Indeed, Lightoller recalled encouraging the frightened passengers by telling them he thought the light was a sailing vessel, and that later in the morning when the wind came up, the vessel would come and pick up the people in the boats. While Lightoller continued observing the vessel's light between his many duties, it did not appear to move.

The Leyland Line's cargo vessel *Californian* departed from Liverpool on 5 April for Boston, Massachusetts, with a general cargo aboard. By 14 April her noon position, by observation, was 42°05' N, 47°25' W. During the afternoon her course was altered after ice reports were received on 9 and 13 April. At 6.30 pm three large bergs were sighted and *Californian*'s captain, Stanley Lord, ordered wireless operator Cyril Evans to advise the Leyland freighter *Antillian*, then in communications range, of the ice.

At 7.30 pm *Californian*'s chief officer George F. Stewart took an observation on the Pole Star and reported to Captain Lord a latitude of 42°5½' N. Because of his vessel's proximity to ice, Lord doubled his look-outs at 8 pm and later took charge of the bridge himself, third officer Charles Groves also being on duty. At 10.15 there was a brightening on the western horizon and Lord concluded that this 'glow' was caused by ice. At 10.21 he ordered the ship to be stopped and the helm put hard a-port. *Californian* swung around to the east-north-east by compass (north-east true) and came to a halt.

Stopped in loose ice about half a mile from the edge of a low ice-field, Lord calculated the vessel's position and entered it in the log: 42°05' N, 50°07' W.

When he left the bridge at 10.30 to go below Captain Lord pointed out to the third officer a light to the eastward. Lord thought it was an approaching vessel. Groves thought it was a star. As he returned to the bridge around 10.55 Lord encountered the wireless operator and asked him if he knew of any other vessels in the vicinity. 'Only *Titanic*,' responded Evans.

'That's not *Titanic*. She's closer to us in size,' replied Lord, indicating the slowly approaching ship. 'You'd better contact *Titanic* anyway and let her know we're stopped in ice.' Wireless operator Evans went immediately to send the message.

By 11.30 pm the other ship's green starboard light could be seen. Lord, still on the bridge, estimated her distance at about five miles and asked that she be contacted by Morse lamp. There was no response from the other vessel, however.

At the midnight watch change Captain Lord asked the relieving watch officer, second officer Herbert Stone, to advise him if the nearby vessel came any closer. He told Stone that he would be resting on the chart room's settee and left the bridge.

To Stone the vessel appeared to be to the south-south-east and dead abeam, starboard of *Californian*. He observed one masthead light and a red sidelight, as well as one or two indistinct lights resembling open doors or portholes. He judged her to be a small tramp steamer about five miles off.

Like Groves earlier, Stone repeatedly tried Morsing the ship, beginning at about 12.10, but also without success.

Around midnight fireman Ernest Gill came on deck after completing his eight-to-twelve watch. Having just come from the lighted engine room, Gill blinked his eyes against the night's darkness as he leaned over the starboard rail of *Californian*'s upper deck. Peering into the night Gill saw '... a very large steamer, about ten miles away. I watched her for a full minute... She was going at full speed.' Gill went below but was unable to sleep. He left his bunk and went up on deck again about 12.30 am. He had been there for about ten minutes when he saw a white rocket, '... about ten miles away on the starboard side. I thought it must be a shooting star. In seven or eight minutes I saw distinctly a second rocket in the same place... It was not my business to notify the bridge or the look-outs... I turned in immediately after.'

At the subsequent American inquiry Gill reported that while he could see stars spangling out from the rockets, he observed no Morse signalling from the vessel, nor could he hear any noise such as escaping steam, concussions from exploding distress rockets, or anything of the sort, though conditions that night were ideal for doing so, especially from the ten-mile distance about which he was so positive.

On the bridge second officer Stone also had observed a flash of light in the sky at about 12.45 am, *Californian*'s time. He then thought nothing of it for several shooting stars had already been plainly sighted. But a short time later he viewed another light, directly over the nearby steamer, appearing to come from a good distance beyond her. Between that time and about 1.15 am he observed three more lights, the same as before and all white in colour.

At 1.15 Stone whistled down the speaking tube to advise Captain Lord of the rockets. Answering from his own cabin, Lord inquired if the rockets were company signals. Stone replied, 'I don't know, but they're all white.' Lord ordered Stone to continue signalling the nearby vessel via Morse lamp, and '... when you do [get an answer], let me know by Gibson.' Again Stone signalled the ship, again without response. The captain returned to the chart room settee.

Californian continued to swing through south and by 1.50 am was heading west-south-west. The other ship had a bearing of south-west-by-west and around 2 am had begun steaming away, bearing SW ½ W. Her red portside light became invisible, and only her stern light could be seen.

As ordered, Stone sent apprentice Gibson to report to the captain. Gibson returned saying he had told the captain not only of the ship's departure but also of the sighting of eight distant rockets. According to Gibson the captain acknowledged his report and then inquired about the rockets: 'Are you sure there were no colours in them?' He then asked Gibson the time and, after telling him, Gibson returned to the bridge to report to Stone. But Lord was unaware of Gibson's visit. In a sworn affidavit he stated, 'I have recollection between 1.30 and 4.30 of Gibson opening the chart room door and closing it immediately. I said "What is it?" but he did not reply.'

Captain Lord was not the only drowsy member of *Californian*'s crew. Telegraphist Cyril Evans, rebuffed by *Titanic*'s operator Jack Phillips during his attempt to contact the liner, had taken off his headphones, shut down his apparatus and gone to bed. His station's mechanically operated detector was unwound, and therefore unresponsive to the distress calls which so soon afterwards began crackling through the night...

At first *Carpathia* sped through a smooth sea on her course of North 52 West. By 2.30 am preparations to receive survivors were completed.

A full head of steam from seven boilers drove her two quadruple expansion engines ever faster. *Carpathia*'s normal top speed was 14½ knots. Never again did the ship attain the 17½-knot speed reached during her dash to *Titanic*. Her frame shuddered, her bedplates vibrated as the engines strained to meet the demand of speed, more speed…

As *Carpathia* approached *Titanic*'s last radioed position (heard more than a full, ominous hour ago, now), there were icebergs to dodge. But by masterful navigation, Rostron guided his 540-foot liner through the ice while never slackening speed. At 3 am, he ordered rockets to be fired at 15-minute intervals to let survivors know help was approaching. By 3.35 am *Carpathia* had reached almost the exact position where *Titanic*, if afloat, would have been visible. But there was only an empty sea punctuated by bobbing ice.

At 4 o'clock the engines were stopped. About 300 yards ahead a green light shone low in the water. *Carpathia* drifted closer. The lifeboat was alongside. Lines were thrown and made fast. At 4.10 am the women from *Titanic*'s lifeboat 2 began to climb through the shelter deck's open gangway. There were only 25 in a boat designed for 40. Fourth officer Boxhall, ordered to look after the boat's all-female complement, climbed wearily on to *Carpathia*'s deck. Captain Rostron sent word asking him to report to the bridge. Still wet and shivering uncontrollably as much from emotion as cold, Boxhall told Rostron that *Titanic* had sunk at 2.20 am.

One by one the lifeboats drew close to *Carpathia*'s towering sides. Many women were hauled up in slings and bosun's chairs, children in canvas ash bags. The men, crew and passengers alike, climbed slowly up the ladders and nets slung over the side. As they reached deck they were taken below where warmth and nourishment awaited them.

Ruth Becker Blanchard remembered the moment of rescue:

> 'From the time we knew the *Titanic* had struck the iceberg until the *Carpathia* came to rescue us, I was not afraid. Every minute was exciting to me. I didn't think for a moment that we wouldn't be saved. It was not until the *Titanic* went down with all those people on the decks – screaming and jumping into the water – that I realized the seriousness of it. My mother, brother and sister had been put into a lifeboat before I was, so I knew they had gotten off the ship.
>
> 'When we rowed up alongside the *Carpathia*, we discovered that we were so cold we could hardly move. Swings were lowered to take us up. I was the first one to be put in the swing and tied in because I was so numb I couldn't hold on. I was pulled up to the top and taken into the waiting room where the survivors were given brandy and hot coffee. Blankets were piled to the ceiling. I thawed out immediately without the brandy and coffee.
>
> 'I had promised the little German lady that I would help her find her baby. I wanted to find my mother, too. Moving around the ship from first to second class, to be sure we didn't miss any of the passengers as they came in, and looking over the deck railing, it seemed like hours had gone by while we watched the lifeboats come in.

'Around 10 o'clock I found my mother. A passenger came up to me and said, "Are you Ruth Becker?" I said "Yes." She said, "Your mother has been looking all over for you." So she took me to Mother and our family was reunited. The little German lady found her baby, too. I never saw anybody so happy in my life!

'The baby happened to be in my mother's boat. Mother said, "It was lucky the child wasn't thrown overboard because it looked like a bundle of clothes – but just in time it started to cry. When they found that the 'bundle' was a baby, everybody wanted to take care of it." The mother and her baby were meeting her husband in New York City.

'Of course, Mother and I were delighted to see each other. She was a nervous wreck, crying when anybody asked her about her experience. And no wonder! Having the responsibility of taking care of the two little children, and not being sure that I had gotten off the *Titanic*. The experience hadn't affected me emotionally at all, so I answered all questions.'

Carpathia's own passengers lined the decks; stewards had been unable to keep them inside. In the half-light of the approaching dawn, they stood mute and uninterfering as *Titanic*'s survivors clambered aboard. There was no sound except the shuffling of feet, an occasional muted sob, a soft word of guidance or support, the squeal of block and tackle as another chair or ash bag was hauled up.

Collapsible C was picked up at 6.15 am. At 7 am boat 14 with fifth officer Lowe in firm command and towing collapsible D was alongside. During the night he had transferred twelve

Lifeboat 14, commanded by fifth officer Harold G. Lowe, approached Carpathia's *side with collapsible D in tow.* (Mr and Mrs George Fenwick)

Collapsible D approached Carpathia's *gangway doors.* (US National Archives)

men and one women (Rhoda Abbott) from half-swamped collapsible A to collapsible D. Having three bodies aboard, Lowe opened boat A's seacocks before setting it adrift.

The breeze Ruth Becker had noticed caused Lightoller difficulty in keeping his overturned boat, collapsible B, afloat and on an even keel. Moving at his command, the two dozen aboard leaned together, first right then left, to keep the balance. The boat was sinking low in the water and Lightoller was afraid that they would not be seen. He repeatedly blew his seaman's whistle to attract attention. Finally *Carpathia* turned towards them, moving slowly now that the wind had begun to influence her own motion. By 8.30 the small boat was alongside and all were taken aboard quickly, including the body of one who had died during the night. Lightoller himself was the last up the ladder, the final *Titanic* survivor to board *Carpathia*.

Four hours earlier, at 4.30 am, Captain Stanley Lord was awakened by chief officer George F. Stewart, then *Californian*'s officer of the watch. Going on deck, Lord saw with the morning's first light some clear water to the west, and at 5.15 he ordered the engines on standby. About this time the chief officer pointed out a four-masted steamer with a yellow funnel, bearing south-south-east from *Californian*. He expressed concern that the ship might be in distress, perhaps with a broken rudder, and said the second officer had told him the ship appeared to have fired several rockets during the early watch.

The captain had the telegraphist roused and ordered him to find out the vessel's name and whether she required assistance. Evans turned on his set and sent a 'CQ' – 'All stations, someone answer'. He was astonished to receive a response almost instantly from the German

Lifejackets lay abandoned in the lifeboat as survivors prepared to board Carpathia. (Mr and Mrs Arthur Dodge)

Photographed from Carpathia's *deck by Mrs James Fenwick, one of her own passengers, the twin-peaked berg is described by surviving* Titanic *passengers and crew as the one with which their vessel collided.* (Mr and Mrs George Fenwick)

steamer *Frankfurt*, which advised him that during the night *Titanic* had sunk at 41.46N, 50.14W, a position Evans immediately took to Captain Lord on the bridge. Lord quickly worked out the location to be S 16 W, about 19½ miles from *Californian*'s estimated position. He immediately ordered *Californian* under way with the entire crew alerted. Thus, for the first time in seven hours, the *Californian*'s engines throbbed to life.

Following zigzag courses between south and south-west, *Californian* pushed through the ice at no more than six knots. Reaching open water at about 6.30, the ship proceeded at full speed – 70 revolutions, or about 13½ knots – southwards, down the icefield's western edge.

Around 7.30 *Mount Temple* was passed, stopped in the wirelessed position of the sinking. There was no sign of wreckage in this location. *Californian* continued south, soon passing a pink-funnelled, two-masted ship heading north – *Almerian*, a vessel lacking wireless. Soon *Californian* sighted *Carpathia* on the ice field's eastern side, abeam and to the south-south-east, and confirmed by wireless that she was picking up survivors. Lord altered course and sped through the ice, stopping alongside *Carpathia* around 8.30 am, their position approximately 41°33' N, 50°01' W.

After circling the area to ensure that there were no more survivors, Captain Rostron ordered *Carpathia* under way, leaving *Californian* to search for any further survivors clinging to rafts or wreckage.

At about 8.30 am Californian *arrived at the spot where* Carpathia *was taking on the last* Titanic *survivors. It had taken the Leyland liner two full hours to avoid the huge ice-field separating her from the disaster site. This dramatic photograph was taken from* Carpathia's *deck by one of her passengers, Mabel Fenwick.* (Mr and Mrs George Fenwick)

Aboard Carpathia *as she sped toward New York,* Titanic's *survivors rested and recuperated from their dreadful ordeal.* (Harper's)

Ruth Becker Blanchard recalls,

> 'When all the lifeboats were in and there was no hope of picking up any more persons, the *Carpathia* got ready to start for New York City at Monday, noon. That was the saddest time of all. That was the time when so many of the women who had been put into lifeboats by their husbands – and told they would meet each other later – realized that they would never see each other again. The women had been watching the lifeboats as they came in, looking for their husbands. They never saw them, they had gone down with the ship. We were so lucky because if my father had been along, he would have gone down with the ship, too.
>
> 'So, we started for New York City, going very slowly because we were still among the ice bergs … The *Californian* came up alongside of the *Carpathia* and offered to take on survivors, but Captain Rostron refused.'

Rostron also arranged for a service of remembrance and thanksgiving to be held in the first class lounge. Following the service he ordered a count of surviving crew and passengers. *Carpathia*'s chief purser Ernest G.F. Brown, RNR and second purser Percy B. Barnett, prepared and checked the list of surviving passengers. *Titanic*'s second officer Lightoller prepared the deck and engine departments' survivor lists, while chief second class steward John Hardy assembled the victualling department list.

A check of the figures brought a chill of reality: of *Titanic*'s 2,225 crew and passengers, there were 705 living survivors aboard *Carpathia*, according to Rostron's handwritten account published later. (Recent research indicates the total number saved to have been 713.)

It was as *Carpathia* left the disaster site that Rostron decided to return to New York. There was insufficient space to transport so many unexpected passengers. Nor were the galley's supplies adequate. The return journey began slowly – it took four full hours to skirt the immense ice pack.

By now survivors' lists were complete. After re-checking them carefully Rostron had them taken to the wireless shack. Telegraphist Harold Cottam had not slept for almost 30 hours. Besieged with requests for information, his temper and his ability to function were beginning to wear thin. To the operator of the Russian steamer *Birma*, in sight, close enough to receive some of the lists via small boat for wireless transmission to shore, Cottam inquired abruptly if *Birma* were a 'Marconi boat', that is, did it use Marconi apparatus? Receiving a negative response (*Birma* had a DeForrest installation), Cottam sputtered, 'Then shut up and stop jamming my signal.'

Competition was very keen among the 15 or more wireless companies in 1912. Operators were instructed not to handle or relay messages involving other companies' traffic. Even now, close to total exhaustion, Cottam would not break the Marconi Company's strict rule.

To maintain communication between *Carpathia* and the outside world, Captain Rostron prevailed upon Harold Bride to join Cottam in the wireless room. Bride had to be carried from the dispensary, where he had been receiving treatment for severely frost-bitten feet. Cottam

Crowds filled lower Broadway seeking news of the disaster at White Star's New York offices. (Washington Evening Star)

In Titanic's *home port, hundreds crowded into Canute Road, the site of White Star's Southampton office, seeking word of her crew's fate.* (Southern Newspapers plc)

snatched a few hours' sleep while Bride continued transmitting. Both Cottam and Bride ignored all information requests from private and public sources. Even a personal request from American President William Howard Taft regarding his close friend Major Archibald Butt went unanswered.

One of the few land stations with apparatus powerful enough to receive *Carpathia*'s signals was on top of Wanamaker's Department Store in New York. Here for many exhausting hours its 21-year-old operator David Sarnoff sat crouched over his receiver, jotting down the names as he received them from the rescue ship and releasing them to the New York press for the world to read.

Interference from amateur and professional stations was so severe that the spellings of many names as received by Sarnoff did not resemble those of *Titanic*'s people. Only after a hasty and impassioned plea to President Taft himself were all wireless stations ordered to cease transmissions and 'give way' to traffic between MPA (*Carpathia*) and MHI (Wanamaker's). Even an attempt by John Jacob Astor's family to use the family yacht *Noma*'s wireless, MJS, in a private inquiry was rebuffed.

Finally a stronger link was established. At President Taft's order, the US Navy scout cruiser *Chester* was dispatched from Nantucket, Massachusetts, to accompany *Carpathia* and to use

An anxious crowd jammed the pavement outside Oceanic House, White Star's London office. (Authors' collection)

Collection boxes for the Lord Mayor's Titanic *Relief Fund were strategically placed throughout London.* (Daily Graphic)

Above, E. H. Rothrock of the Chronicle, and below, Charles Aleck, who murdered him causelessly. As a "joke" fellow workmen of Aleck, who could not read, showed him the glaring headlines of the Titanic disaster and told him he was the subject. So Aleck came to Spokane from a logging camp and killed the editor.

Titanic's loss resulted in a murder. Charles Aleck (bottom), an illiterate logger in the state of Washington, was shown the Spokane Chronicle's *screaming* Titanic *headlines, and told they pertained to him. Enraged, Aleck went to Spokane and killed the newspaper's editor, E.H. Rothrock (above).* (Portland *[Oregon]* Journal)

The rescue ship Carpathia *off-loaded 13 of* Titanic's *lifeboats upon her arrival at New York on the night of 18 April.* (Harper's)

Crowds awaited the appearance of Titanic's *survivors at Pier 54's entrance.* (Illustrated London News)

its more powerful transmitter to augment *Carpathia*'s weaker signals. (Bride later complained about the *Chester* operator's competence.) But by 17 April, as *Carpathia* neared New York, most survivors' names were known.

Carpathia's voyage to New York had not been particularly pleasant, with severe thunderstorms and a dense fog putting everyone's nerves on edge. But the warm reception survivors received from *Carpathia*'s passengers and crew certainly helped. Said Ruth Blanchard,

> 'The *Carpathia* was on its way to Europe when it picked up our distress call and came to our rescue, so it was [partly] full of its own passengers. Therefore the 705 extra survivors had no place to sit except in the dining saloons and [on] the decks. The children sat on the floor. I remember we children ate sugar lumps off the dining room table. At night our family slept in the officers' quarters, which were in the bottom of the ship. I didn't like that at all. It scared me to be way down there.
>
> 'There was really nothing to do. Everybody just sat around talking, telling about their experience, and crying.
>
> 'The *Carpathia* passengers were wonderful. They couldn't do enough for us. One lady gave Mother a dress. We wore our coats over our night clothes.'

All that remained of the world's largest liner were the 13 lifeboats moored at Pier 59. Pillaged by souvenir hunters, the boats are thought to have rotted away later at a Brooklyn, New York, boatyard. (Authors' collection and New York World)

At New York elaborate preparations were made to receive survivors and expedite their arrival with minimal red tape. Even sacrosanct United States customs regulations were suspended. To spare survivors from a crush of reporters and well-intentioned curious, the public was barred from *Carpathia*'s pier and from two adjacent blocks.

While apparently the idea met with government approval, the Cunard Company forbade *Carpathia*'s boarding by reporters and families while she neared New York. Thus, as *Carpathia* reached the lower reaches of New York Harbor on the evening of 18 April, she was surrounded by a flotilla of yachts and small boats. Each bore shouting newspaper reporters who held up large cardboard banners asking questions (or making offers to pay for 'exclusives'). Frequent explosions of magnesium flares for photograph-taking added to the confusion.

Carpathia soon outdistanced these boats, but as she slowed near Quarantine to take aboard the port doctor, several reporters who had bribed their way aboard the tender *Governor Flower* tried to clamber aboard, and had to be manhandled away by *Carpathia*'s third officer Rees.

As *Carpathia* continued up the harbour, she was buffeted by strong winds and heavy rains. Angry lightning flashes illuminated the eerie scene as she quickly passed the Battery at Manhattan's southern tip, where more than 10,000 had gathered to observe her arrival. Around 8.30 pm she approached her pier, number 54, at the foot of West 14th Street. But she wheeled to port, then made a starboard circle in the Hudson River, finally coming to a stop near White Star piers 59 and 60, at the foot of West 19th and West 20th Streets. Here *Titanic*'s lifeboats were lowered from *Carpathia*'s davits and decks. The Merritt and Chapman wrecking lighter *Champion* stood by as seven were placed in the water and four were lowered to her deck. (Two boats remained overnight aboard *Carpathia*.) Then as *Champion* towed the boats to the bulkhead between piers 58 and 59, their attendant crews tied them up in the water.

Carpathia slowly retraced the last few hundred feet to her own pier where she tied up at 9.30 pm.

Welcomed by tears and hugs of joy the survivors stepped wearily down the gangway and headed towards the street. Many departed for hotels, some to their own homes, and more than 40 by ambulance to city hospitals for treatment of various minor complaints.

The 174 third class survivors disembarked around 11 pm, long after the others had departed. Many had lost all in the disaster and were destitute. White Star provided temporary aid, with assistance from numerous municipal and private relief agencies.

In contrast, several first class survivors departed from New York aboard private trains. Mrs Charles M. Hays, widow of the Grand Trunk Railroad's president, boarded a special train at Grand Central Station, while the Thayers and Mrs George Widener each had private trains awaiting at Jersey City, New Jersey, for transport to their Philadelphia homes. The line separating rich and poor, which had become non-existent during the hours of tragedy and the tumultuous days which followed, again was drawn.

Unemployed and unpaid since Titanic's *loss, the crew gathered on the steps of the Institute of the Seaman's Friend in New York, where they attended a memorial service and received a distribution of clothing and tobacco.* (Authors' collection)

Twelve-year-old Ruth Becker, her mother, brother and sister were well cared for:

'Finally, Thursday night, three days after the *Carpathia* rescued us, we landed in New York Harbor in the pouring rain. Good friends met us there and took us to a hotel. The next day Mother went shopping with friends and bought us clothes to wear. Luckily she had saved some money which she had pinned on her clothing.

'The hotel made us honorary guests and would take nothing for food and lodging. Everybody was wonderful to us!

'When we boarded the train to go to Indiana, Mother took me aside and said, "Ruth, don't you dare tell anybody that we are survivors of the *Titanic* disaster." Mother was so inundated with reporters bothering her, and they made her very nervous. And, too, she was afraid the passengers on the train would question her. I assured her I wouldn't tell a soul. But, when we got on the train, we were showered with candy and cookies and gifts for my little brother and sister from the passengers. So our trip to Indiana was a pleasant one. We were glad to be on dry land again!'

In May 1912, Denver socialite Margaret Tobin ('Molly') Brown presented a silver loving cup from the grateful Titanic *survivors to* Carpathia's *Captain Arthur Rostron.* (Library of Congress)

Conditions for some had begun to return to normal. For others, things would never again be the same. Events had already begun to alter many lives, and indeed would leave their mark on an era. From this time and for ever, the name of *Titanic* never would be forgotten.

Yet there had been a time when the name *Titanic* was unknown, a time when the men who designed and built her and the yard in which she was launched did not exist. But destiny's relentless, unalterable flow brought time, place and men together, and what had been unknown became a dream, and the dream became a reality…

CHAPTER THREE

A Burst of Cheering

The shipbuilding firm of Harland and Wolff is situated at Queen's Island in Belfast, Northern Ireland, on the River Lagan. Its origins can be traced to 21 September 1858 when Edward James Harland purchased the yard for £5,000 from his employer, Robert Hickson. On 11 April 1861, Harland took on as his full partner Gustav Wolff, nephew of G.C. Schwabe whose financial assistance had permitted Harland to purchase the company. New Year's Day 1862 saw the establishment of the company's name, Harland and Wolff, under which it has continued ever since.

Joining the firm in 1862 as a 15-year-old apprentice draughtsman, William James Pirrie soon became head designer and in 1874 was admitted to the partnership. With Sir Edward Harland's death in 1896 and Gustav Wolff's retirement in 1906, Pirrie became the company's controlling chairman.

Under Pirrie's planning and direction the yard underwent modernisation during 1906–8. Two enlarged building slips, numbers two and three, were constructed in an area previously occupied by three slips. An immense gantry, designed by the shipyard and constructed by Sir William Arrol and Company Ltd, Glasgow, was erected over the two new slipways and covered an area of 840 by 240 feet.

The construction of the two new slips followed an agreement between Pirrie and Joseph Bruce Ismay, chairman of the Oceanic Steam Navigation Company Ltd which owned and operated the ships of Britain's great White Star Line.

Since construction of the first *Oceanic* in 1870 Harland and Wolff had built ships for White Star. The freighters and great liners all bore the stamp and the integrity of builder and owner, and helped immeasurably to make the name White Star respected throughout the shipping world.

Before his death in 1899, White Star's founder and president Thomas Ismay had planned four large liners, to be constructed and operated for comfort rather than speed. His successor and eldest son Joseph Bruce Ismay carried on his illustrious father's traditions. With the successive appearances of *Celtic* (1901), *Cedric* (1903), *Baltic* (1904) and *Adriatic* (1907) the White Star Line appeared to own the most modem and luxurious fleet of North Atlantic liners.

The 20,904-ton *Celtic,* almost 681 feet long, was the first vessel to exceed the size of the

Joseph Bruce Ismay (1862–1937). (The Shipbuilder)

William James Pirrie (1847–1924). (The Shipbuilder)

Alexander Montgomery Carlisle (1854–1926). (Illustrated London News)

Great Eastern (1860). But within a mere six years *Celtic* herself was surpassed by all three of her own sisters, culminating in the 709-foot long, 25,541-ton *Adriatic*.

Even these liners, the 'Big Four', were dwarfed by the 1907 appearance of the great new Cunard Line ships *Lusitania* and *Mauretania*. Constructed in response to five large German vessels built between 1897 and 1907, and heavily subsidised by the British government, the 790-foot *Lusitania* and *Mauretania* featured innovative propulsion, the steam turbine, which proved immediately and immensely successful.

The White Star Line's management immediately saw the advantages of the steam turbine's power and economy. In 1909 the company completed two liners, *Megantic* and *Laurentic*, identical except for their engines: *Megantic* was fitted with conventional piston-based reciprocating engines while *Laurentic* had a combination of reciprocating and turbine engines. *Laurentic* proved to be far more economical to operate, so White Star managers decided to adopt combination engines for the much larger ships then being planned.

With completion of Cunard's *Lusitania* and *Mauretania*, White Star had an urgent need to match the level of service and facilities provided by its British rival.

In late 1907, during an after-dinner conversation with J. Bruce Ismay, Lord Pirrie proposed the concept of three huge liners – two to be built first, followed by a third. The vessels, each 50% larger than the Cunarders, were to be in keeping with White Star tradition of 'comfort rather than speed', emphasising great elegance within while providing safety for passengers and economy of operation.

The names of the three sister ships later were chosen to be *Olympic, Titanic* and *Gigantic*. Both the shipyard and White Star positively, even vehemently would deny the selection of *Gigantic* as the third ship's name. No official or written source for the name can be found. Yet, in newspaper reports before and after *Titanic*'s loss, the name appears again and again in such prestigious publications as the *New York Times* and *Lloyd's List and Shipping Gazette*.

Nor was this the first time the name *Gigantic* had been selected for a White Star Line ship. The following news story, reproduced here in its entirety, appeared in the *New York Times* dated 17 September 1892:

> 'London, Sept. 16 – The White Star Company has commissioned the great Belfast shipbuilders Harland and Wolff to build an Atlantic steamer that will beat the record in size and speed.
>
> 'She has already been named *Gigantic*, and will be 700 feet long, 65 feet 7½ inches beam and 4,500 horsepower. It is calculated that she will steam 22 knots an hour, with a maximum speed of 27 knots. She will have three screws, two fitted like *Majestic*'s, and the third in the centre. She is to be ready for sea in March, 1894.'

This vessel was never built.

Following the disaster to *Titanic*, the third vessel's name was quickly and officially changed to *Britannic*, a name always regarded as 'lucky' for the White Star Line. She was the second of their liners to be so named.

Plans for the three giant new vessels were drawn up by a team of designers. Prominent among these was Alexander Carlisle, Lord Pirrie's brother-in-law, who was responsible for the ships' internal arrangements, their decorations and their life-saving appliances.

The basic design was presented to White Star management during a special trip which J. Bruce Ismay made to Belfast on 29 July 1908. He approved the design, and a letter of agreement was signed on 31 July. (These 'letters of agreement', one for each ship, were the only contract, *per se*, ever signed between White Star and Harland and Wolff. It was each company's understanding that all White Star vessels were to be built on a cost-plus basis with only the finest materials and workmanship used. All bills from the shipyard were paid promptly and without question upon presentation.)

Plans for Titanic *and her sister-ship* Olympic *were completed in the draughting room at Harland and Wolff's Queen's Island yard in Belfast, Ireland.* (Harland and Wolff Ltd)

During the summer and autumn of 1908, working plans were completed, special supplies and equipment were ordered. The keel for Harland and Wolff's 400th commission – yard number 400, *Olympic* – was laid in slipway number two on 16 December 1908.

Now, Lord Pirrie's foresight in developing the shipyard, in constructing the special slipways, in building the huge gantry became evident. Just a bit more than three months later, on adjacent slip number three, the keel for yard number 401 – *Titanic* – was laid on 31 March 1909.

Perhaps about this time a persistent folk legend began, perhaps in Belfast. *Titanic*, on Harland and Wolff's books officially as yard number 401, allegedly had also been assigned a hull number of 3 9 0 9 0 4, supposedly engraved or painted on a keel plate. The number, if hastily written and then read as a mirror image, spelled what to some were the ominous, even insulting words, 'N O P O P E.' The legend continued that the hundreds of pious, working-class Catholic shipyard workers were deeply indignant until assured by management that the choice of number was strictly a coincidence. But lingering doubts about the ship's future were, according to the legend, fully validated by *Titanic*'s tragic fate. While the legend persists, the reality is prosaic: Harland and Wolff did not issue hull numbers to its vessels.

Work on the twin giants proceeded rapidly, so rapidly that a rumour began to spread among yard workers. It is likely that it began at the end of a work day when, with all else quiet throughout the yard, an inspector was inside the hull checking a riveting crew's output for the day, tapping with his hammer to test the soundness of the rivets.

And perhaps a worker, leaving the yard late, perhaps resentful at having been driven too hard that day by an ambitious foreman, experienced a flash of superstitious insight and imagined he was hearing the attempts of a worker trapped inside the hull to attract attention, to get out of his prison …

And so the rumour began that workers were trapped into the hull because of the speed with which they were being impelled. This, too, some thought, doomed the ship.

October, 1910: Olympic *(right) neared completion while work on* Titanic *(left) continued.* (Engineering)

Titanic *is seen under the great Arrol Gantry just prior to launch.* (Harland and Wolff Ltd)

Titanic's construction safety record was about average, essentially matching the 'one for every £100,000' spent, which was the rule of thumb in shipyards of the period. Eight fatalities from keel laying to launch can be confirmed.

As the twin hulls grew, so did the public's interest. The *Olympic*'s launch on 20 October 1910 was described in great detail in all the scientific and shipping journals, just as it was in the popular press. While the fitting out of *Olympic* proceeded, work on *Titanic*'s great hull continued. Through the winter and spring of 1911 most purveyors of shipbuilding supplies and equipment included in their advertisements, 'As supplied to the great new liners *Olympic* and *Titanic*'. As the date for *Titanic*'s launch drew near even manufacturers of consumer goods such as soap and beer exploited either the new vessel's name or the fact that their product was used aboard.

Spectators entered the shipyard to witness Titanic*'s launch on 31 May 1911.* (Illustrated London News)

The launch day – 31 May 1911 – was clear and mild. From early morning onwards yard workers and their families, visitors and distinguished guests began to fill the shipyard. Stands for special guests and the press had been built near the spot where the immense bows towered towards the blue sky. Earlier in the morning the specially chartered

Leaving a remarkably small wake for so large a mass . . . (Harland and Wolff Ltd)

boat *Duke of Argyll* had brought from Fleetwood, Lancashire, to Belfast a party of reporters and important guests, including John Pierpont Morgan, the American financier whose International Mercantile Marine controlled the White Star Line.

Titanic *entered the water shortly after 12.15 pm.* (Belfast Telegraph)

As the hour for launching approached every seat in the stands was filled, as were all vantage points near the yard and up and down the River Lagan. It was later estimated that more than 100,000 people were present to view the event.

Shortly before noon a red rocket was fired from the yard to indicate that launch was imminent. On top of the front of the gantry the American flag flew on one side, the British Union Jack on the other. At the centre fluttered a large red company pennant with its five-pointed white star. A row of signal flags below spelled out the word SUCCESS. From the hull's stern flew the red launch flag.

All was ready. At 12.13 pm a second rocket shot into the air. The roar of the crowd stilled to an expectant murmur. Pirrie gave a quiet order to the launch foreman. There was no ceremony, no formal naming of the vessel. (The absence of a christening, some later said, was another reason for the vessel's demise. In reality, it was merely a continuance of standard White Star Line policy. *None* of their ships was christened.)

The knocking loose of the last timber supports was followed by a general shout of 'There she goes!' A burst of cheering rent the air as *Titanic*, her passage eased by 22 tons of soap and tallow spread to a one-inch thickness on the ways, slid gently into the water. Reaching a speed of 12 knots, the hull was gently stopped in about its own length and held in place by special anchors embedded in the river bottom and connected by seven-inch steel wire hawsers to eye-plates riveted to the hull's plating.

Having viewed the floating hull – the largest movable object yet built – for some time, the crowds strolled back into Belfast's streets. The hull itself, after being detached from the restraining anchors, was towed to its berth by five Liverpool tugs.

Lord and Lady Pirrie entertained a group of distinguished guests at the Queen's Island yard. Luncheon was served and congratulations were extended on all sides. The press and other favoured guests were served luncheon at Belfast's Grand Central Hotel, after which they were addressed by Harland and Wolff and White Star representatives.

At about 4.30 that afternoon, *Olympic* departed from Belfast, accompanied out of the Lough by the company's new Cherbourg tenders *Nomadic* and *Traffic*. At the mouth of the Lough, the tenders turned south for a direct voyage to the French port. *Olympic*, carrying among others J.P. Morgan and J. Bruce Ismay, headed across the Irish Sea to Liverpool, her

Shipyard workers grappled for the ends of the drag chains used to slow and stop Titanic *after her launch.* (Cork Examiner)

port of registry and White Star's headquarters city, where, at Ismay's express wish, she was to be opened for two days of visits by local citizens.

From all parts of the British Isles came supplies and equipment for *Titanic*: tools, steel for plating and rivets, plumbing supplies, generators and electrical fixtures; wood for decking and panelling; caulking and cement and rivers of paint. Arriving by ship, train and truck, the thousands of components converged at the Belfast shipyards of Harland and Wolff.

Irish workers fabricated these varied materials into the great ship's developing form. Though her owner was American and her nominal owner English, *Titanic* was an Irish ship, built with the care, skill and integrity of Irish workers and craftsmen, built (as history would demand) to endure, in form, the cruellest indignity a ship can suffer.

But this was in the unforeseeable, unpredictable future.

Through the summer and autumn of 1911, as *Titanic*'s fitting out proceeded, the graceful though massive hull took on the trim look of a great liner. Deckhouses and superstructure were completed, individual cabins' bulkheads were installed, swimming pool tiles were laid, air ducts and electrical cables were threaded through the complex structure.

On 18 September 1911 the date for *Titanic*'s maiden voyage was announced through the publication of the company's 1911/12 winter sailing list: her debut was scheduled for 20 March 1912. But two days later an unforeseen event forced White Star to change this date and, in so doing, they altered the course of history.

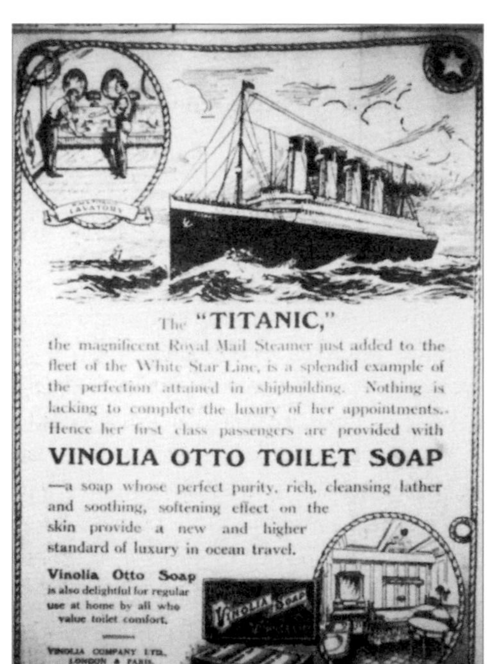

Great public interest was generated by the new liner, as evidenced by newspaper advertisements. (Belfast Telegraph)

On 20 September 1911, while departing from Southampton on her fifth voyage to New York, *Titanic*'s sister ship *Olympic* was rammed by the Royal Navy cruiser HMS *Hawke*. The collision apparently resulted from a misunderstanding of the two vessels' intended courses. But a then little-known element also played a role in the accident, an element which – almost seven months later – would have a similar, nearly tragic bearing on *Titanic*'s maiden voyage departure: the attraction which the hull of a vessel under way in confined waters can have for another vessel's hull.

Though damage to both vessels was fairly severe there were no injuries to passengers or crew. *Olympic* was laid up for two weeks at Southampton while temporary patches – wood above the waterline, steel plates below – were installed to cover the large hole in

During a late February crossing from New York, Olympic *broke a propeller blade. Between 1 and 7 March she returned to Harland and Wolff for repair while completion of* Titanic *proceeded.* (Merseyside Maritime Museum)

her starboard hull aft. Departing from Southampton on the morning of 4 October, *Olympic* returned to Harland and Wolff, which had the only dry dock large enough to accommodate her for repairs. She arrived in Belfast two days later.

To make room for the damaged liner, *Titanic* was removed on 4 October from the Thompson Graving Dock and tied up at the Alexandra Wharf. *Olympic*'s dry docking on 6 October permitted an accurate estimate of the time needed for her repair. It was also decided that, as long as she was at the yard, it would be as good a time as any to make minor modifications to certain first class areas, based upon her 'in-service' performance.

Titanic's construction had to be slowed as workers were diverted to complete *Olympic*'s repairs. In several days it became apparent to the White Star management that *Titanic* couldn't be completed and adequately tested to meet the announced 20 March maiden voyage date. On 10 October the company released a new date: Wednesday 10 April 1912.

Her repairs completed, *Olympic* left Belfast and resumed service on 30 November. *Titanic* was returned almost immediately to the Thompson Graving Dock and fitting out continued with fully staffed work crews.

By the end of January, her funnels now in position, *Titanic* had assumed a nearly-finished form. In early March *Olympic* returned to Belfast for replacement of a propeller damaged on 24 February during an eastbound crossing. She was at the Harland and Wolff yard from 1–7 March. Photographs of the two sister ships show *Titanic* with lifeboats in place but the forward part of her promenade deck not yet enclosed. The alteration that would forever distinguish *Titanic* from her sister ship was completed at the very last moment.

The Titanic *left the shipyard and proceeded down the Victoria Channel on 2 April 1912.* (Private collection)

Monday 1 April was crisp and cool. But a brisk north-west wind swept across the region. It would complicate trials by making *Titanic* difficult to manage in the narrow confines of the River Lagan. Trials were postponed until the following day, and 'black gang' members received an extra five shillings pay for the delay.

Under tug escort she entered Belfast Lough for her speed and manoeuvring trials. (Harland and Wolff Ltd)

Tuesday 2 April was a fine, clear and calm day. In addition to the 78 stokers and trimmers, 41 officers and senior crewmen (engineers, cooks and stewards) were aboard. Bruce Ismay couldn't attend because of family obligations; the White Star Line was represented by Harold Sanderson, a senior member of the company's board of directors. Illness prevented Lord Pirrie from attending; Harland and Wolff was represented by Thomas Andrews, Pirrie's nephew, a managing director of the shipyard, and by Edward Wilding, a marine architect, as well as a nine-member 'guarantee group'.

Those who hadn't slept on the ship came aboard at a very early hour. By 6 am, with tugs fast, *Titanic* moved slowly away from her dock, out of the shipyard and into the Victoria Channel which led to the Belfast Lough.

Crowds of spectators lined the channel's landward side as *Titanic*, gleaming in the rising sun, swept majestically past, under control of the straining tugs: *Hornby* on the starboard bow line, *Herald* out in front on the forward line; *Herculaneum* and *Huskisson* on the starboard and port lines, respectively.

There was little sound except the excited approval of the spectators and the chug of the tugs' engines. *Titanic*'s own engines were not yet operating, although billows of black smoke from her funnels showed that the ship's firemen were busy getting up steam.

Through the Channel and into the Lough, *Titanic* glided slowly, silently into the open water, still propelled by the tugs. Several miles down the Lough, about two miles off the Irish

The sitting room of a C-deck parlour suite, similar to the accommodations occupied by Mr and Mrs John Jacob Astor and Mr and Mrs Isidor Straus. (Authors' collection)

The second class smoking room was found aft on B deck. (The Shipbuilder)

The third class dining room set new standards of comfort for those travelling in steerage. (The Shipbuilder)

The new liner's cabins reflected the owners' penchant for comfort. A de luxe cabin on B deck cost £300 ($1,500) for two passengers and their servant. (The Shipbuilder)

town of Carrickfergus, the procession came to a standstill. The tugs cast off and returned to Belfast harbour as *Titanic* stood alone, poised for the start of her trials.

The blue and white signal flag for the letter 'A' ('I am undergoing sea trials') was run up the halyard. On the bridge Captain Edward J. Smith issued a brief order. Fourth officer Joseph Boxhall grasped the handles of the engine room telegraph and thrust them forward. From the engine room far below the jangle of the repeater's bell sounded across the still water, breaking the early morning silence.

Titanic's engines had been turned by her builders and engineers on several occasions during fitting out. But they had never exerted any power, nor had they been used to move the vessel. Now, as steam was fed into the great triple-expansion engines and the centre turbine, *Titanic* moved for the first time under her own power. The smooth waters of the Lough parted before her as, slowly but steadily, the ship got under way, her wake an immense 'V' ever widening behind her.

Through the morning *Titanic* steamed through her trials: stopping, starting and stopping again; turning in various circles at various speeds; helm over, back, then over again in a serpentine course; several combinations of her three propellers involved in making speed and turning calculations . . .

The owners' and builders' engineers and representatives, the Board of Trade official and senior ship's officers all gathered for lunch in the first class dining room to compare notes and observations. First impressions were optimistic and enthusiastic. The ship was functioning well, even better than predicted.

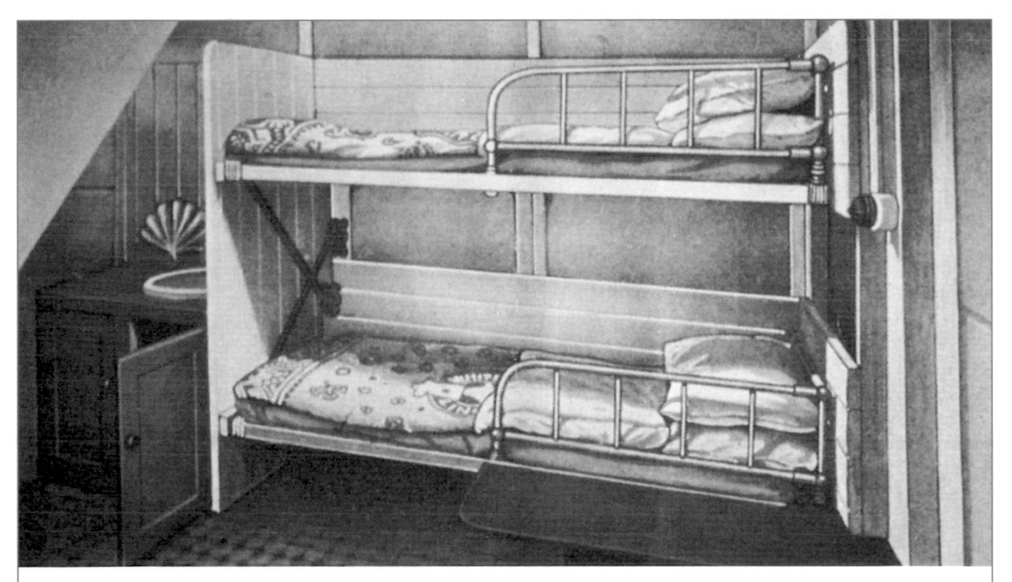

The decor of third class cabins was considerably less elaborate, although provision of two-berth cabins was unusual for the pre-war period. (Authors' collection)

After lunch the major stopping test was conducted, with the engines reversed while the ship travelled at high speed. At 20 knots, *Titanic* took a bit less than half-a-mile – about 850 yards – to come to a complete stop.

With crew and officers at their respective stations, *Titanic* headed for the mouth of the Lough and the open waters of the Irish Sea. Turning south, the vessel travelled a straight course for about two hours down, about 40 miles, and two hours back to the Lough's mouth, at an average 18-knot speed.

Entering the Lough *Titanic* sailed towards the setting sun and Belfast. Still some distance from the shipyard, she stopped at about 6 pm. One more test was conducted for the Board of Trade's representative, Mr Francis Carruthers: dropping and raising the port and starboard anchors. Satisfied that the new liner met all British government requirements, Carruthers signed *Titanic*'s passenger certificate, 'good for one year from today 2.4.12'.

With Board of Trade certification at hand *Titanic* was handed over by her builder, represented by Thomas Andrews, to her owner, represented by Harold Sanderson. Yard workers who were not to accompany the vessel to Southampton were lightered ashore. Brought out from shore and taken aboard were fresh food supplies, some last-minute galley equipment and several special chairs for the first class reception room.

A few minutes after 8 pm, lights ablaze, *Titanic* turned and passed into the night, departing from Belfast for the last time. Down the Lough, again into the Irish Sea, heading for Southampton where she was due on the midnight tide on 3/4 April. Crew watches were set. There was little sleep for the shipyard representatives, who moved throughout the ship, examining, testing and adjusting. During this passage, under actual sea conditions, she briefly reached 23¼ knots, the highest speed she would ever attain.

On through the night and into the morning *Titanic* shaped her course: the Irish Sea, St George's Channel, the Cornish coast. Late morning and early afternoon: around Land's End and into the English Channel. Later afternoon and early evening: approaching the Isle of Wight as darkness began to fall. Into Spithead, past the Nab Light Vessel; more slowly, now, into Southampton Water where the pilot came aboard.

It was nearly midnight, the time of high tide, when *Titanic* approached the White Star Dock. Here she was met by five Red Funnel Line tugs: *Ajax*, *Hector*, *Vulcan*, *Neptune* and *Hercules*. The tugs assisted the immense ship as, engines stopped, she entered the turning circle at the river end of the dock area and swung around to enter the dock stern-first. (Her 10 April departure would coincide with the noon low tide; a more convenient port turn from the dock would be permitted by the 'bow outward' position, to say nothing of a more handsome public presentation.)

After her 570-mile journey *Titanic* was warped into her mooring at Berth 44.

CHAPTER FOUR

From the Four Corners of the Compass

Preparations to receive and service the '*Olympic* class' of White Star liners had been completed on both sides of the Atlantic. The new tenders *Nomadic* and *Traffic* had been constructed at Harland and Wolff especially to serve the needs of *Olympic* and *Titanic* (and the forthcoming third sister ship) at the French port of Cherbourg.

At New York City, piers 60 and 61 of the Chelsea pier complex – between 14th and 23rd Streets along the Hudson River (or, as it was known locally, the North River) – had been extended and enlarged to accommodate the new vessels.

At Southampton, 78 miles south-west of London, the new White Star Dock had been

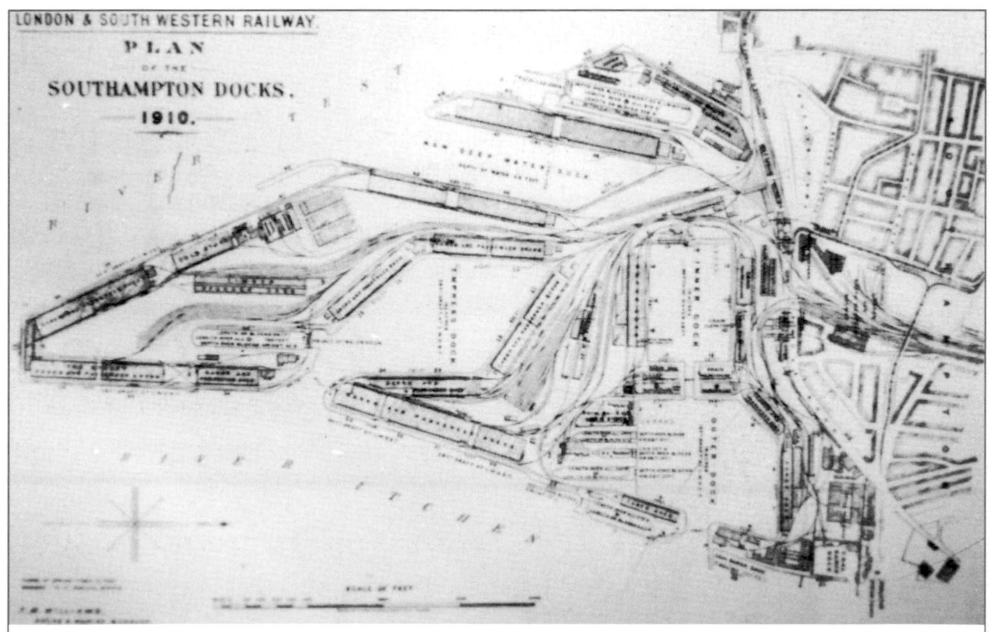

Southampton's new deep water mooring facility was named the White Star Dock in recognition of the company for whose ships it had been especially constructed. (Railway Magazine)

constructed for the weekly service the line planned to establish with its three sister liners. (*Oceanic* of 1899 was to be the service's third ship until completion of *Gigantic*, planned for 1915.)

Fresh from her sea trials, it was to Southampton that *Titanic* came for provisioning, staffing and the boarding of her first passengers, transforming her into the floating city of her owners' proud dream.

Provisions. Staff. Passengers. No matter how beautiful a liner's interior, no matter how trim her lines or how smart her appearance, she is not alive until she has passengers aboard, a staff to attend them and food from her kitchens to feed them. Just as equipment and pieces of her fabric came to Belfast from the four corners of the United Kingdom for the new ship's construction, supplies and foodstuffs for her larders now came to Southampton from the four corners of the compass ...

Titanic's 'shopping list' was as impressive as the ship herself.

Fresh meat	75,000 lb	Oranges	180 boxes (36,000)
Fresh fish	11,000 lb	Unions	50 boxes (16,000)
Salt and dried fish	4,000 lb	Hothouse grapes	1,000 lb
Bacon and ham	7,500 lb	Fresh milk	1,500 gals
Poultry and game	25,000 lb	Fresh cream	1,200 qts
Fresh eggs	40,000	Condensed milk	600 gals
Sausages	2,500 lb	Fresh butter	6,000 lb
Sweetbreads	1,000	Grapefruit	50 boxes
Ice cream	1,750 qts	Lettuce	7,000 heads
Coffee	2,200 lb	Tomatoes	2¾ tons
Tea	800 lb	Fresh asparagus	800 bundles
Rice, dried beans, etc,	10,000 lb	Fresh green peas	2,250 lb
Sugar	10,000 lb	Onions	3,500 lb
Flour	200 barrels	Potatoes	40 tons
Cereals	10,000 lb	Jams and marmalade	1,120 lb

Good Friday, 5 April 1912, was the only day upon which Titanic *was 'dressed' in her flags.* (Private collection)

The special rooms on *Titanic*'s orlop deck designed for storage of liquid refreshments were also fully stocked:

Beer and stout	20,000 bottles	Mineral waters	15,000 bottles
Wines	1,500 bottles	Spirits	850 bottles

Taken aboard at Southampton between 4 April and sailing day on 10 April were great quantities of glassware, cutlery and tableware:

Breakfast cups	4,500	Salt shakers	2,000
Tea cups	3,000	Salad bowls	500
Coffee cups	1,500	Pudding dishes	1,200
Beef tea cups	3,000	Sugar basins	400
Cream jugs	1,000	Fruit dishes	400
Breakfast plates	2,500	Finger bowls	1,000
Dessert plates	2,000	Butter dishes	400
Soup plates	4,500	Vegetable dishes	400
Pie dishes	1,200	Entrée dishes	400
Beef tea dishes	3,000	Meat dishes	400
Cut tumblers	8,000	Dinner forks	8,000
Water bottles	2,500	Fruit forks	1,500
Crystal dishes	1,500	Fish forks	1,500
Celery glasses	300	Oyster forks	1,000
Flower vases	500	Butter knives	400
Ice cream plates	5,500	Sugar tongs	400
Dinner plates	12,000	Fruit knives	1,500
Coffee pots	1,200	Fish knives	1,500
Tea pots	1,200	Table and dessert knives	8,000
Breakfast saucers	4,500	Nut crackers	300
Tea saucers	3,000	Toast racks	400
Coffee saucers	1,500	Dinner spoons	5,000
Soufflé dishes	1,500	Dessert spoons	3,000
Wine glasses	2,000	Egg spoons	2,000
Champagne glasses	1,500	Tea spoons	6,000
Cocktail glasses	1,500	Salt spoons	1,500
Liquor glasses	1,200	Mustard spoons	1,500
Claret jugs	300	Grape scissors	100
Asparagus tongs	400		

The ship's linen stores were no less extensive:

Aprons	4,000	Double sheets	3,000
Blankets	7,500	Pillow-slips	15,000
Table cloths	6,000	Table napkins	45,000
Glass cloths	2,000	Bath towels	7,500
Cooks' cloths	3,500	Fine towels	25,000
Counterpanes	3,000	Lavatory towels	8,000
Bed covers	3,600	Roller towels	3,500
Eiderdown quilts	800	Pantry towels	6,500
Single sheets	15,000	Miscellaneous items	40,000

A national coal strike which had lasted six bitter weeks was settled on 6 April, not soon enough for coal to be sent from pithead to Southampton for *Titanic*'s voyage. Coal from five IMM ships in port, and coal left over from fuelling *Olympic* (which had departed from Southampton only hours before *Titanic*'s 3 April midnight arrival), was taken on board. Some 4,427 tons were added to the 1,880 tons already in the bunkers. (The week in port alone consumed 415 tons for steam to operate cargo winches and to provide heat and light throughout the vessel.)

The foremast's shadow fell across the ship's bridge while she was moored at Southampton. (Illustrated London News)

Heavy hawsers linked Titanic *to Southampton's Berth 44.* (Bob Forrest Collection)

A rare postcard shows the liner's stern and the Blue Ensign. (Bob Forrest Collection)

Titanic's officers had come aboard at Belfast before the sea trials, as had the engineering officers and many senior crew members, such as department chiefs. Also boarding at Belfast were the two Marconi wireless telegraphers, senior operator John Phillips and junior operator Harold Bride. During the trials and the voyage to Southampton they had been busy fine-tuning their powerful new radio equipment and transmitting and receiving many messages for the owners and builders. The wireless operators were actually employed by the Marconi Company, and not by White Star, yet they did sign the ship's articles, indicating that they were under Captain Smith's command.

The staff of the *à la carte* restaurant, a separate concession, were recruited from among employees of Luigi Gatti's two London restaurants, Gatti's Adelphi and Gatti's Strand. While far from being White Star employees, they also signed the ship's articles and received from White Star the nominal wage of one shilling for the voyage.

Titanic's eight bandsmen were not White Star employees, nor did they sign the ship's articles. Their employer was a Liverpool firm of musical directors, Messrs C.W. and F.N. Black, who supplied orchestras for the liners of several companies, including White Star. The musicians boarded at Southampton as second class passengers on ticket number 250654. Five bandsmen shared an unnumbered cabin adjacent to E106; the three restaurant musicians berthed in an interior cabin forward of the reciprocating engine room and inboard of E63.

As chief officer of *Olympic*, Henry T. Wilde was familiar with the structure and operation of the new class of vessels. To utilise his knowledge the company transferred him from *Olympic* to *Titanic* to serve only during her maiden voyage, since he was soon due for his own command. But his presence caused a realignment of *Titanic*'s senior officers: William. M. Murdoch, the previous chief, was moved to first officer; former 'first' Charles H. Lightoller became second officer, a place held previously by David Blair. The remaining officers – Herbert J. Pitman (third), Joseph G. Boxhall (fourth), Harold G. Lowe (fifth) and James P. Moody (sixth) – were unaffected.

(It may be imagined that Blair, known to his friends as 'Davy', departed from *Titanic* with considerable reluctance. There is no public record of his reaction following the ship's loss. His only public appearance during later White Star service is as navigator aboard *Oceanic* when, on 8 September 1914, she became a total loss through grounding off Foula Island in the Shetlands.)

A majority of the crew – seamen, stewards, stokers, trimmers, greasers and kitchen helps – were signed on during Saturday 6 April. The prolonged coal strike had caused great hardship among Southampton's working class. Now there was not only an employment opportunity, but it was one aboard the newest, largest White Star ship under the command of Edward J. Smith, well known and liked by the workers. Hiring halls were crowded and the several seamen's unions, only lately influential in the shipping world, were well represented among those employed.

Thought for many years to have signed aboard on this day was a greaser from Liverpool named Frank Tower. Subsequently nicknamed 'Lucky' or 'Lucks' Tower because of his alleged presence aboard *Empress of Ireland* and *Lusitania*, as well as *Titanic*, Tower's reputation (and that of his supporters) suffers a small blemish when one vainly searches for his name or any approximate spelling of it on *Titanic*'s official crew signing-on list.

(Two who did sign aboard on 6 April have associations almost beyond belief with all the *Olympic*-class vessels: both stewardess Violet Jessop and fireman John Priest were aboard *Olympic* in 1911 when she collided with the *Hawke*; each survived *Titanic*'s loss, and that of the third sister, *Britannic*, when that vessel was sunk in the Aegean Sea by enemy action in 1916. John Priest's remarkable saga continued with his survival of the war losses of *Alcantara* and *Donegal*. Forced to retire from work at sea because no one wished to sail with him, he died of pneumonia in 1935.)

A curious legend later related to the signing-on period. It was reported in the Liverpool *Daily Post* in May 1912, and then picked up by *The New York Times*. Among those signing ship's articles as a fireman on 6 April, the story went, was a man who produced the 'Certificate of Continuous Discharge' book bearing the name Thomas Hart, 51 College Street, Southampton. The man was placed on the eight-to-twelve watch and was lost in the sinking. Hart's aged, grieving mother, the account continued, was officially notified by the company that her son was dead. She saw his name posted on the list of lost outside the company's

Canute Road offices. But she received the shock of her life on 8 May when her son entered their Southampton home alive as ever. He sheepishly admitted, first to his mother and later to authorities, that he had lost his discharge book in a pub while drunk. He had wandered about in confusion since the disaster. But the newspapers had it wrong; no one named Thomas Hart was among *Titanic*'s crew; a hastily written 'J. Hart' on the sign-on list had been mistakenly read as 'T. Hart'. In reality it was Liverpudlian James Hart, 53, a temporary resident of Southampton, who had signed on as a fireman, producing his own discharge book to the authorities witnessing the sign-on process. He died aboard *Titanic*.

Supplies and cargo continued being taken aboard. Most crew had signed on. (A total of 909 in 'working capacities' were aboard when *Titanic* departed from Southampton; one was to desert at Queenstown.) By Wednesday 10 April, on schedule, *Titanic* stood ready to receive passengers.

It is well known that there were premonitions of disaster regarding *Titanic*: Morgan Robertson's prophetic 1898 novel *The Wreck of the Titan* is one of literature's most unbelievable coincidences. William T. Stead, a first class passenger on *Titanic*, had not only written of a liner sunk by ice, but in another story had told of passengers aboard a sinking vessel unable to be saved because there were insufficient lifeboats. An 1874 work by American poet Celia Thaxter likewise described the unalterable fate of a collision between a ship and an iceberg.

But no premonition or paranormal experience can match the truth, the number of passengers who, for various reasons, cancelled passage aboard the ill-fated liner: documentation exists for the cancellation of more than 55 bookings.

Henry Clay Frick, an American steel baron, booked a suite in February 1912 but cancelled it when Mrs Frick sprained her ankle during an excursion to Madeira. John Pierpont Morgan took over the booking but cancelled when his business interests lengthened his stay abroad. The same suite was then booked by another wealthy American, J. Horace Harding, who later cancelled and changed his passage to the *Mauretania*. (While no record exists of the suite in question, it was likely suite B52, the one occupied by J. Bruce Ismay during the voyage. It was, after all, available.)

With his wife and daughter, Robert Bacon, the American ambassador to France, had booked passage aboard *Titanic* from Cherbourg. Their sailing, however, was postponed due to the delay in the arrival of his successor, Myron T. Henrick. But the Bacon family did enjoy maiden voyage excitement, rescheduling their passage to the first trip of the *France* on 20 April.

Mr and Mrs George W. Vanderbilt had booked passage aboard *Titanic* but cancelled it at the request of Mr Vanderbilt's mother, Mrs Dressler, who had an aversion to all maiden voyages. ('So uncomfortable. So much can go wrong…'.) She had no actual premonition of disaster, but her reasoning was persuasive. Though their luggage had been sent aboard, the Vanderbilts cancelled their booking. Their servant, Frederick Wheeler (himself a second class passenger) stayed aboard to tend the luggage and was lost.

Most cancelled bookings were more prosaic. Mr and Mrs James V. O'Brien were delayed when a lawsuit they had begun in an Irish court took longer than expected. Several passengers didn't like their accommodation, while others couldn't obtain the accommodation they desired. The Reverend J. Stuart Holden, vicar of St Paul's, Portman Square, London, cancelled his passage on 9 April due to his wife's illness.

Indeed, there were premonitions: Mr and Mrs E.W. Bill of Philadelphia, staying at London's Hotel Cecil, were anxious to sail on *Titanic*. A day or two before sailing Mrs Bill had a dream in which the vessel was wrecked. They cancelled their passage and sailed on *Celtic* instead.

And so it went: for reasons of health, for business, for lack of suitable accommodation, upwards of 55 passengers altered their plans.

Even among those who did not cancel there were forebodings. Walter Harris, of Enfield, and Percy Thomas Oxenham, of Ponder's End, had booked for New York aboard *Philadelphia*. That sailing was cancelled due to the coal strike and the men transferred to *Titanic*. Before sailing, Harris visited some friends, among whom was a young lady who practised palmistry. After examining Harris' hand she declined to say what she had read, remarking only that she did not like it. Harris' little son suddenly asked, 'Is Daddy going to be drowned?' (Harris was lost, Oxenham saved.)

But 1,317 passengers did not cancel – passengers who became featured players in one of history's most dramatic disasters. Among them was eight-year-old Marshall Briles Drew, who recalled shortly before his passing in June 1986 the circumstances leading to his *Titanic* voyage:

> 'My Uncle Jim (James Vivian Drew) and Aunt Lulu and I went to Cornwall, England, in the fall of 1911. My father and his brothers were Cornish. We went to Cornwall to visit with Grandma Drew and other relatives. The oddity here is that we crossed on the *Olympic*, sister ship to the *Titanic*.
>
> 'As we were returning anyway, I assume my Uncle Jim decided on the *Titanic*'s maiden voyage, with all the hoopla!'

For Marshall, his aunt and uncle, and for the others on board, the hoopla was to turn to horror in five days.

CHAPTER FIVE

Park Lane and Scotland Road

Titanic's officers and senior crew had been aboard during the ship's entire stay at Southampton, standing regular watches and overseeing the loading of supplies, stowage of cargo and final preparations for sailing. The general crew – engine room men, stewards, seamen and the like – were not due aboard until sailing day. The official signing-on list bore the notation, 'Date and hour at which he [each crew member] is to be on board: 6 am 10.4.12.'

Sailing day, 10 April 1912. The sun rose over Southampton at 5.18 am to a generally fair morning with north-west to west winds, fresh and sometimes gusty. Daylight's first hour saw *Titanic*'s crew streaming from all parts of Southampton, converging upon the dockyard gate. Showing their discharge books there and passing through, they proceeded towards Berth 44, where *Titanic* lay sparkling in the rising sun, her black-capped buff funnels glowing in the early-morning light.

Again showing their books at the gangway, the crew hurried aboard and were directed to their quarters by petty officers and assistant department heads. Their bunks were found on four decks:

D deck	forward, at bow	108	firemen
E deck	forward, at bow	72	trimmers
	port side, a bit aft	44	seamen
	port side, further aft	62	second class stewards
		106	saloon waiters
		24	bedroom stewards, miscellaneous cooks and kitchen staff
	port side, just aft of amidships		entire *à la carte* restaurant staff
F deck	forward	53	firemen
	port side, amidships	42	third class stewards
	starboard, amidships		engineer officers
G deck	forward	15	leading firemen
		30	greasers

The balance of the crew, those who performed miscellaneous functions – printers, bell-boys, clothes pressers, Turkish bath and hospital attendants, masters-at-arms, lamp trimmers, post office workers – were scattered in many small enclaves throughout the ship, near the locations where they were to perform their duties. This was especially true of the first class stewards and stewardesses, whose tiny cabins holding two, three or four were wedged into odd corners among the wide corridors and spacious cabins of first class.

The crew were happy as they came aboard, laughing and calling to one another, shoving in a friendly way to be first along the deck, through corridors and into quarters. Many had not worked since the coal strike which had begun more than six weeks earlier. All were happy to be aboard a brand-new ship commanded by the well-known and paternal Captain E.J. Smith.

Also aboard at 6.30 am was Thomas Andrews of Harland and Wolff. During *Titanic*'s construction Andrews (Lord Pirrie's nephew) was a managing director and head of the draughting department. With the intimate knowledge of the ship he thus gained, and with Alexander Carlisle's 1911 departure, Andrews was aboard on this maiden voyage to represent the builders, to determine whether adjustments in the ship's structure or machinery were necessary, and to superintend the Harland and Wolff workers (the 'guarantee group') who would effect this work.

Andrews worked on board almost the entire time she lay at Southampton. His notes of suggestions for improvement filled many pages. These were not major adjustments; the ship certainly was soundly constructed and capable of fulfilling her function. Rather, Andrews' notes related to improvement of *details* whose modifications would set *Titanic* apart and create a new standard of excellence and luxury the entire world would envy.

Andrews occupied cabin A36, at the port side of the after first class entrance. This cabin had been installed almost as an afterthought. It did not appear on *Titanic*'s cabin plans dated as late as January 1912. The room was added during last-minute modifications which included the forward promenade deck's enclosure. Centrally located, it was an excellent spot from which Andrews might oversee 'his' ship.

Captain Edward John Smith, 'E.J.' as he was affectionately known among more than a generation of ocean travellers, came aboard *Titanic* on sailing day at about 7.30 am and prepared to meet and assist the various officials whose approval would permit the vessel to go to sea. E.J. had served his apprenticeship aboard the *Senator Weber*, an American-built sailing vessel owned by A. Gibson & Co of Liverpool. Joining the White Star Line in 1886 Smith served aboard the company's major vessels – freighters to Australia, liners to New York – and quickly assumed command. As the ships grew in size, so did the importance of Captain Smith's presence. He worked his way up through *Adriatic*, *Celtic* and *Coptic* (the latter for experience in the Australian route) and *Germanic*, among others. He was *Majestic*'s captain for nine years commencing in 1895, during which period he made two trooping voyages to South Africa during the Boer War. For this service he was awarded the Transport Medal. In addition he was an honorary commander of the Royal Naval Reserve and, as such, had been granted warrant number 690 allowing him to fly the Blue Ensign on any merchant vessels he commanded.

Captain Smith was regarded as a 'safe captain' and, for the period, he probably was. Certainly there had been incidents over Smith's long career – a grounding, a shipboard fire, a boiler explosion, an engine derangement, delays from dangerous storms – almost all beyond a master's control. But he had commanded *Olympic* when she had been damaged in collision with HMS *Hawke* in September 1911. Earlier, in June 1911, while manoeuvring *Olympic* into her New York pier, he had damaged a tugboat with the thrust from one of the liner's propellers. It seemed that Captain Smith – along with most contemporary liner captains – had much to learn about the displacement effects of so huge a hulk as the vessel he now commanded.

At age 62, Smith was close to retirement. Since *Baltic* of 1904 he had taken out the company's newest liners on their maiden voyages. After *Baltic* came *Adriatic* in 1907, then *Olympic* in 1911, and now *Titanic*. It was generally thought that he would retire from White Star service upon completion of *Titanic*'s first trip. But an article appearing on 19 April 1912 in the Halifax, Nova Scotia, *Morning Chronicle* quoted White Star officials as announcing that he would have charge of *Titanic* until the company completed the larger and finer steamer then under construction. There is no further evidence to support this statement. Yet, *Gigantic* was expected to be ready for her own first voyage by 1915. By the time he was 65 Smith would not have been the oldest captain commanding a transatlantic liner. Perhaps he might have been considering staying on, at least for three more years…

At 8 am the Blue Ensign was hoisted at the stern and the crew, under direction of petty officers, began to assemble on deck for muster. The ship's articles – the 'sign on list' – for each department was distributed to respective department heads. Captain Benjamin Steele, White Star's marine superintendent, supervised the muster as each man was scrutinised by one of the ship's doctors. A company representative further examined each department's final rosters, then handed them to Captain Steele who, in turn, took them to Captain Smith for examination and approval.

Not appearing on the muster lists were the names of several groups of workers – not company employees, yet surely not passengers: the five postal workers (three American, two British); the eight members of the ship's orchestra (travelling as, though not accorded the courtesies due to, second class passengers); the nine-member Harland and Wolff 'guarantee group' (Thomas Andrews would make a total of ten). Three of the group, including Andrews, were booked in first class, the remaining seven in second class… A total of 22 names were not on the 'crew list' but, nevertheless, were gainfully employed aboard ship.

While the crew was being mustered, the Board of Trade's final inspection was conducted by its Southampton representative, Captain Maurice Clarke. His major concern appeared to be the lifeboats. He examined them carefully and observed the manning, lowering and raising of two boats, numbers 11 and 15 on the starboard side, under the supervision of fifth officer Harold G. Lowe and sixth officer James P. Moody. Satisfied that the boats were in proper working order and their crews proficient, Clarke repaired to the bridge. There, with *Titanic*'s commander, he reviewed the ship's papers. He was handed the 'Report of Survey of an Immigrant Ship', the same sheet on which the Board's Belfast representative

Francis Carruthers had certified *Titanic* seaworthy for one year from 2 April 1912. Clarke signed the report twice, indicating that he had observed a satisfactory boat drill and that *Titanic* carried 5,892 tons of coal, sufficient to take her to her intended destination, New York.

The final formality came and went as Captain Smith handed to White Star's marine superintendent Steele the 'Master's Report to Company': 'I herewith report this ship loaded and ready for sea. The engines and boilers are in good order for the voyage, and all charts and sailing directions up-to-date. Your obedient servant, Edward J. Smith.'

There were handshakes all around, offers of congratulation and 'good voyage' as the two officials left the bridge.

They were replaced almost immediately by Thomas Andrews and the owner's proud managing director, Joseph Bruce Ismay. White Star's president had motored with his family to Southampton from London the day before; they had stayed overnight at the South Western Hotel, overlooking the docks. Mrs Ismay and the children were not going on the voyage, so it was with special interest that they examined the ship's luxurious interior as Mr Ismay conducted them on a personal tour.

Leaving the family in care of a ship's petty officer, Ismay and Andrews ascended the steep steps to the bridge where they, too, offered congratulations to the ship's commander. Neither Ismay nor Andrews would appear again on the bridge until almost exactly 96 hours later…

The boat train from London bearing second and third class passengers had left Waterloo Station at 7.30 am, arriving at the dockside shortly after 9.30 am. Passengers detrained and immediately boarded *Titanic* through the second class entrances, aft on C deck, and the pair of third class entrances, one further aft on C deck, the other at the forward bulkhead of the forward well deck.

Many of the 494 third class passengers embarking at Southampton were Scandinavians. The White Star Line advertised extensively throughout Norway and Sweden, and employed a large network of ticketing agents throughout the region. White Star competed with the Cunard Line for southern European immigrants, particularly on routes between Trieste and Genoa and Boston and New York. But in 1912, White Star ships from Liverpool and Southampton carried many Scandinavians to the United States, most of whom booked third class passage 'aboard the first available ship'. And today, 10 April 1912, the first available ship was *Titanic*.

Anderson and Andersson (Alfrida, Anders and five children, all lost); Berglund and Birkeland; Hagland and Hansen; Johnson and Johnsson; Alma Pålsson and her four children (mother and all children lost); Anna and William Skoog with four children (all six lost); Johan Svensson and Severin Svensson (Severin would survive and reach his destination in far-off South Dakota … altogether, 176 adults and 30 children.

Scandinavians did not have the monopoly on large families. Of approximately 140 British third class passengers, 19 were members of two families: Frederick and Augusta Goodwin and six children, including baby Sidney; and John and Annie Sage with their nine children. (All 19 were lost.)

Also on board were Frank and Emily Goldsmith, with their son Frank J., on their way to Detroit, Michigan; Leah Aks, booked through to Norfolk, Virginia, to join her husband; with Mrs Aks her ten-month-old son, Frank, better known as 'Filly'.

Third class cabins were located on D, E, F and G decks with entrances forward and aft. The only connection between forward and after sections was a wide corridor running almost the entire length of the ship on E deck's port side. Stewards' accommodation lined this corridor, called 'Park Lane' by the officers and 'Scotland Road' by the crew. There were no connecting fore-to-aft passageways for third class passengers on other decks.

Veitchi-covered stairways in third class entrances opened on to linoleum-tiled, steel-walled corridors. Third class cabins ranged from tiny two-berth rooms to six- and even eight-berth rooms. *Titanic* was not designed to carry large numbers of immigrants, and thus had just a single area of open berths, on F deck near number two hatch. Many liners of the period still maintained a number of these dormitory-like open spaces for immigrants' berths.

An arrangement not unique to White Star ships but incorporating dividers built to 'White Star design' was an area on G deck between numbers two and three hatches. This space was given over to portable rooms whose movable steel walls enclosed variable spaces according to the number of third class passengers on board. Except for these portable rooms, almost all third class staterooms were panelled in pine and had veitchi floor coverings, a far cry from the bare metal walls and floors of earlier (and some contemporary) liners.

Now, for the first time since the Harland and Wolff workers had departed, the third class areas were filled with people, the walls resounding to the bustle, joy and sorrow of departure. There was confusion, too, as passengers tried to locate their cabins and, even when correctly directed by harassed stewards, wandered aimlessly about.

The boarding of second class passengers was more sedate and better organised. Their cabins were centrally located aft on D, E and F decks; there were two almost adjacent entrances. One was equipped with an elevator that ran from G deck to the boat deck. Corridors' floors were covered in linoleum tiles, and the walls were wood-panelled.

Second class staterooms aboard *Titanic* rivalled first class accommodation aboard almost any other ship of the period. The well-lit two-, three- and four-berth cabins, many of them outside rooms open to the sea air, were panelled in white. Each room was tastefully fitted with mahogany furniture and comfortable upper and lower berths, with sofa beds providing the 'odd berth', as needed. Cabins had linoleum tile floors.

As passengers boarded and were directed to their cabins, second class corridors filled with people: eight-year-old Marshall Drew, travelling with his aunt and uncle, eagerly anticipating his second Atlantic crossing in less than a year. Young Marshall and his Uncle Jim were permitted to enter the first class areas while the ship was loading; after walking the upper decks they visited the gymnasium. Returning to their own quarters they stopped at the first class barber's shop, which doubled as the ship's souvenir and gift shop, where Uncle Jim bought Marshall a ribbon similar to those worn by sailors on their uniform caps: 'RMS *Titanic*', it proclaimed in gold threads.

Seven-year-old Eva Hart and her parents Benjamin and Esther were on their way to Winnipeg, Manitoba, where Mr Hart was to start a business. Eva and her father were seldom separated, and together they travelled all over the liner. Mrs Hart was uneasy about the sea voyage and very apprehensive of the 'unsinkable' label which had been given to the new liner by the press. Once in her cabin, she never left it except for meals, spending her time reading and knitting. During daylight hours she slept, for she felt that the source of her foreboding would become known at night and she wished to be awake and alert then.

A 'Mr Hoffman', a single gentleman travelling with two small children, seemed furtive and unwilling to mingle with other passengers. Mr William Harbeck was travelling with two superb motion picture cameras and 110,000 feet of exposed film, much of it relating to the *Titanic*. Mr Lawrence Beesley, a Dulwich College science master, busied himself by examining all accessible areas of the ship with an objective eye.

Time passed. 10.30 … 11 o'clock came and passed. There was scarcely an hour remaining before departure. Moments before 11.30 am the boat train arrived, bearing many of the 193 first class passengers boarding at Southampton. It had left London's Waterloo Station at 9.45.

Many 'glamorous' passengers would board later that day at Cherbourg. But the first class passengers boarding at Southampton were surely exciting enough …

Isidor Straus, American merchant prince, and his wife Ida (active in many charitable causes), with Mrs Straus' maid Ellen Bird and Mr Straus' valet John Farthing; the famous theatrical producer Henry B. Harris and his wife Irene ('Renée'); Col Archibald Gracie, historian, author of a book about the American Civil War, returning to his Washington home with notes about the War of 1812 that he had completed after researching in England … Mrs Ida Hippach of Chicago and her daughter Jean. (More than eight years earlier, on 30 December 1903, Mrs Hippach had lost two of her sons, Robert, age fourteen, and John, age eight, in the fire which destroyed Chicago's Iroquois Theatre and claimed 602 lives.)

Perhaps the most famous (and certainly the richest) passenger aboard was Col John Jacob Astor (his military title stemming from his command during the Spanish-American War), aboard with his bride of exactly seven months, Madeleine Force Astor (her age 19, his 48). Col Astor's personal fortune was estimated at between £15,465,000 and £20,620,000 ($72 million to $100 million). The Astor entourage included Mr Astor's manservant Victor Robins, Mrs Astor's maid Rosalie Bidois and, because Mrs Astor was 'in a delicate condition', a trained nurse, Miss Caroline Endres, a graduate of St Luke's Hospital School of Nursing, New York.

This tidy little group, almost an entity in itself, occupied the 'parlour suite' on C deck, amidships (C62). It consisted of a sitting room, two bedrooms, a private bath and toilet, and two wardrobe rooms for trunks. Miss Endres occupied her own cabin, C45, where she presumably was on 24-hour call to Mrs Astor's 'condition'.

The parlour suites occupied by Mr and Mrs Astor and, across the ship, by Mr and Mrs Straus (C55) were of 'period' design: C62 was in Louis XIV style, while C55 was in Regency style. The furniture was oak, the carpeting deep blue. One might think there could be nothing more elegant afloat: yet there was, and it was aboard the same ship.

The two 'promenade suites' on B deck, just aft of the forward first class entrance and designated B51 (starboard) and B52 (port) each contained not only the parlour suites' amenities, but also had its own private promenade deck, extending the entire length of the suite and open to the sea's air and light. For each suite, the occupant received at no additional cost an inside cabin for his or her servant(s) – B101 for suite B51, B102 for suite B52.

Also on B and C decks were cabins which could be interconnected to form suites of two, three or even more cabins. Luxuriously fitted in period design with panelled walls and the finest styles of oak or mahogany furniture, they surely were in keeping with White Star's well-known partiality for comfort.

Other first class cabins were situated forward and amidships on D deck, and amidships on E deck's starboard side. Even this 'secondary' accommodation was very comfortably, if not luxuriously, fitted and surpassed similar rooms on other transatlantic liners.

11.30… 11.45 am. Departure time was near. Trinity House pilot George Bowyer was already aboard, as indicated by the red-and-white striped pilot flag flying from the halyard. As noon approached the Blue Peter was run up the foremast, signifying 'Imminent Departure'. On the bridge Captain Smith gave a quiet order to the quartermaster on duty, who gently pulled downward on the whistle lanyard. The roar of *Titanic*'s triple-valved whistles reverberated through the cool Southampton air… a second time… then a third.

From their positions at docking stations – Wilde and Lightoller at the bow, Murdoch and

As Titanic *moved out into Southampton's River Test, the displacement of water caused by her passing broke the hawsers of the* New York *(left). The American vessel's stern drifted towards* Titanic *as the tug* Vulcan *(centre) succeeded in preventing the impending collision.* (L'Illustration)

Titanic *passed the bow of* Oceanic *moored at Berth 38, the collision with* New York *having been narrowly averted.* (Daily Graphic)

Third class passengers lined the poop deck's rails as Titanic *moved down Southampton Water towards the English Channel.* (Daily Graphic)

Pitman at the stern – the ship's officers reported by telephone to the bridge, where fifth officer Lowe relayed their messages to Captain Smith and Pilot George Bowyer.

'Tugs all fast,' came the report.

'Let go all lines,' was the command from the bridge.

The immense hawsers splashed into the water and were quickly drawn ashore by the pierhead gang under the dockmaster's direction. *Titanic* drifted gently from her dock.

Not yet under her own power, she was pushed, pulled and nudged out of the enclosed dock area by five straining tugs of Southampton's Red Funnel Line – *Ajax*, *Hector*, *Neptune*, *Hercules* and *Vulcan* – the same tugs that had assisted her upon arrival from Belfast.

Having left the crew muster for some last-minute, land-side recreation, including visits to at least two pubs, eight members of *Titanic*'s 'black gang' sped down the pier at the mighty whistles' first blast. Only two of them managed to scramble aboard before the crew's gangway was raised. The remaining six, including three brothers named Slade, stokers Shaw and Holden, and trimmer Brewer, were left at the dockside, frustrated in their attempts to reboard the departing liner. However, the situation had been foreseen: a group of substitutes was on board, and as *Titanic* departed from the pier, an adequate number were immediately signed on to round out each watch's roster.

At the dock's entrance *Titanic* nosed into the newly dredged turning circle and was manoeuvred by the tugs into a position facing down the River Test. The tugs cast off. An order from the bridge preceded clangs from the engine-room telegraphs. The two mighty bronze wing propellers began to turn slowly. Against the incoming tide, *Titanic*'s bow knifed ahead, slowly at first, then faster as more power reached her propellers.

On her starboard side the turbulence caused by the huge vessel's forward passage swept harmlessly into the River Test. To port, however, the Test Docks' bulkheads impeded the dispersal of the turbulence. *Titanic*'s immense bulk made it impossible for the displaced water to find an outlet.

Tied up at Berth 38 were *Oceanic* and *New York*, still temporarily out of service after the coal strike. Moored in tandem, they faced downstream, with *New York* outboard. Water displaced by the passing *Titanic* caused *New York* to bob, first up, then down as *Titanic* passed. The motion put such a great strain on *New York*'s mooring lines that they snapped with loud reports. As *Titanic* moved past, her speed was increasing and she was drawing water behind her. *New York*'s stern, now loose, began to arc out towards *Titanic*, passing broadside to her.

The alert Captain Charles Gale of the tug *Vulcan* managed to get the second of two wire ropes aboard *New York*'s stern as the unmanned American liner veered to within four feet of striking *Titanic*'s own stern. On *Titanic*'s bridge, instinctive reactions of Captain Smith and Pilot Bowyer also prevented the collision. The order 'full astern' was given quickly. *Titanic*'s forward movement was checked and, as the reverse force took hold, the vessel moved very slowly backwards towards the mouth of White Star Dock. Her entire length moved past *New York*'s stern, still quite close but under the restraint of *Vulcan*'s line.

New York had now broken fully loose from her mooring. But with more tugs at the scene and with more lines aboard, the wayward liner now drifted around the head of the Test Docks,

The new liner passes a yacht moored off the Isle of Wight. (Peter Pearce)

her forward movement finally ceasing. Additional lines were placed on *Oceanic*, so that when *Titanic* passed again there would not be a repetition.

Titanic's departure had been delayed more than an hour. An ill omen, some thought. An inauspicious start. Did the delay and the near-collision mean *Titanic* was ever to be a 'late' as well as an 'unlucky' ship? Time would tell, perhaps…

Through the ocean channel, into Southampton Water, past the Isle of Wight to starboard, and around Calshot Spit's intricate turn *Titanic* glided. Pilot Bowyer's experienced skill guided the liner safely to the Nab Light Vessel, where he handed over to Captain Smith. Likely Bowyer disembarked here as usual, no doubt wishing his friends on the bridge a Good Voyage before descending Titanic's side by ladder to the awaiting pilot vessel. (Bowyer's descendants, however, say that on this occasion he elected to disembark at Cherbourg.)

Cherbourg, *Titanic*'s next port, now lay less than 70 miles away. Then it would be on to Queenstown for a brief, noon stop. The open sea would be next, for an uneventful and, hopefully, smooth crossing to an arrival on the morning of Wednesday, 17 April, at White Star's Pier 60 in New York.

A three-day turn-around. A New York departure at noon on Saturday, 20 April…

The American flag, denoting her ultimate destination, fluttered from her forward mast, *Titanic* picked up speed as she headed southwards in the afternoon sun, into the open waters of the Channel.

CHAPTER SIX

Westwards to Destiny

Without exception the 142 first class, 30 second class and 102 third class passengers boarding *Titanic* at Cherbourg arrived on the *Train Transatlantique*. The train, which took a little more than six hours to make the trip from Paris, departed from the Gare St Lazare at 9.40 am, almost at the same time that the London & South Western Railway's boat train left Waterloo Station on its 100-minute trip from London to Southampton.

Cherbourg had been used by White Star as its Continental port of call since 1907, when the company inaugurated its Southampton–New York service. Cherbourg had a splendid harbour enclosed by a long sea wall, but it did not have docking facilities for large ships.

Continental passengers arrived at Cherbourg's Gare Maritime *aboard the* Train Transatlantique *after a six-hour journey from Paris.* (Authors' collection)

White Star's two Cherbourg tenders brought passengers from the station to Titanic, *anchored out in the roadstead.* Nomadic *(left) took the first and second class passengers while* Traffic *accommodated third class passengers and mail.* (Authors' collection)

Visiting liners had to anchor offshore while passengers and mails were ferried out aboard tenders from the maritime land station.

To provide this service, White Star had two tenders constructed at Harland and Wolff's Belfast yard. Completed in time to serve *Olympic* on her 1911 maiden voyage visit to Cherbourg, the two tenders *Nomadic* and *Traffic* were now to serve the same function for *Olympic*'s sister, *Titanic*, on her own maiden voyage.

The *Train Transatlantique* arrived at the trackside marine terminal on time. Embarkation was scheduled for just after 4 pm, but *Titanic*'s near collision at Southampton had delayed her Cherbourg arrival until after 6 pm. ('... Would the passengers be so kind as to be ready for embarkation at 1730 hours?') Fortunately the weather was good. Had it been cold or raining the passengers would have had to wait inside, on the two tenders' confining decks.

It was a most interesting group of passengers who milled about inside and around the tiny terminal. The 'season' was nearly over and in addition to the customary business travellers, many socially prominent passengers were on the Cherbourg manifest.

Mrs Charlotte Drake Cardeza and her son Thomas of Philadelphia were accompanied not only by Mr Cardeza's valet, Gustave Lesueur, and Mrs Cardeza's maid, Anna Ward, but also by fourteen trunks, four suitcases and three crates of baggage, on which Mrs Cardeza would later place a value of £36,567 2s ($177,352.75). The Cardezas were booked for suite B51, the three-room complex with its own promenade on B deck's port side for which, according to a White Star brochure, they paid $4,350 (almost £890).

The notables also included American mining magnate Benjamin Guggenheim and his valet, Victor Giglio. (Mr Guggenheim's chauffeur, René Pernot, was aboard, too, travelling separately on his own second class ticket.) And there were Sir Cosmo and Lady Duff-Gordon, with Lady Duff-Gordon's secretary, Miss Laura Francatelli. (Lady Duff-Gordon was the internationally known dress designer 'Lucile'. For some reason she and her husband were booked under the names of 'Mr and Mrs Morgan' and they occupied separate cabins.)

Mrs James Joseph Brown, better known to her friends as 'Margaret' or 'Maggie' (and after her 1932 death as 'Unsinkable Molly'), had been on holiday in Egypt where she met the Astors; eager to make the transatlantic crossing with them, she was able to re-book her White Star reservation to the earlier ship – *Titanic*.

Among the second class passengers, a young man booked as 'Baron von Drachstedt' found his accommodation unacceptable. He paid for and was assigned a cabin in first class, D38. (Later, during a hearing in the United States, the 'Baron' was to confess to being plain Mr Alfred Nournay.)

Another second class passenger was Samuel Ward Stanton, the well-known American marine editor and illustrator. Stanton was returning from Grenada, in Spain, where he had been sketching the Alhambra for murals and other decorations he was commissioned to do for the Hudson River Day Line's new steamboat *Washington Irving*.

Third class passengers boarding at Cherbourg included Syrian, Croatian, Armenian and other Middle Eastern nationals who had been routed from eastern Mediterranean ports via Marseilles to Paris and, now, to Cherbourg. The 102 third class passengers were tired from their long trips and confused by the strange tongue in which announcements were made. Boarding could not come too soon for them.

By 5.30 those not already waiting on the tenders were asked to board. The 176 first and second class passengers and their luggage filled less than a fifth of the space on *Nomadic*, while the mails and 102 third class passengers with their luggage filled scarcely a quarter of *Traffic*.

Though *Titanic*'s commander had not tried to make up the time caused by the near-collision at Southampton, late afternoon sun greeted the liner's approach to Cherbourg. As *Titanic* moved majestically but cautiously through the opening in the port's sea wall, her length and height were reflected in the roadstead's calm water. It was 6.30 pm when the liner dropped her anchor at Cherbourg.

The two tenders fussed out to the immense ship's side. Fifteen first class and seven second class passengers prepared to disembark. (These 'cross-Channel' passengers had been transported for £1 10s (£1.50 or $7.50) first class and £1 ($5) second class; their names do not appear on any printed or official list, but are on *Titanic*'s ticketing manifest. Also carried were seven 'local' first class passengers to Queenstown, at a rate of £4 ($20) each.)

Mails were transferred, 278 passengers and their luggage were taken aboard, some freight – four cycles, eight cases, and a canary consigned to a Mr Meanwell – were taken off. Within 90 minutes the ship was ready for departure. For the second time that day the mighty voice of

By the time Titanic *had embarked her passengers and departed Cherbourg, night had fallen.* (L'Illustration)

Titanic spoke. Three times the deeply pitched three-tone whistle resounded through the low hills around Cherbourg, announcing to all that the giant was now ready to depart.

At 8 pm, the tenders having left for shore, the powerful windlass gear whirred and strained, hauling in the clanking chain and its dripping anchor. By 8.10 pm, all secure, the liner made a tight turn using her wing propellers, and was under way.

Passing through the Grande Rade and leaving the winking lights of Cherbourg far behind, *Titanic* passed into open water. The pulse of her engines quickened as through the night she moved across the Channel, around England's south coast and into the lower reaches of St George's Channel and the Irish Sea.

Morning found *Titanic* approaching the Irish coast, a brilliant sunrise off her starboard quarter. During the trip up St George's Channel adjustments to the ship's compass were made, necessitating several wide, sweeping turns. But the main wake and course lay towards Queenstown. Passing the Daunt Light Vessel and pausing to pick up the pilot, *Titanic* continued to the harbour opening at Roche's Point, her sounding line in constant use. At 11.30 am the great anchor was again lowered and *Titanic* prepared to take aboard passengers and the Irish mails.

From the shore about two miles away chuffed the two side-wheel, black-funnelled tenders *America* and *Ireland*. When serving White Star liners, the tenders usually loaded from the White Star wharf, located between Scott's Quay and the railway station at the western end of town. But today the volume of mail and passengers was abnormally large. The tenders tied up at the pierhead adjacent to the railway station so that passengers and mails could be taken aboard directly from the train. The tenders took about half an hour to make the trip from shore. Ferried out were 113 third class, eight second class and three first class passengers. A total of 1,385 mail sacks was also taken aboard.

Disembarking at Queenstown were the 'six adults in Mr Odell's party', among whom was Francis M. Browne, a Belvedere College teacher and a candidate for priesthood. He had accepted Mr Odell's invitation to travel aboard the new ship from Southampton to Queenstown. Now, as the 32-year-old teacher boarded the tender for shore, he clutched a packet of exposed photographic plates, pictures he had taken the previous day and earlier that morning around the liner's decks and public rooms.

Also debarking were a Mr E. Nichols, and one John Coffey. When the 24-year-old Coffey signed on *Titanic* as a fireman he gave his home address as 12 Sherbourne Terrace, Queenstown. It is possible that he signed on to get a free trip home. He came ashore hidden under some empty mail bags. (Coffey's next, and last, appearance is his signing aboard *Mauretania* as a fireman when that liner made her westbound call at Queenstown on Sunday, 14 April. How he explained the blank space in his seaman's book is not recorded.)

Coffey was not the only crew member with a fondness for Ireland's green hills. While passengers were boarding from the tenders, a member of *Titanic*'s 'black gang' – perhaps a stoker, perhaps a trimmer – took a brief, unauthorised break to climb the ladder inside the dummy fourth funnel. His blackened, soot-covered face peering down at the clean, breeze-swept decks from on high caused thrills of revulsion and even fear to run through the minds of some passengers and crew who glimpsed him. The face quickly withdrew, yet the appearance of this infernal-looking fellow was sufficient to serve, many said, as an evil omen,

Because of her immense size, Titanic *anchored some two miles from town, off Roche's Point. Passengers boarded by way of way of tenders* Ireland *(centre) and* America *(foreground), moored at Queenstown's railway station. Emotional farewells were the order of the day.* (Cork Examiner)

With all passengers and mail aboard, fourth officer Joseph Boxhall (centre) and second officer Charles Lightoller prepared to order the closing of the gangway door for the last time. (Cork Examiner)

a sign of impending doom. (Those who now laughed at the superstitious fears of their fellow passengers had good reason to recall their own derision 3½ days later.)

Embarking from the tenders through the second class entrance aft on E deck came the additional passengers. Those travelling third class were quickly conducted across the entrance lobby to two portside doors that opened into a corridor in their own accommodations. Second class passengers remained in their area. First class passengers Dr. William E. Minahan, his wife Lillian and his sister Daisy were greeted and respectfully escorted to a lift and thence to their cabin, C78.

Among the third class passengers were Daniel Buckley; Katie Gilnagh; Eddie Ryan; Nora O'Leary; John Kennedy; Mary and Kate Murphy; Margaret Rice and her five sons, Albert, George, Eric, Arthur and Eugene (mother and five sons… all would be lost); James Moran; Agnes, Alice and Bernard McCoy; Eugene Daly…

Accompanying the tenders out from land were several small boats with merchandise draped over their bows and sides – soft

As the tenders returned to shore (with Titanic's *fireman John Coffey and seven cross-channel passengers aboard) the liner stood poised for her Queenstown departure.* (Cork Examiner)

goods, mostly: tweeds and laces which could be effectively displayed in the minimal time available to set up shop. The enterprising merchants were pleased to come aboard, by way of the tenders' decks, and allow their goods to be examined more closely. From one of these 'bumboat' men, and on the merest whim, Col Astor purchased for his young wife a fine lace shawl, paying £165 (more than $800) for it.

Again departure time approached. Again *Titanic*'s powerful voice spoke three times and the echoes resounded from the hills around the harbour. The tenders headed back towards land, the merchants' small boats dispersed. The anchor came up, dripping. With the American flag fluttering from the foremast, the company's red pennant with its white star at the mainmast's peak, and the Blue Ensign waving from the stern flagstaff, *Titanic* began her stately departure.

From a spot on the third class promenade deck, aft, passenger Eugene Daly sounded his own note of departure. Coming out on the tender he had played some lively airs on his bagpipes, taking the edge off the sorrow of parting. Now, however, he saluted the receding land with the mournful dirge, 'Erin's Lament'. It was a fitting and nostalgic farewell to the beautiful country which so many would never see again. The great bronze wing propellers began to revolve slowly, then faster as more steam was fed to the engines.

There was a brief slowing down to drop the pilot, John Cotter, at the light vessel, then a broad turn to starboard. Down the Channel, ever faster now that the centre turbine was cut in. The low green hills of Ireland swept past, became a blue line on the horizon, then a thin black thread which vanished astern as *Titanic* reached the open sea's swells. Now, irrevocably, her course was westward to destiny. Her destination ... disaster.

* * *

On the North Atlantic the winter of 1912 was the mildest in more than 30 years. It allowed immense fields of sheet and floe ice to break off and drift further south than was normal, into the east-west shipping lanes. But the winter had been severe enough to drive the Gulf Stream and its moderating temperatures southwards, where its warmer currents no longer melted the ice pouring down from the north.

With the sheet ice came huge bergs, immense chunks of ice and debris 'calved' from Greenland's awesome glaciers, floating in silent solitude as great, ghostly presences. Some bergs resembled mountain ranges or great buildings or palaces; others resembled full-rigged ships.

Fully four-fifths of an iceberg's mass lies below water. As portions of the submerged mass melt, the berg's centre of gravity shifts, eventually causing the entire berg to capsize and present a new surface to the air. When this occurs the water still in the upper portion of the berg makes its face dark and especially difficult to sight at night.

As the water drains out of the berg's top portion, it once again assumes its pure-white guise. But even this colour change does not make it safe to approach. For below the water's surface pinnacles of ice have now become rock-hard spurs that protrude from the berg's main body, extending outwards to trap the unwary vessel that approaches too closely.

As many ships (most without wireless) reached port following the *Titanic* disaster they reported having sighted or having actually been in ice during the week of 7 April. A plotting of the positions reported by these vessels shows an immense ice field extending from 46° N to 41°31' N, and from 46°18' W, to 50°40' W, moving southwards and slightly westwards as the week passed.

After departing from Queenstown *Titanic* quickly entered the North Atlantic lane for westbound steam vessels. Commencing on 15 January 1899, an agreement among the major shipping companies set the route for the 'summer season' (from 15 January to 15 August) as follows:

> (Westbound): 'Steer from Fastnet or Bishop Rock, on the Great Circle course, but nothing South, to cross the meridian of 47° West in Latitude 42° North, thence by either rhumb line or Great Circle or even North of the Great Circle, if an easterly current is encountered, to a position South of Nantucket Light Vessel, thence to Fire Island Light Vessel, when bound for New York, or to Five Fathom Bank South Light Vessel, when bound for Philadelphia.'

One can tell at a glance that a course which takes a vessel to a position of 42° N, 47° W will place it almost in the middle of the ice reported between 7 and 12 April. Even with wireless reports available to him and to his company, Captain Smith did not, nor was he advised by his company to, alter *Titanic*'s course from the season's established westbound route.

Titanic surged steadily onwards.

12 noon Thursday (11 April) to 12 noon Friday (12 April) 386 miles logged
12 noon Friday (12 April) to 12 noon Saturday (13 April) 519 miles logged
12 noon Saturday (13 April) to 12 noon Sunday (14 April) 546 miles logged

During these days, too, many eastbound and westbound ships reported heavy ice conditions along the lanes. On the night of *Titanic*'s departure, the French Line's *Niagara* reported being stopped and damaged by ice at 44°07' N, 50°40' W. She requested assistance and *Carmania* left her own course to stand by until it was determined that aid was not actually required.

President Lincoln, *Corsican*, *Montrose*, *Lackawanna*, *Saint Laurent*... all stopped in or passing heavy ice on 11/12 April...

Avala, *California*, *East Point*, *Manitou*. All encountering ice on 12 April, ice which lay along the sea lane...

Borderer, *Minnehaha*, *Hellig Olav*. Involved with ice during 13 April...

14 April... *Trautenfels*. *Montcalm*. *Canada*. *Corinthian*. *Lindenfels*. *Memphian*. *Campanello*... All reporting ice which lay ahead, directly in *Titanic*'s intended course.

* * *

As *Titanic* sped westwards the days passed calmly for passengers and crew alike. For the former, there were no formal activities, no general parties or organised recreation. Passengers were left to their own devices. The crew kept regular watches, pleased to be working on a clean new ship.

Third class passengers were provided with a general room, aft in the poop, on C deck. The cheerful room was panelled and framed in pine with a white enamel finish. Tables and chairs were teak, as were the comfortable contoured benches which lined the room.

For the men there was a smoking room adjacent to, but separate from, the general room. It was panelled and framed in oak, with furniture similar to that in the general room. There was a bar next to the smoking room and yet another third class bar forward on D deck.

Second class public rooms were aft on B and C decks. In appearance and comfort they rivalled first class rooms aboard most liners of the period.

Titanic's second class smoking room (aft on B deck) was handsomely panelled in oak. The comfortable oak furniture was upholstered in dark green morocco leather. The second class library, one deck below, was panelled in sycamore. Its mahogany furniture was tapestry-covered, and its windows were hung with green silk draperies.

The large oak-panelled dining room on D deck contained mahogany tables and chairs, the latter covered in red leather. The floor was linoleum tile. The dining room could seat 394 passengers.

The difference in rates paid by second class and first class passengers reflected not only the size, furnishings and fittings of cabins and public rooms, but also the number of amenities offered to first class passengers. They included a gymnasium; a plunge bath; a Turkish bath with Moorish decor, a verandah and palm court; a smoking room and a lounge (high on A deck, with its raised roof); and a stylishly furnished reading and writing room. There were not just one, but three elevators to speed passengers from the spacious public rooms on A and B decks to their cabins, amidships on B, C and D decks. The immense first class dining saloon on D deck with its adjacent reception room was one of the largest apartments afloat: seats for 532 passengers were placed about the numerous small tables seating from two to eight people – a far cry from the long rows of single tables with their closely-adjacent, bolted down seats found aboard many liners.

Dining hours were one of the few scheduled events in shipboard routine: 8.30 to 10.30 am for breakfast, 1 to 2.30 pm for luncheon, 6 to 7.30 pm, perhaps a bit later, for dinner. The *à la carte* restaurant was located on B deck, just aft of the fourth funnel. Its staff, recruited from Luigi Gatti's two London restaurants, worked for the Gatti concession and not for the White Star Line. The restaurant, with its light fawn-coloured French walnut panelling and two-tone Dubarry rose carpeting, seated 137 diners at 49 tables. It was open from 8 am to 11 pm daily for first class passengers with special tastes.

One of the special amenities which second class passengers shared with first class was the fine ship's orchestra. Consisting of eight talented musicians recruited from other ships, British restaurants and music halls the ensemble was led by 33-year-old Wallace Hartley, himself an accomplished violinist who came to *Titanic*'s 'band' from the Cunarder *Mauretania*.

The orchestra was divided into two sections, and members played interchangeably in each: a blue-jacketed trio consisting of piano, violin and viola or cello played daily in the second class entrance foyer, aft on C deck. In addition to providing luncheon, dinner and after-dinner music in the first class reception room on C deck, the trio performed in the lobby adjacent to the *à la carte* restaurant, dressed in their blue uniform jackets with green facings, and dark blue trousers. Each player was expected to know from memory the 352 songs in the White Star 'music book' and to recognise them 'by the number' when called for by their leader.

Somehow the time passed quickly. There never seemed to be enough time to fulfil goals set early in the day. By nightfall, as passengers deserted the public rooms and sought the comfort of their staterooms late in the evening, there still seemed to be things to do, things to think about…

High on the bridge second officer Lightoller was relieved at 10 pm by first officer Murdoch. Lightoller made the rounds of the ship before turning in to his cabin aft of the wheelhouse on the port side. Perhaps before falling asleep he reviewed in his mind the cargo, the contents of the holds whose loading he had supervised. Nothing of any great value: pharmaceuticals, botanicals, opium instead of gold in the specie room. (Smiling, perhaps) 'Spices instead of specie…'

In his office on C deck starboard of the first class forward entrance, purser Hugh McElroy checked the day's receipts from the bars and the Marconi room before placing them in his safe. He noted the special packages in the vault, given into his personal keeping, instead of being consigned to the cargo holds.

'Nothing special here,' he mused. He leafed through his own copy of the cargo manifest. 'Nor here. Just routine express cargo. Certainly nothing that's heavily insured. No instructions for special handling, either. Well, one good thing… It won't take long to unload.' McElroy folded the manifest and placed it in the safe with the package list. He closed and locked the safe door. Securing the office, he crossed the first class forward entrance and went towards his unmarked cabin next door to C53.

In the controller's office just off the *à la carte* restaurant entrance, manager Luigi Gatti was also tallying the day's receipts. He briefly recalled his wife's premonition. She had not wanted her husband to make this trip and told him that she 'felt strange about it'. He had shrugged off her fears, telling her that nothing could happen to him, that he was an expert swimmer and could easily get to land. 'You worry too much,' he told her. 'Didn't I get through the collision aboard the *Olympic* last year without a scratch?' Gatti stepped into the restaurant to dismiss the remaining staff for the night; among them were several of his cousins. He then descended to his C deck cabin, between those of chief steward Andrew Latimer and ship's assistant surgeon J. Edward Simpson.

In the first class dining saloon, a group of men had gathered earlier that evening for dinner. At the table was the English journalist and editor William Thomas Stead, going to America to address a peace conference at President William Howard Taft's request. Stead also was a believer in mysticism and spiritualism. He frequently consulted mediums and investigated psychic phenomena. (Today he would be called a 'ghost chaser'.)

In 1886 he had written a fictional article for the *Pall Mall Gazette* in which he described a ship's loss through collision with another ship. Great loss of life resulted because there were insufficient lifeboats to accommodate passengers and crew. In 1892 Stead wrote a lengthy article for the *Review of Reviews* entitled 'From the Old World to the New', depicting a journey from England to the United States. The voyage is made aboard the White Star liner *Majestic*. During the crossing the liner rescues survivors from a fictitious craft sunk after collision with ice. *Majestic* herself must steer south to avoid striking the ice-field. During the past several years, Stead repeatedly had been advised by mediums to avoid ocean travel. He himself had recently given a talk in which he described himself in a shipwreck, calling for help. Now, in the spring of 1912 he was making his own crossing 'from the old world to the new' aboard a White Star liner, captained by the man who had once been master of the *Majestic*.

During dinner on the second or third evening out, Stead regaled table companions with stories of travel and spiritualism. One of the party, Fred Seward, recalled Stead relating a story of an Egyptian mummy carrying a curse that brought sickness, death and destruction to its owners. (The mummy in question – actually an inner coffin cover for a priestess of Amun-Ra – was currently on exhibit at the British Museum in London.) The look of terror and anguish in the painted eyes of the cover's main figure caused many who saw it to believe the occupant had suffered a tormented life, and there were some who wished to try to exorcise the evil spirit captured in the mummy's soul.

That Stead's tale of the mummy's curse left a great impression is beyond doubt. Seward, in a 19 April interview with a *New York World* reporter, related the dinner party incident involving Stead's story. In the emotion, exaggeration and distortion that followed the disaster, this tale of the mummy's curse became that of a real mummy aboard *Titanic* – one whose powerful spell had actually caused the wreck.

(The 'mummy saga' allegedly continues with its wealthy owner, also aboard *Titanic*, paying an immense bribe to have the case placed in a lifeboat, from which – presumably upon payment of another immense bribe – it was taken aboard *Carpathia* and secretly landed at New York. Its presence in the wealthy American's collection caused such devastation that the decision was made to return it to England; the case was taken to Canada where, on 28 May 1914, it was placed aboard the *Empress of Ireland* ...)

Neither administrators nor trustees of the British Museum are empowered to sell or trade items from its collection to private individuals, no matter how wealthy.

The entire tale is one of fabrication and hysteria caused by the disaster's deep emotional impact. But because the story is directly related to an authoritative journalist who was also a believer in spiritualism, it was given credibility from the start.

A mummy case in whose painted eyes there is a look of anguish still exists, still owned by the British Museum. Its number: 22542 ...

The *Titanic* night moved on ...

In her cabin Esther Hart sat knitting, 'looking after the ship' as her husband and daughter slept soundly after a day of exploration together.

In cabin E101 Miss E. Celia Troutt (later, better, known by her married name Edwina MacKenzie) chatted with her voyage room-mates, Nora Keane and Susie Webber. Before retiring, Nora related a conversation she'd had earlier with Nellie Hocking from Cornwall. Nellie said that as night fell she had heard the sound of a cock crowing. Cornish folklore called this a sign of impending disaster. ('... Of course it's true. Listen! You can almost hear it yourselves!')

And well might the room-mates and Nellie have heard a rooster crowing. Among the items in first class passenger Mrs Ella White's claim for loss of property were 'live poultry: roosters and hens from Chasse ile rage, Jardin d'Agriculture' valued at $205.87 (£42 4s, or £42.20).

In the third class butcher's care (as were all domestic pets, the remainder aboard *Titanic* being five passengers' dogs), the 'live poultry' would have been comfortably crated, carefully marked (to prevent their becoming a chicken stew) and kept near the dog kennels on F deck just aft of the third class galley. Naturally, the rooster(s) would have crowed, and it is quite likely that the sound might have travelled through the after area of the ship's lower decks ...

On G deck, near the bow on the starboard side, the five postal clerks had finished their day's sorting. The three American clerks, William Logan Gwinn, John Starr March and Oscar Scott Woody, and the two British clerks, James Bertram Williamson and John Richard Jago Smith, had worked hard on the piles of mail and the huge, cloth sorting bags. The men were pleased to enjoy a relaxing evening in their salon, amidships on C deck, which they shared with the two Marconi operators.

Gwinn had been scheduled to 'work' the *Philadelphia* but when news of his wife's illness reached him he had requested and received assignment to *Titanic*'s earlier crossing. Woody was looking forward to his 44th birthday on Monday 15 April. Aware that he would be celebrating it away from his wife, his postal colleagues had planned a little party for him ...

It was a routine night aboard *Titanic*, similar to those aboard all ocean liners. Soon the night would pass, dawn would come, a new day would follow, and then another routine night ...

The dawn of 15 April 1912 was not to come for *Titanic*. In a cataclysmic encounter with one of nature's most awesome creations, the newest and largest of man-made objects was destroyed, sunk in a matter of two hours and forty minutes.

The grief and sorrow *Titanic*'s loss engendered has never fully disappeared: man's memory for grief is long. Immediately following the disaster, this mourning was most intense, for it was during these days that the bodies of the lost were recovered. And it soon became apparent that the vast majority of the victims never would be found. They would sleep for eternity in the sea which now claimed them as her own ...

CHAPTER SEVEN

City of Sorrow

Within hours of *Titanic*'s loss, much of Canada had witnessed an eclipse of the sun, 'the greatest this country has seen in 53 years,' according to a Halifax, Nova Scotia, newspaper. To some it seemed to be a celestial reflection upon the passing of a giant. Even as the *Carpathia* made her way to New York, the White Star Line had begun preparations with Halifax as the focal point. The arrangements there concerned *Titanic*'s passengers and crew, but the reunions that would result would be far less joyous than those at New York's Pier 54.

By 15 April, *Titanic*'s owners had arranged for an attempt to recover the tragedy's victims. A.G. Jones and Company, White Star's Halifax agents, chartered the Commercial Cable Company's cable ship *Mackay-Bennett* to search the Atlantic's wide waters. John Snow and Company Ltd, the province's largest undertaking firm, was asked to oversee funeral

Workmen loaded a hundred coffins on to the cable ship Mackay-Bennett, *first of four White Star-chartered ships to depart from Halifax in search of* Titanic's *victims.* (Philadelphia Inquirer)

Tons of ice were also a requisite for Mackay-Bennett's *grim voyage.* (Halifax Morning Chronicle)

arrangements. More than 40 members of the Funeral Directors' Association of the Maritime Provinces agreed to assist Snow's in preparing the recovered dead for burial.

By Wednesday, 17 April, the necessary supplies – tons of ice, embalmer's tools, and more than a hundred coffins – had been stowed aboard *Mackay-Bennett* at her Halifax pier. The all-volunteer crew, under Captain F.H. Larnder's command, would receive double wages for the unpleasant task they faced and the vessel left port at noon.

Most other ships were already giving the scene of *Titanic*'s loss a very wide berth. What captain wished to show his passengers a grim panorama of wreckage, ice and bodies buoyed by white life-jackets, giving the appearance of seagulls on the surface? 'It's a hoodoo area,' some captains said. 'Best to keep the living away from the dead.'

Other captains became censors. On board the Uranium Line's *Volturno* westbound from Rotterdam, Captain Nelson learned of the disaster from his wireless operator. Only these two men knew of it until the liner reached port, the captain deciding to withhold the terrible news even from his officers. (Eighteen months later, *Volturno* herself would be in the news with her destruction by fire.)

The primary reason for vessels to avoid the disaster area was more basic: the North Atlantic passenger steamship companies had already shifted the shipping lanes far to the south, belatedly reacting to the now obvious dangers of ice. Nevertheless, several vessels were passing through the area where *Titanic* had gone down, and these ships' wireless reports now guided the *Mackay-Bennett* to the disaster site. The North German Lloyd liner *Rhein* reported bodies and wreckage in latitude 42.01 N, 49.13 W. The *Bremen* sent word that she had passed more than a hundred bodies at latitude 42.00 N, longitude 49.20 W.

One of *Bremen*'s first class passengers, Mrs Johanna Stunke, later told the press, 'We saw the body of one woman dressed only in her night dress, and clasping a baby to her breast. Close by was the body of another woman with her arms tightly clasped round a shaggy dog ... We saw the bodies of three men in a group, all clinging to a chair. Floating by just beyond them were the bodies of a dozen men, all wearing lifebelts and clinging desperately together as though in their last struggle for life.' To the north was the glistening bulk of a low-lying iceberg. The ocean's surface was covered with deck chairs and other wreckage.

Mackay-Bennett arrived on the scene at 8 pm on Saturday 20 April and recovery operations began the following morning. The cable ship's boats were lowered, and 51 bodies were recovered despite heavy seas. As each body came aboard, a square of canvas with a stencilled number on it was attached. Valuables and personal property were placed in canvas bags bearing the same number. A full description of the victim, including hair colour, height, weight, age, birthmarks, scars and tattoos was recorded in a ledger on the corresponding page number, along with a complete inventory of jewellery, clothing and pocket contents. These details, it was hoped, would permit identifications to be made.

After almost a week in the sea, many of the bodies were in poor condition. Some showed signs of injuries sustained during the *Titanic*'s sinking. Others had been badly disfigured by sea life. At 8.15 pm a burial service was held on *Mackay-Bennett*'s forecastle deck as 24 bodies, wrapped in canvas weighted with iron grate bars, were recommitted to the sea. The remainder were embalmed for return to Halifax.

The fourth body found brought tears even to the eyes of *Mackay-Bennett*'s sea-hardened crew. It was that of a fair-haired boy about two years old, found amid a mass of wreckage. His entry in the ledger book was tragically brief. 'No identification. No effects.' The only child found during recovery operations, he, too, was prepared for entry into Halifax.

Names of the identified dead were sent ashore immediately via wireless. Others would have to await arrival of next-of-kin for identification.

Word of *Mackay-Bennett*'s mission spread, and a succession of ships began reporting bodies, icebergs and wreckage. The debris field was extensive: 'cabinet furniture, including chairs, writing desks, and stools' said one report; 'bedroom furniture and fittings, a considerable quantity of white woodwork and framing amongst which was a cabin door and its adjoining partitions', said another; 'an oak newel post; hats, polished and white painted woods, and a great square of probably forty feet dimensions which may have been part of the ill-fated steamer's deck' said a third.

By 23 April, *Mackay-Bennett* had 80 bodies on board, and had received additional supplies of canvas and burlap from the Allan liner *Sardinian* passing through the area. The following day found the ship in heavy seas and dense fog. Nevertheless, recovery operations began at 4.30 am and continued for 14 hours. Eighty-seven additional victims were recovered, searched and tagged.

Aware that he and his ship soon would be overwhelmed through sheer numbers, Captain Larnder contacted White Star's New York office for assistance. On 21 April the company's Halifax agents chartered *Minia*, a cable ship owned by the Anglo-American Telegraph Company Ltd. A coffin shortage delayed her departure, but fully stocked with ice,

The cable ship Mackay-Bennett *re-entered a silent Halifax Harbour with 190* Titanic *victims on board. Her flag flew at half mast.* (Harper's)

grate bars, the coffins and embalming supplies, *Minia* left at midnight on 22 April to join the *Mackay-Bennett*. At 6.15 am on Friday 26 April the two cable ships began searching together. Fourteen were found by noon, and these were placed aboard *Mackay-Bennett*, now filled to capacity. Her crew had found 306 bodies. Of these, 116 had been buried at sea. The cable ship now returned to Halifax with 190 victims on board, a hundred in all the available coffins, the rest in canvas.

Minia continued the search. Bad weather persisted, and after recovering 17 more victims, Captain William George Squares DeCarteret advised the White Star Line that the gales had swept the remaining bodies into the Gulf Stream. Fifteen of those found by *Minia* were returned to Halifax on 6 May, among them Charles M. Hays, president of the Grand Trunk Railway. As *Minia* left the area, yet a third recovery vessel, the Canadian Ministry of Marine and Fisheries' *Montmagny* was despatched on 3 May from Sorel, Quebec.

Upon *Mackay-Bennett*'s 30 April arrival at HM Naval Dockyard's north coaling wharf number four, the off-loading of the dead began under the watchful eyes of 20 sailors from the Canadian cruiser *Niobe*. The stout concrete walls surrounding the dockyard effectively shielded the proceedings from view. One enterprising journalist who tried to photograph the off-loading immediately had his camera confiscated under orders from Halifax's police chief.

The first to come ashore were the bodies that had been on the foredeck, mainly crew for whom there had been no embalming or other preparation. Then came the second and third class passengers, whose remains were swathed in canvas. Finally came the bodies of the first class passengers, all embalmed, most identified, and all in coffins on the stern.

As the last of the dead left the dockyard on horse-drawn hearses, Captain Larnder reluctantly gave in to reporters' requests for interviews. Squeezed into the captain's dayroom, the session went smoothly until a table collapsed and Captain Larnder ended the press conference. Yet another bad omen, some said.

At least one reporter decided to change it to a *Titanic*-related omen and wrote his report of the incident so that the table collapse occurred during a reception aboard the liner before her Southampton departure. 'This was much commented upon, the hope being expressed that no mishap would happen to the mammoth liner after she left port,' his account concluded. (Because much work remained to be done while *Titanic* was in port, no visitors – press included – had been permitted aboard at Southampton.)

Mackay-Bennett's arrival also set into motion the procedures designed by the Halifax authorities and White Star Line's Percy VanGelder Mitchell, transferred from Montreal to supervise arrangements, to ensure strict decorum, expedite the return of loved ones to next-of-kin, and comply fully with provincial and city regulations.

The Mayflower Curling Rink on Agricola Street was turned into a temporary morgue. Where curlers normally engaged in spirited contests, 67 canvas-enclosed cubicles were constructed, each large enough to enclose three coffins. After embalming behind partitions at the rink's western end, the coffins were brought to the cubicles where, under escort, family or friends could attempt identification. Only those bearing proof of their own identity and authority to act were admitted to the rink. The dead were to be kept at the rink for two weeks. Where faces were distinguishable, photographs of the deceased and additional descriptive details were taken to assist with future identification efforts.

The curling rink's second floor was converted into the coroner's headquarters, and the staff worked hard to process the required documents leading to the issuing of death certificates

First class passengers' remains were embalmed and placed in coffins stowed on Mackay-Bennett's *stern.* (Harper's)

Vincent Astor (right) arrived in Halifax to identify the body of his father, millionaire John Jacob Astor. (Harper's)

– small, crimson-coloured squares bearing the usual spaces for name, sex, age, date of birth, address and occupation. For 'cause of death' it noted, 'accidental drowning, *SS Titanic*, at sea'. Valuables of the deceased were recorded and stored for safe keeping by the coroner's staff.

Body number 124, that of John Jacob Astor, was the first to be claimed and released from the rink. Identification had been relatively easy. His record noted that he wore a blue serge suit, a blue handkerchief with 'A.V.' on it, a belt with gold buckle, brown boots with red rubber soles, and a brown flannel shirt with 'J.J.A.' in its collar. Astor's effects included a

In Halifax's non-sectarian Fairview Cemetery were buried 121 Titanic *victims.* (Authors' collection)

The gentle, curving rows of Titanic*'s dead filled a hillside at Fairview Cemetery.* (Authors' collection)

gold watch, gold cuff links with diamonds, a diamond ring with three stones, £225 in English bank notes, $2,440 in American bank notes, £5 in gold, 7 shillings in silver, 50 francs, a gold pencil and a pocketbook.

Based upon relatives' instructions or, in some cases, upon outright guesswork about a victim's religion, those not claimed from the Mayflower Curling Rink were designated for interment at one of the city's three cemeteries – the non-sectarian Fairview Cemetery, the adjacent Baron de Hirsch Cemetery for the Jews, or the Mount Olivet Cemetery for the Catholics. Henry L. Mulligan from White Star's Boston agency was placed in charge of burial arrangements.

Mistakes did occur. Michel Navratil, a Catholic from France, had been travelling with his two sons aboard *Titanic* under the assumed surname of 'Hoffman'. Unclaimed by his estranged wife, his body was buried in the Jewish cemetery based on the assumed name.

Rabbi Jacob Walter decided unilaterally that ten bodies designated for interment at Fairview Cemetery actually belonged in the Baron de Hirsch Cemetery. As memorial services proceeded in the city, he had several workmen move the ten in question. White Star and provincial authorities discovered the unauthorised transfer, and upon further investigation, learned that four of the dead had been Catholics, while others were subjects of family instructions already in hand. As the *Halifax Evening News* pointed out, 'The coffins were somewhat damaged in the frequent changes to which they were subjected and it is said that someone will have to pay for new ones'. The identity of the party financially responsible is not recorded. The unauthorised transfers were cancelled.

Burials began on Friday, 3 May, at all three cemeteries. At Fairview, long trenches had been dug, and into these 50 coffins were placed. Graves were individually dug at Mount Olivet and Baron de Hirsch for 14 additional burials that day. On Saturday, 4 May, there was a single burial service, but it brought out all the concern and sympathy Halifax could muster. The little boy, unclaimed and seemingly forgotten, was to be laid to rest after all efforts at identification had failed.

His plight had deeply touched so many people that White Star and provincial authorities were swamped with offers to sponsor the little fellow's funeral. The decision was made easier when Captain F.H. Larnder requested that he and the crew of the *Mackay-Bennett* – the people who had found the young one – be permitted to accept responsibility for the boy's burial. His request was granted.

St George's Anglican Church was filled to overflowing with flowers and mourners. Following the service, the boy's small white casket, covered with flowers, was carried from the church on the strong shoulders of six *Mackay-Bennett* crewmen and taken by hearse to Fairview Cemetery. There, on a hillside overlooking Fairview Cove, he was laid to rest with the others from *Titanic*. Captain Larnder and his crew paid for a granite marker, larger than most others, and bearing the inscription, 'Erected to the Memory of an Unknown Child Whose Remains Were Recovered after the Disaster to the Titanic, April 15, 1912'.

(After receiving permission from family, local and provincial authorities to exhume his remains, scientists using DNA analysis announced in 2002 that the 'unknown child' was a Finnish boy, Eino Viljami Panula. After further investigation and testing, however, they reported in 2007 that the child unquestionably was 19-month-old Sidney Leslie Goodwin of Melksham, Wiltshire, England, the only one of his eight-member family whose body was recovered.)

Meanwhile, *Montmagny*'s search had not been very successful. A dense fog still enveloped the area, and just four bodies were recovered. On Friday, 10 May, steerage passenger Harold Reynolds was found clinging to a life ring. Later that afternoon, a Syrian girl about 15 years old was discovered and, ten minutes later, the body of Charles Edward Smith, a bedroom steward, was taken aboard. The next afternoon, an unidentified crewman was found and buried at sea 'with

The Pålsson family's sad story was recorded on their gravestone in Fairview Cemetery. Only Mrs Pålsson was found and buried here. Until 2002, it was thought that her son, Gosta Leonard Pålsson, had been buried in an adjacent grave as 'the unknown child'. The inscription on the doomed family's gravestone in Halifax's Fairview Cemetery reflects the officially recorded but incorrect 1912 spelling of her surname. (Authors' collection)

Titanic's violinist 'Jock' Hume was interred under a gravestone whose design was identical to most other victims' markers. (Authors' collection)

suitable services'. As the service proceeded, *Montmagny*'s bell began to peal eerily, seemingly of its own accord, though its ringing was actually caused by the stiff winds buffeting the ship.

On Monday, 13 May, *Montmagny* off-loaded the three coffins at Louisburg, Nova Scotia, for shipment by train to Halifax, and within 24 hours resumed her search. On her second trip only small pieces of wood were found, scattered to the east of the disaster site. Reaching the Gulf Stream as the eastern boundary of her search, she left the area late on Sunday, 19 May.

White Star made one last attempt to locate additional disaster victims. On 14 May the company chartered Bowring Brothers' *Algerine*, which departed from St John's, Newfoundland, one day later. During the voyage a single body, that of saloon steward James McGrady, was recovered.

The six weeks of searching by four ships had yielded 328 dead, of which 119 had been buried at sea. Of the 209 returned to Halifax, 59 were claimed and shipped to other locations, while 150 were buried in the city's three cemeteries. A further ten bodies were found and buried at sea by crews aboard *Carpathia*, *Oceanic*, the tanker *Ottawa* and the freighter *Ilford*, bringing the total recovered to 338.

Soon dark grey granite tombstones were installed over each victim's grave. Most were of identical size and shape. On their sloping top surfaces were engraved the names (if known), the words 'Died April 15, 1912' and the body numbers. In many cases the line reserved for the name was never filled in.

The transatlantic voyage that had begun in Southampton, Cherbourg or Queenstown with such excitement and anticipation had ended for these people, not in the United States, the land of dreams and hopes, of friends and family, but in the compassionate city of Halifax, in whose care their eternal rest would be assured.

For 2,016 others, the eternal sea would serve as well.

CHAPTER EIGHT

Questions and Answers ... and Questions

That there had been a great disaster there was no doubt. That *someone* was responsible there also was no doubt. To establish responsibility – to say nothing of liability – there certainly was no doubt that official investigations were required.

Though *Titanic* was a British ship she was owned by an American trust. Though she sank in international waters, her destination was New York, and there her survivors had landed. In the United States Attorney General's opinion, jurisdiction did exist for a Congressional investigation with the right to subpoena British subjects to testify.

Michigan's Senator William Alden Smith chaired the United States Senate's investigation into Titanic*'s loss.* (Library of Congress)

William Alden Smith, Republican from Michigan and a member of the Senate Committee on Commerce, was selected by his fellow senators to chair a sub-committee to investigate *Titanic*'s loss.

Smith hastily assembled a six-man committee whose members lacked comprehensive knowledge of ships or shipping. Smith himself asked most of the questions, sometimes piercingly correct and at other times almost bumbling. Smith opposed the Morgan interests which owned the International Mercantile Marine and, through it, controlled the White Star Line, *Titanic*'s operators. Yet throughout the hearings he maintained an objectivity that caused many Americans to accept his results.

The Harter Act of 1898 permitted steamship disaster victims to sue ship owners if it were proved the vessel had been

Guglielmo Marconi, inventor of wireless (left, in tie), watched and listened intently as Titanic's *junior wireless operator Harold Bride (right and below centre) testified in Washington.* (Philadelphia Inquirer)

carelessly operated and that the owner or operators were aware of the negligence. Senator Smith hoped to prove negligence and thus provide his American constituency with such a right to sue *Titanic*'s owners and operators for damages. To this end he relentlessly questioned one witness after another in an exhausting marathon investigation.

Perhaps it was because Smith represented a Midwestern state and not one from the

White Star's American vice-president Philip A.S. Franklin (left) and attorney Charles C. Burlingham (centre) escorted J. Bruce Ismay (right) to another day of intense questioning by Senator Smith's committee. (Private collection)

Titanic's *crewmen gathered, awaiting their turns to testify before the Senate committee in Washington.* (New York Times)

more prestigious, industrial East. Perhaps it was the American press, taking its cue from its British colleagues, consciously or unconsciously questioning Smith's (and America's) *right* to investigate. Perhaps it was the grey, ubiquitous power of the Morgan interests, whose sworn enemy Smith was, initiating and then spreading rumours of his incompetency. Perhaps it was Smith himself – his direct, abrupt manner – and his haste in finding the truth of the matter. Whatever the cause, Senator Smith was quickly labelled a fool and his honest efforts mocked by the American and British press.

But Smith was no fool. He was an attorney, a builder and operator of railways, owner and publisher of a moderately sized newspaper. In addition he was a board member (and later chairman) of a company operating a fleet of Lake Michigan steamboats. Physically vigorous and mentally alert (his 53rd birthday occurred 12 May 1912, towards the hearings' conclusion), Smith's background and condition fully qualified him to serve as the *Titanic* disaster's chief investigator.

Bruce Ismay had been anxious to return *Titanic*'s crew to England as soon as possible. In wireless messages sent as *Carpathia* steamed towards New York with *Titanic*'s survivors, Ismay had requested that *Cedric*'s impending New York departure be held until surviving crew could be transferred to her. Ismay's intent was widely misinterpreted. Most thought he wished to shirk his and the company's responsibilities to ensure crew appearances at an American investigation.

In fact, the crew had no money and only the clothing on their backs. Their pay had stopped the moment *Titanic* sank, and Ismay knew well the heart-rending anguish the survivors' families were experiencing, awaiting the return of their loved ones. Thus, in the haste and emotion of the moment, Ismay had acted in what he thought was the crew's best interests.

Philip A.S. Franklin, International Mercantile Marine's American vice-president, was aware of Senator Smith's pending investigation and dissuaded Ismay from expediting his own and the crew's return to England. To avoid adverse public opinion and complex legal problems, Ismay was forced to accept detention until released by Senator Smith and his committee.

Smith wasted no time in exercising the United States Senate's authority to detain *Titanic*'s surviving officers and crew. On Saturday, 20 April, the Red Star liner *Lapland*, on which *Titanic*'s crew had stayed since their New York arrival, was to leave for England. Just before her 10 am departure, Federal marshals served subpoenas on 29 *Titanic* crewmen and four officers to appear as witnesses before the Senate committee. *Lapland* then sailed down the North River, past the Statue of Liberty, and was well through Lower New York Bay before it was discovered that five additional crew with important testimony had left without being subpoenaed.

Senator Smith himself made a hasty telephone call to the Brooklyn Navy Yard, and a wireless message was sent to *Lapland* to stop and await a boarding party. A Federal marshal pursued the ship by tug. His mission was successful: five more were detained to testify. Escorted by private detectives, they and the other subpoenaed crew were lodged aboard White Star's *Celtic* until the afternoon of 21 April, when they were herded on to a train to Washington, DC, for Smith's hearings.

Between 19 April and 25 May the hearings occupied 17 days – the first two at New York's Waldorf Astoria Hotel, the remainder at the new Senate Office Building in Washington. Testimony and affidavits would fill 1,145 printed pages. Altogether the investigation cost the American taxpayers $6,600 (approximately £1,360).

A century later, the forcible detention of *Titanic*'s crew may seem little more than incarceration. Yet while in New York, some crew escaped the steely glares of White Star's hired detectives to refresh themselves and tell their stories to patrons of bars along Manhattan's West Street, across from the *Lapland*'s pier. They attended a memorial service at the Institute of the Seaman's Friend for their fallen shipmates, and were given full outfits of clothing, toiletries and tobacco. Some even managed to visit friends or relatives in New York City's environs. While in Washington, they were honoured guests at an Elks' Club spring festival and visited George Washington's home, Mount Vernon, in Virginia.

Despite White Star's efforts to limit their public comments, some even appeared on stage at Washington's Imperial Theatre, a vaudeville house, in matinee and evening performances, a newspaper advertisement promising that able-bodied seamen Walter Brice, Edward Buley, Frederick Clench and Frank Evans 'will detail the most graphic features of the wreck. Their comrades also will be given an opportunity to tell their experiences' – and share in the box office receipts.

On 24 April, the *Brooklyn Daily Eagle* published a one-column photograph of dining room steward Frederick Dent Ray. Its caption read, 'This is the steward who waited on Major Archibald Butt aboard the *Titanic* and who was called to the White House by President Taft.' An uncropped version showing Ray flanked by two unidentified *Titanic* crew soon appeared in

AFTER INTERVIEW WITH PRESIDENT

In late April and early May 1912, several American newspapers published this photograph of first class dining saloon steward F. Dent Ray (left) and two unidentified Titanic *crew members, its caption reporting a purported meeting of Ray with US President William Howard Taft. No evidence can be found that the meeting ever took place.* (Postville (Iowa) Review/Authors' collection)

several newspapers in America's Midwest. Had Ray been interviewed by Taft about Butt's final moments? The President's own appointment calendars for the period contain no mention of such a meeting, despite their minute detail. Washington's five largest newspapers did not report the event, and Ray himself apparently never spoke of what appears to have been a mythical meeting.

Senator Smith's final report to the United States Senate, dated 28 May 1912, was 19 pages long; exhibits filled another 44 pages. It included a summary of his committee's activities:

> 'We examined 82 witnesses upon various phases of this catastrophe, including 53 British subjects and 29 United States citizens … , 2 general officers of the International Mercantile Marine … all surviving officers, 4 in number … and 34 members of

the crew... We took the testimony of 21 passengers of all classes and 23 other witnesses on subjects relating to our inquiry. We held our sessions in New York and Washington.'

His report praised Captain Rostron and his heroic dash to save *Titanic*'s passengers; he dealt with shortcomings of wireless and telegraph services in the hours and days following the disaster. In the report's most strongly worded section he soundly condemned Captain Stanley Lord, *Californian*'s master, for his failure to respond to apparent distress signals from the sinking *Titanic*, thus establishing the tone for ensuing years of controversy.

Smith's recommendations were few but far-reaching.

Lifeboats: increased capacity, with a seat for each person aboard; adequate manning of lifeboats; lifeboat drill for crew and passengers.

Wireless: 24-hour manning of wireless equipment; action against amateur interference; reliable auxiliary power sources; maintenance of secrecy with all messages.

It would not take the United States Congress long to study and pass legislation embodying these recommendations.

As the hearings in Washington began, the 167 surviving crew aboard *Lapland* were eagerly anticipating reunions with friends and families. After an uneventful crossing she arrived at Plymouth shortly after 7 am on Monday 29 April. After an agonising wait while mail and other passengers were off-loaded, *Titanic*'s surviving crew were ferried ashore aboard the tender *Sir Richard Grenville*.

While the tender slowly steamed for the dock, members of the Board of Trade were already taking depositions and preparing affidavits. Not permitted to board the tender, some British Seafarers' Union members pulled alongside in a small boat and through a megaphone advised the crew to withhold statements until they could consult with their union representatives.

Titanic's crew believed they would be released upon landing. Not so. The Board of

In Plymouth Harbour, Titanic's *crew lined the tender* Sir Richard Grenville's *rail as* Lapland's *passengers watched from above.* (Daily Sketch)

A six-foot-high fence separated Titanic's *detained crew from relatives, the press and curiosity seekers at Plymouth.* (Lloyd's Deathless Story)

Trade wished to question each before releasing them to go home. Accordingly, bedding and provisioning has been provided in the dock's third class waiting room, sealed off behind a high iron fence. As friends and family vainly waited outside, the crew were interrogated inside by the Board's representatives.

Public pressure and, perhaps, humanitarian instincts prevailed. Instead of holding the entire crew overnight, the Board released 85 seamen and firemen at about 1.30 pm after extracting from each an oath that they would not talk to reporters. Leaving behind the cooks, stewardesses and stewards, the seamen and firemen departed from Plymouth for Southampton at about 6 pm aboard a special train.

At Southampton, even as the men were being released, an open-air service celebrating the crew's return was being held at the Marlands, a city commons and park. Territorials, army and navy reserve men, and 50,000 civilians attended. Prayers of thanksgiving for the saved, of remembrance for the lost were offered – the same bittersweet mix of prayers said earlier on 19 April at St Paul's Cathedral in London, during the national mourning service.

As the shadows deepened and evening fell over Southampton hundreds of friends, family and well-wishers gathered at West Station. The train's arrival, 45 minutes ahead of schedule, was greeted with cheers and tears. Almost lost in the crush of the crowd, the surviving crewmen pushed through the pressing throng to join their waiting families. The station platform was illuminated frequently by photographers' flash powder.

Crewmen marched to a Southampton memorial service for their fallen comrades.
(Lloyd's Deathless Story)

Cheers died to a murmur as the crowd realised almost simultaneously that there were many crew absent. A brief moment of near silence gave way to mixed sobs and cheers as the men – families, wives, children, parents in tow – departed from the station and walked up the hill to the town and home. The train departed from West Station and moments later arrived at the Docks Station, where the frenzied scene of welcome was repeated.

The night of 29 April at Southampton was one of joy and gladness, of sorrow and recollection. Nowhere else in the world that night could be found within a single block joyous parties in parlour and pub celebrating a loved one's return, while several houses away widows and bereaved mothers mourned for loved ones who would never come home.

The second group of *Titanic* survivors, 86 stewards, stewardesses and kitchen staff, were released from Plymouth on Tuesday 30 April. Most boarded a special train for Southampton, where they arrived around 9 pm. The previous night's scenes were again repeated, this time with an air of finality. Except for the 34 crewmen and four officers being detained at Washington for the American inquiry, whose names were known, the crew members arriving this night at Southampton were the last. There would be no more. And a sense of loss, a great wave of shock and sorrow descended upon the city, as it had upon the world ...

The remaining crew, including look-outs Lee and Fleet and quartermaster Hichens, arrived at Liverpool aboard White Star's *Celtic* on 6 May. Though on a smaller scale than that at Southampton, the celebration was no less joyous.

A weary Bruce Ismay managed a tight smile but his wife Florence beamed as the crowd welcomed them home upon their Liverpool arrival aboard Adriatic. (Daily Sketch)

Bruce Ismay and *Titanic*'s four officers arrived at Liverpool on 11 May aboard *Adriatic*. Mrs Ismay had journeyed to Queenstown to board the liner on its inbound voyage, and as Bruce Ismay walked down the gangway, his wife followed, beaming, for in contrast to his treatment in America, Ismay was greeted with cheers from the large crowd gathered at the Liverpool landing stage. Mr and Mrs Ismay could scarcely press through the crowd to reach their motor car. Hands reached out to touch him amid cries of recognition. It was almost a hero's welcome. And as Ismay and his wife left the dock for Sandheys, their home just outside Liverpool, they appeared quite affected by the greeting.

Titanic's surviving officers were also greeted at the dock by relatives. But they were tight-lipped when it came to answering the press's questions. There were questions to be asked and answers that had to be given. Though nominally owned by an American corporation, *Titanic* was a British-registered ship, built under British standards, sailing under British regulations with a British crew. And it was to be a British commission whose Court of Inquiry would investigate the disaster and ensure that no other British ship would ever meet a similar fate. The American hearings had asked 'How?' The British investigation would ask 'Why?'

The British Board of Trade regulations defining ships' structure had last been revised in 1894 when the largest vessel afloat was the 12,950-ton Cunarder *Campania*. By 1911, *Titanic*'s completion saw size increased to more than 46,000 tons, with even larger British ships coming. With development of the 'super liners' (*Lusitania*, *Mauretania*, *Olympic* and *Titanic*) some political figures – among them the populist Horatio Bottomley – questioned the regulations, particularly regarding adequate lifeboat provision.

Indeed the Board had already considered this question. An advisory committee had met early in 1911 to discuss lifeboats and their relation to increased ship size and passenger-carrying capacities. While there were points remaining to be considered, the committee found no reasons for changing existing regulations, which were based upon cubic footage allotted to passenger accommodation. *Titanic*'s original designer, Alexander Carlisle, was so pleased that the committee would even *consider* the question of adequate lifeboats that he signed its final report with only the mildest protest.

Titanic's final plan included 16 lifeboats. With seating capacity for 980 persons these met then-current regulations. Four Englehardt collapsible boats, with seating for 196 persons, were added by *Titanic*'s designers and builders and represented capacity beyond the Board's requirements.

The 'Order for Formal Investigation' into *Titanic*'s loss, which granted authority to the inquiry under the Merchant Shipping Act of 1894, was initiated by the Board of Trade and signed on 30 April 1912. The Wreck Commissioner, Lord Mersey – John Charles Bigham, Baron Mersey of Toxteth (Lancashire) – had already received his authority through a 23 April warrant signed by the Right Honourable Robert Threshire, Earl Loreburn, Lord High Chancellor of Great Britain. The names of the five assessors to assist Lord Mersey were approved by the Home Secretary on 23 April.

A formidable battery of attorneys represented the hearing's many parties. Principal among them were Sir Rufus Isaacs, KC, the Attorney General, counsel to the Board; the Right Honourable Sir Robert Finlay, KC, MP, who headed the White Star Line's counsel, and Mr Thomas Scanlan (instructed by Mr Smith, solicitor), who represented the National Sailors' and Firemen's Union.

John Charles Bigham, Lord Mersey, was appointed wreck commissioner for the Board of Trade's investigation into the Titanic *disaster. He is shown here with his son, who was the commission's secretary.* (Daily Sketch)

The Attorney General presented 26 questions to the commission to prove and for which they had to try and find answers. They concerned construction, navigation and ice warnings received by *Titanic*. A final question was added, though hearings were already under way, concerning the steamer *Californian*'s possible proximity to the sinking.

The hearings were conducted in the Scottish Drill Hall, near Buckingham Palace, where the acoustics were abominable. Sounds were subdued and dispersed as barely-heard, muffled echoes. The addition of sound reflectors to the front of the hall had little effect. Spectators, counsel and commissioners all strained to hear the testimonies.

Among the hearings' highlights: early testimony of *Titanic*'s officers and crew describing the wreck's details; Captain Rostron's account of the rescue and Guglielmo Marconi's testimony regarding wireless' role in maritime safety; Captain

Workmen prepared a large half-model of Titanic *to assist Lord Mersey and his assessors in visualising the night's events.* (Daily Mirror)

Stanley Lord, *Californian*'s master, who appeared only as a witness, and who was accused of no wrongdoing during the hearings; Sir Cosmo Duff-Gordon and his wife (well-known as clothing designer 'Lucile'), who satisfactorily explained to the commissioners how they managed to depart from the sinking *Titanic* in a lifeboat with a 35-person capacity but bearing only an even dozen; Bruce Ismay, who explained, again to the commissioners' satisfaction, that he had nothing to do with *Titanic*'s navigation, and that he left the sinking ship only after he saw no other passengers in the lifeboat's vicinity.

The hearings' concluding public sessions were occupied with technical testimony and evidence about *Titanic*'s construction and how it compared with other ships; about the Board of Trade's own lifeboat rules (and how the Board was diligently pursuing modification of them, an effort begun early in 1911, more than a year before ...); about stopping and turning tests conducted with *Titanic*'s sister vessel *Olympic*. The testimony and public sessions ended on Friday 21 June. Eight days of summations and closing arguments followed. To determine guilt or innocence was not the commission's purpose. It was to establish right or wrong; to accept and praise right; to criticise wrong.

As a jury retires to consider its verdict, so did Mersey and his assessors then retire from public view to study the records of testimony, the exhibits and counsels' arguments. And

Sir Cosmo Duff-Gordon (to the left of model's fourth funnel) listened intently as George Symons described lifeboat 1's departure from Titanic *with only 12 on board.* (Daily Mirror)

Lord Mersey ('X') and his nautical assessors observed the lowering of an Olympic *lifeboat at Southampton on 6 May.* (Daily Sketch)

a vast amount of information it was: the transcript of testimony alone consisted of 25,622 questions and answers, which filled 959 double-column folio-sized pages.

On 30 July the Mersey Commission presented its findings. Summarised in the briefest form they were:

> That the collision of *Titanic* with the iceberg was due to the excessive speed at which the ship was navigated; that a proper watch was not kept, that the ship's boats were properly lowered but insufficiently manned; that the Leyland liner *Californian* might have reached *Titanic* if she had attempted to do so; that the track followed was reasonably safe with proper vigilance; and that there had been no discrimination against third class passengers in the saving of life.

The Commission exonerated J. Bruce Ismay and Sir Cosmo Duff-Gordon from allegations of improper conduct. The judgement recommended more watertight compartments on

Look-out Archie Jewell ('X', top left) completed his testimony, and earned a rare 'thank-you' from Lord Mersey. The hearing room's seats were filled with press and spectators. (Daily Mirror)

ocean-going ships, provision of lifeboat capacity for all aboard, and tighter rules regarding ships' look-outs.

Lord Mersey praised the general conduct of passengers and crew, but regretted that none of the lifeboats – especially number 1 – had attempted to save the drowning. He highly praised *Carpathia*'s Captain Rostron. He was convinced that those aboard *Californian* had

Lady Lucile Duff-Gordon was one off just two passengers to testify at the British inquiry. (Her husband was the other.) (Daily Graphic)

seen *Titanic*'s signals at a distance of from eight to ten miles and could have reached her without risk, thus saving the lives of many or all. In conclusion, Mersey severely blamed the Board of Trade for its failure to give earlier consideration to revising the Merchant Shipping Act of 1894.

Following the release of Mersey's findings, the London *Daily Telegraph* said this of the inquiry's report:

> 'It must be borne in mind that Lord Mersey's court was not in the ordinary sense a court of justice, and the results of its deliberations must not be regarded as a judgement...
>
> 'Technically speaking, the report is not the last word, but in practice it would probably be treated as though it were. It is difficult to suppose, for instance, that any court which had to inquire into the responsibility of the owners of the ship would disregard the expression of opinion by Lord Mersey and those who sat with him, and this particular point is one of vital importance. For if "fault or privity" can be brought home to the owners of *Titanic* the limitation of liability laid down by the Merchant Shipping Act – £15 per ton for loss of life, £8 per ton for loss or damage to goods – is wiped out and the damages of sufferers are left at large...'

According to the Merchant Shipping Act, *Titanic*'s owners were liable for freight losses of about £123,711 (about $600,000). Claims in American courts by relatives of those who lost

Californian's *Captain Stanley Lord (centre) arrived at the Board of Trade inquiry to give testimony as a witness. Only after he left the stand did the Board of Trade introduce a question implying allegations of Captain Lord's inaction while* Titanic *sank.* (Daily Graphic)

Californian's apprentice James Gibson testified against his captain, Stanley Lord, at the British inquiry. (Daily Graphic)

their lives and businessmen who lost their goods ran into millions of dollars. The ship's owners, therefore, brought suit in American courts to limit liabilities under American law, which meant the value of 13 recovered-but-used lifeboats, a small amount for pre-paid freight, and the value of passengers' tickets, or about £20,159 ($97,772.02) in all. It was against this amount that claims totalling £3,464,765 ($16,804,112) were filed.

The United States District Court, Southern District for the State of New York had jurisdiction over the case, mainly because *Titanic* had been sailing towards the Port of New York and because White Star's principal American office was there. Assigned to hear the case was District Court Judge Charles M. Hough. Early in the proceedings and in a separate decision, District Court Judge George C. Holt ruled that British law applied to the total claim limit.

Between the action's initiation and the start of hearings (September 1912 to June 1915), Judge Hough withdrew due to ill health. Judge Julius M. Mayer thus heard the case.

The claimants wished to prove negligence; the White Star Line wished to limit its liability

Lord Mersey (second from left, top row) and his assessors presided over the British Board of Trade's inquiry into Titanic's *loss, which received answers to more than 25,000 questions.* (Daily Graphic)

J. Bruce Ismay answered more than 800 questions during his testimony before Lord Mersey. (Sphere)

by proving that negligence had no part in the disaster. Meanwhile, in the case of *Ryan v Oceanic Steam Navigation Co Ltd*, a British jury found for the claimants. White Star appealed. But on 9 February 1914 Lord Justice Vaughan Williams dismissed the case and thus upheld negligence in *Titanic*'s navigation. Following this decision, many claimants withdrew their actions in the United States District Court and refiled them in British courts.

There were still a sufficient number of claimants – and claims – to make the American hearings

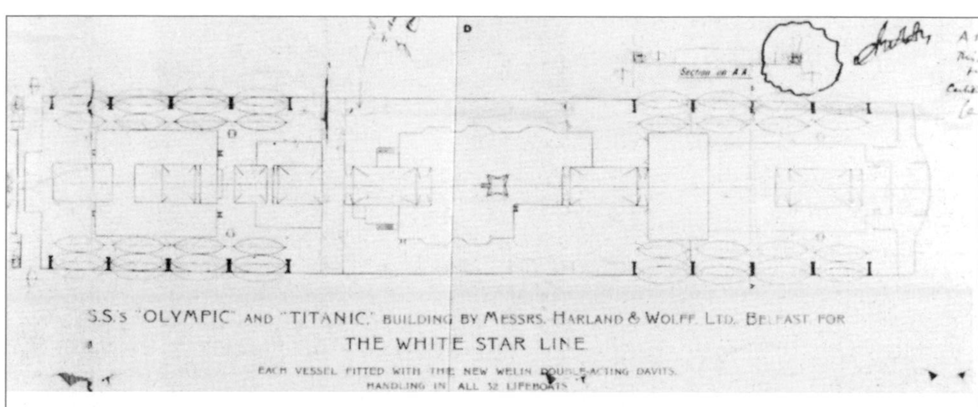

It was shown at the New York limitation of liability hearings that even while Titanic *and* Olympic *were under construction, White Star had considered equipping the two ships with 32 lifeboats each, more than enough to have saved everyone on board* Titanic. (US National Archives)

At the limitation of liability hearings in New York, Mrs Charlotte Drake Cardeza filed a 14-page, $177,352.75 (£36,567) claim against the White Star Line for loss of her personal property. (Philadelphia Inquirer)

Among the evidence presented at the hearings was Titanic's *freight list, showing money White Star had received for carriage of cargo aboard the lost liner.* (US National Archives) more than mere formality. Harland and Wolff's naval architect Edward Wilding described in detail *Titanic*'s construction and safety features. Alexander Carlisle, in a sworn deposition made at London, reiterated his British inquiry testimony about *Titanic*'s inadequate lifeboat capacity. Far more passengers appeared and testified than had at either the Senate or Board of Trade investigations, including John B. Thayer, Karl Behr, William J. Mellors, Mrs Jacques Futrelle ...

Claims had been filed for loss of life and property. The largest for loss of life – $1,000,000 (£206,185) – was filed by the widow of New York theatrical producer Henry B. Harris. Mrs Charlotte Cardeza, wife of a Philadelphia, Pennsylvania, millionaire, submitted the largest claim for lost property – $177,352.74 (£36,567). The government of the United States filed one of the smaller claims: $41.04 (£8 10s 5d) for lost registered mail.

The diversity of property claims reflected the variety of passengers aboard *Titanic*. Among the hundreds of claims for lost clothing, jewellery and personal items were the following:

Eugene Daly	Set of bagpipes	$50.00
Emilio Portaluppi	Picture of Garibaldi, 'signed by him and presented by him to my grandfather'	$3,000.00
William Carter	One Renault 35 hp automobile	$5,000.00
Ella Holmes White	Roosters and hens from Chasse ile rage Jardin d'Agriculture [total, 4 fowl]	$207.87
Edwina Troutt	Marmalade machine	8s 5d
Håkan Björnström-Steffansson	Oil painting by Blondel, 4x8 feet, 'La Circassienne au Bain'	$100,000.00
Stuart Collett	Hand-written college lecture notes, two year course	$50.00
Hersh L. Siebald	Seven parcels of parchment of the Hebrew Holy Scrolls [Torah]	$250.00
Margaret Brown	Three crates of ancient models for Denver Museum	$500.00
Annie May Stengel	Copy of *Science and Health*	$5.00
Robert W. Daniel	Champion French bulldog, named Gamin de Pycombe	$750.00

The total for all claims, £3,464,765 ($16,804,112) had to be divided pro rata among all claimants. By December 1915 barristers on both sides reached a tentative settlement. On 28 July 1916, more than four years after the disaster, Judge Mayer signed the decree ending all *Titanic* lawsuits. The amount distributed among the claimants was £136,701 ($663,000).

Thus were responsibilities investigated and assigned. Some who were responsible bore no blame; others were assigned blame not rightfully theirs. Liabilities were set, many believed, far below their actual value. But the law, in all its infallible majesty, had spoken. Only time's passing would bring questions for which no answers had been provided, and answers whose questions had yet to be asked ...

CHAPTER NINE

With Time's Passing

There is perhaps no more fitting conclusion to any *Titanic* story than to look both backwards and forwards. Backwards to a very brief consideration of three lives touched by their *Titanic* associations. Forwards to the discovery of *Titanic*'s broken wreck and what this discovery means to the ship and its memory, as well as to those who would exploit the wreck for their own selfish ends.

Joseph Groves Boxhall was born in Hull, Yorkshire, on 23 March 1884. He died on 25 April 1967. Prior to his joining *Titanic* at Belfast as her fourth officer, Boxhall had been 13 years at sea. He served his apprenticeship with William Thomas, Liverpool, and later served as an officer with the Wilson Line of Hull. Passing for his master's certificate at Hull in 1907, he joined the White Star Line and had served for five years prior to joining *Titanic*. He had by that time gained his extra master's certificate.

Following the *Titanic*, Boxhall served briefly as fourth officer aboard *Adriatic*. He was a sub-lieutenant in the Royal Naval Reserve and shortly before the outbreak of the First World War was commissioned in a battleship for a year's training. When the war began he remained for a time with this ship, HMS *Commonwealth*, and was then sent to Gibraltar where he commanded a torpedo boat. He became a staff member of Gibraltar's commanding admiral, and remained at that post until the end of the war.

Returning to White Star, Boxhall continued to serve until well after that line's 1934 merger with Cunard. He served as first officer aboard several Cunard liners, including *Berengaria* and *Aquitania*, and eventually became chief officer aboard *Ausonia*, *Scythia* and *Antonia*. Of all the junior officers aboard *Titanic*, Boxhall stayed longest at sea, retiring due to ill health in 1940.

He maintained an interest in the sea and in *Titanic*, although he never participated actively in any public discussions of the disaster. While he did not encourage debate concerning his role that night, he was not reluctant to declare that he was always certain the position he calculated for *Titanic* was correct and there could be no reason for him to change his view.

When Walter Lord's book *A Night to Remember* was made into a film Commander Boxhall came out of semi-retirement to assist in the production as joint technical adviser with Commodore Harry Grattidge. He found it '... very interesting to see myself as I was 46 years ago'. It was Commander Boxhall's wish that, upon his death, he be cremated and his ashes scattered at the site of *Titanic*'s loss.

Commander Joseph Groves Boxhall on the occasion of his serving as technical adviser in the 1958 film A Night to Remember. (Courtesy of William MacQuitty)

The following extract is from the log of the Cunard motor vessel *Scotia*:

> 'MV *Scotia*, New York to Southampton, June 12, 1967, at 0938, Lat 41°46' N, Long 50°14' W, the cremated remains of the late commander J.G. Boxhall were scattered on the sea during a brief ceremony.'

Yet another to be touched very profoundly by the *Titanic* was Joseph Bruce Ismay. Born at Enfield House, Great Crosby, on 12 December 1862, he was the eldest son of Thomas Henry Ismay and the former Margaret Bruce. Thomas Ismay had begun the White Star Line, officially known as the Oceanic Steam Navigation Company Limited, in 1867. It was managed by his own firm of Ismay, Imrie and Company, and upon his death on 23 November 1899 its control passed to 36-year-old Bruce Ismay.

On 1 January 1900 Bruce Ismay took on as partner Harold Arthur Sanderson, an old friend who had been the company's general manager for the past five years. Under Bruce Ismay's leadership, with Sanderson's support and assistance, the White Star Line flourished. Plans were made to enter the Australian and New Zealand trades with several new steamships. Construction also began on three large liners to complement the 21,000-ton

Joseph Bruce Ismay, in one of his last photographs, which remained a favourite of Mrs Ismay's. (Courtesy of Wilton J. Oldham)

Celtic. (Launched on 4 April 1901, *Celtic* was Thomas Ismay's last ship and the first to exceed *Great Eastern* in tonnage. She was the first of the 'Big Four' liners – *Cedric*, *Baltic* and *Adriatic* were the other three.)

Ismay also presided over White Star's sale to the American-controlled International Mercantile Marine. This great combine was formed in 1893 from the American, Red Star and Inman Lines and through recent purchases or control of the Atlantic Transport, Dominion and Leyland lines. Reaching an 'understanding' with the major German Atlantic shipping companies, the combine dominated the North Atlantic freight and passenger trades.

(Resisting Morgan's offers, the Cunard Line had remained British. For their loyalty – and to preserve British interests in liners which might serve as transports and armed merchant cruisers in war time – the British government extended low-interest loans to Cunard, enabling the company to build *Lusitania* and *Mauretania*, the largest and fastest liners of the day.)

Perhaps fear of this government-subsidised competition caused White Star shareholders to accept the Morgan offer. The sale, for more than £10,000,000, was readily accepted by shareholders, though personally painful for the Ismay family. In essence, White Star became an American-owned company on 1 January 1904. At Morgan's request, J. Bruce Ismay assumed the chairmanship of International Mercantile Marine, which he effectively managed along with his own company's operations.

White Star's fortunes were never better. During the next eight years many new freighters and liners were completed. An expanded New Zealand and Australian service was established. And to the already popular and profitable 'Big Four' were added the great *Olympic* and *Titanic*, with a third sister, *Gigantic*, well advanced in her planning.

With the company's success thus assured, Ismay wished to retire as IMM chairman to devote more time to his own company and to personal pursuits. In an Autumn 1911 exchange of letters, Bruce Ismay and Harold Sanderson reached an understanding that Ismay was to retire at the end of 1912 and that Sanderson would head IMM.

This proposal was acceptable to the combine's American interests, though there was some bickering about the actual date. Ismay himself had some second thoughts, particularly about the season in which his departure would occur. But finally a letter dated 26 February 1912 was sent to J.P. Morgan and Company at New York, citing 30 June 1913 as the date of Ismay's retirement and Sanderson's succession as chairman.

In April 1912 Ismay's presence aboard *Titanic* was twofold: to observe the liner on her maiden voyage and also to visit IMM's main American office in New York to discuss details of his forthcoming retirement. His 1.40 am departure from the sinking *Titanic* was fully vindicated by the British inquiry. It was established beyond doubt that there were no women or children – indeed, no other passengers – in the vicinity of the boat as it was being lowered. As Lord Mersey stated:

> 'The attack on Mr Ismay resolved itself into the suggestion that, occupying the position of managing director of the steamship company, some moral duty was imposed upon him to wait on board until the vessel foundered. I do not agree. Mr Ismay, after rendering assistance to many passengers, found "C" collapsible, the last boat on the starboard side, actually being lowered. No other people were there at the time. There was room for him and he jumped in. Had he not jumped in he would merely have added one more life, namely his own, to the number of those lost.'

Certain segments of the American press maligned Ismay. In a horrendous display of irresponsible journalism, the Hearst-owned newspapers, led by the *New York American*, displayed his photograph surrounded by small pictures of women whose husbands had been lost. The picture's caption read, 'J. Brute Ismay'.

The British press was more kind. Several witnesses to Ismay's behaviour during the sinking testified on his behalf during the American inquiry. Their evidence was generally acceptable to the British public. To many, he had acted heroically during the liner's evacuation. When he returned to England aboard *Adriatic* on 11 May 1912, a large crowd of well-wishers cheered his arrival at Liverpool.

The British inquiry found him personally clear of fault. Yet he was never really happy again. Each anniversary, particularly, caused him great sorrow and self-recrimination. He was especially troubled by survivors' accounts, many over-dramatised to the point of untruth, which appeared continually in newspapers. His family was supportive, but his wife Florence would not allow the subject to be discussed or even mentioned. Bruce Ismay lived the rest of his life haunted by his own feelings of guilt.

He had wished to remain as White Star's chairman following his resignation from IMM, but the combine's American interests blocked his wish. However, he did remain a member of IMM's British committee until he resigned from even this post in 1916.

After leaving International Mercantile Marine and White Star, Ismay continued to serve actively as a board member with numerous companies, particularly the London & North Western Railway. When that firm became part of the London, Midland and Scottish Railway, Bruce Ismay was asked repeatedly to be the new system's chairman. But he always refused, never again wishing to be in a position of public prominence.

Following the First World War he sold Sandheys, his country home near Liverpool, but still spent time each week in that city attending company board meetings. During the 1920s he spent much leisure time at his Irish estate, The Lodge, at Costelloe, County Galway, on Ireland's west coast.

While he withdrew from his active role in business, Bruce Ismay did not become reclusive. He enjoyed walking in London's parks and attending concerts. His house at 15 Hill Street, Berkeley Square, became a meeting place for friends and family at small dinner parties. Until his eyesight began to fail, he spent several successive seasons at a rented lodge near Gleneagles, in Scotland, where he engaged in his two favourite sports of shooting and fishing.

His own children – Margaret, Tom, George and Evelyn – were married now. There were grandchildren to brighten summer holidays. When The Lodge at Costelloe was gutted by a mysterious fire in September 1922, Ismay had the house rebuilt (it was completed in 1927) and took a lively interest in its redecoration.

In 1934 Bruce Ismay retired from active business life. The shipping company his father had founded, and whose fortunes he, himself, had helped to ensure, had merged with its great rival, the Cunard Line. Within two years, all but two of the ships bearing White Star's black-topped buff funnels had gone to the scrapyard, judged superfluous by the new management.

Late in 1936 a circulatory illness forced the amputation of Bruce Ismay's right leg. He was confined to a wheelchair, and could walk only with the aid of crutches. He was able to spend the summer of 1937 at a house in the country, returning to his Hill Street home in early autumn. Far to the north, the great *Olympic*, upon which he had lavished so many hours and so many hopes, was towed to Inverkeithing, Scotland, for final demolition. On 14 October 1937 he suffered a severe stroke and died three days later. His cremated remains were buried in Putney Vale Cemetery, near London.

Stanley Lord was born at Bolton, Greater Manchester, on 13 September 1877. Of all the figures in *Titanic*'s story, perhaps none is so tragic as that of the master of the Leyland steamship *Californian*. As alleged by the Mersey commission, Captain Lord was aware – or should have been – of *Titanic*'s plight, but did nothing to save her passengers and crew, though his vessel was in a position to do so.

During the Board of Trade hearings, Captain Lord had appeared solely as a witness. He was not indicted (rightly or wrongly) for his role, and therefore was unable to appear officially and publicly in his own defence. The press, in accepting Lord Mersey's opinion, vilified Lord and his supposed callous indifference. He was forced to resign from the Leyland Line, for whom he had worked more than 14 years. The Board of Trade refused to reopen investigation into the matter in 1912 and again in 1913.

Little credence was given to evidence presented during the original Board of Trade hearings: *Californian*'s estimated position, stopped in ice, from 17 to 20 miles away from the sinking site, the fact that the vessel seen from *Titanic* during the sinking was *moving*; that the nearby lights of yet another ship were seen from *Californian*'s bridge; that several other vessels were in *Titanic*'s vicinity during and immediately after the disaster...

With the advent of the First World War, Captain Lord abandoned efforts to have his case

Titanic's *swimming bath, first class.*

Turkish bath, first class.

First class dining saloon.

Reading and writing room, first class.

À la carte *restaurant, first class.*

Typical cabin, second class.

Dining room, second class.

Nautile *is taken aboard* Nadir *following completion of her 17 June 1993 dive.* (Photo by Dik Barton, © 1993 RMS Titanic Inc)

The brass pedestal of Titanic's *steering telemotor stands out starkly in* Nautile's *powerful lights.* (© 1987 RMS Titanic Inc)

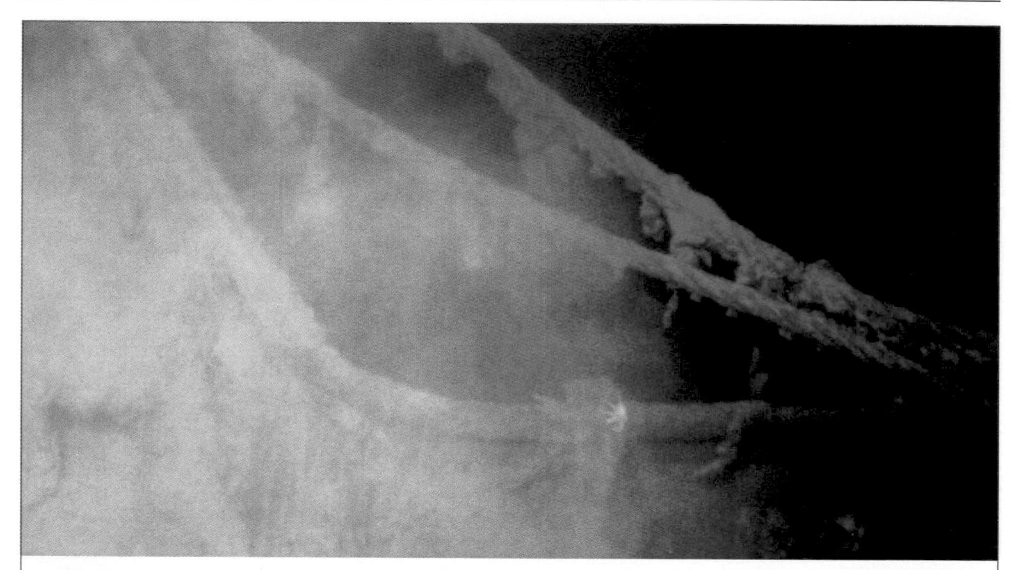

Cables from Titanic's *foremast drape the corner* of *number two cargo hold's hatchway. A fog* of *sediment disturbed by* Nautile's *motions clouds the left* of *the photo.* (Authors' photo, © 1993 RMS Titanic Inc)

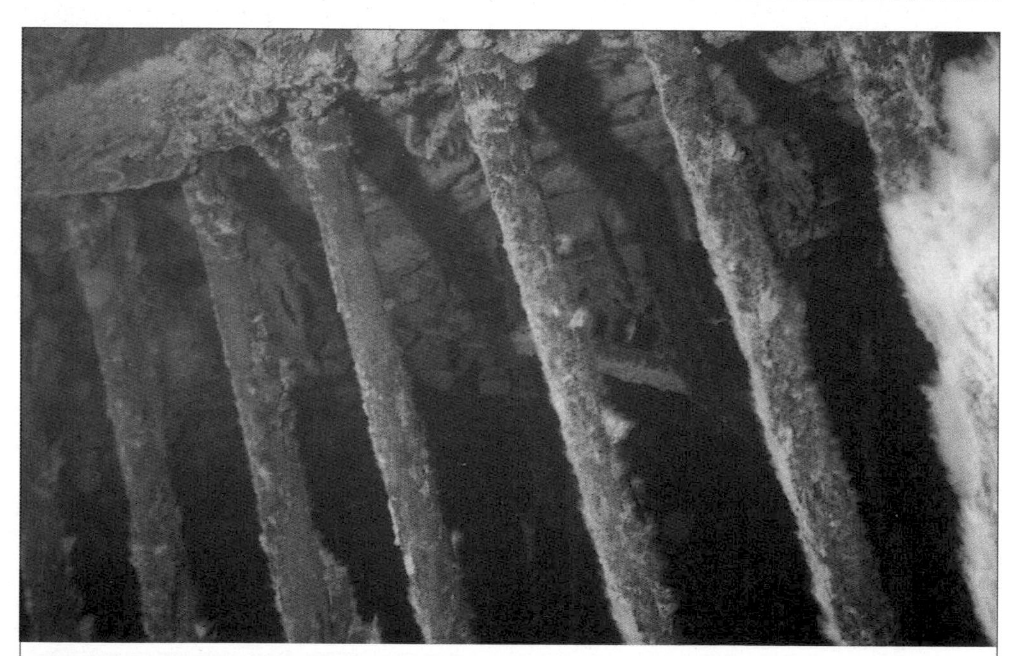

The remote-operated vehicle Robin *snapped this view* of *the barrier that separated the number two hatchway from the surrounding cargo hold.* (© 1993 RMS Titanic Inc)

While they survived impact with the sea's bottom, these au gratin dishes faced two new threats: burial and corrosion. (© 1987 IFREMER/RMS Titanic Inc)

Saved from destruction by the conservators' art, a small stack of the au gratin dishes awaits display. (© 1987 RMS Titanic Inc)

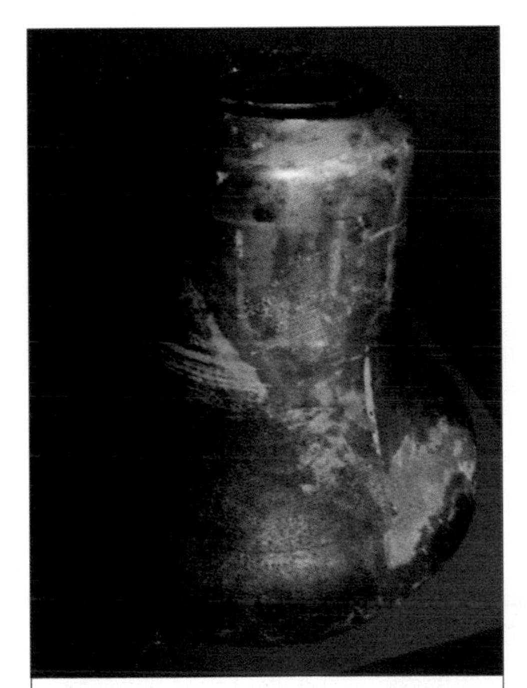

Corrosion on its sides and a heavily rusted mounting support at its top confirm the long years spent on the ocean floor by Titanic's *bell.* (Robert M. DiSogra)

Titanic's *voice: beauty combined with utility. The liner's whistles are placed on temporary exhibition following their arrival in Norfolk, Virginia, in July 1993.*

The accumulated impurities and corrosion of more than 80 years on the sea's bottom are removed by careful electrolysis in a French laboratory. The cherub's arms once held a candelabra at the foot of Titanic's *after grand staircase on A deck.* (© 1987 Electricité de France/RMS Titanic Inc)

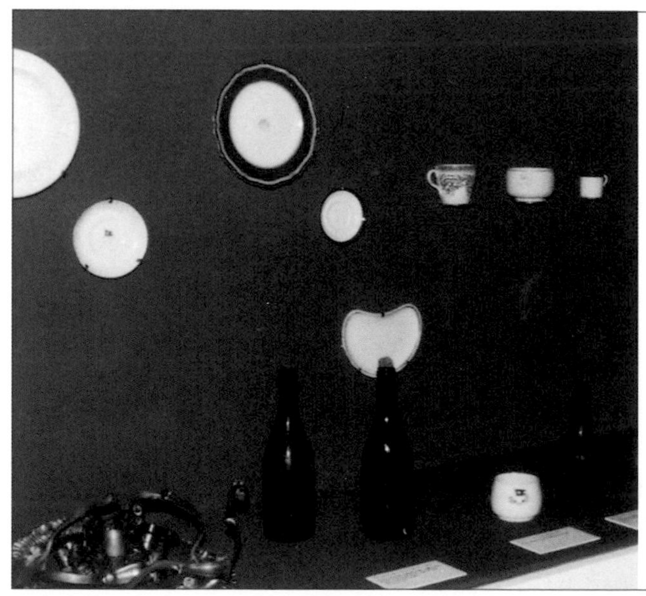

One portion of the 1994-95 National Maritime Museum Titanic *artefact exhibition featured dinnerware in several patterns, a variety of bottles, and a gilded chandelier, which was seen by nearly 750,000 people during the exhibition's year-long run.* (Robert M. DiSogra)

Captain of the Californian *in 1912, Stanley Lord in a photograph taken by his son on 13 September 1957, Captain Lord's 80th birthday.* (With kind permission of his son, Stanley T. Lord)

reheard. With the assistance of Frank Strachan, the Leyland Line's American agent, Captain Lord obtained a command in the fleet of the London-based Nitrate Producers Steam Ship Co Ltd (Lawther, Latta & Co). He entered their services in February 1913 and held command until March 1927, including sea service during the war. While still deeply hurt by Mersey's allegations, Lord found that his association with the *Titanic* inquiry did not affect him personally or professionally during this period. He let the matter drop.

After his 1927 retirement Stanley Lord had little awareness of the public's continued interest in *Titanic*. He was not an avid reader. When the 1955 book A *Night to Remember* was serialised in the *Liverpool Daily Echo*, Lord – no relation to the book's author Walter Lord – read parts of it. But the parts he read contained no reference to *Californian* and made little impression on him.

However, with the 1958 release of the film based on *A Night to Remember*, Captain Lord became aware that, in his words, 'the film gave great prominence to the allegation that *Californian* stood by in close proximity to the sinking *Titanic*'.

In efforts to clear his name and present publicly the facts not brought out by the British inquiry, Captain Lord enlisted the services of W. Leslie Harrison, general secretary of the British Mercantile Marine Service Association, of which Lord had been a member continuously since 1897. Acting on behalf of *Californian*'s former master, Harrison corresponded with the book's author and the film's producer, requesting that they grant consideration to the captain's side of the story. But both author and producer maintained that the British inquiry findings were authoritative and provided sufficient justification for the references to *Californian* in their respective works.

With the active participation of Captain Lord, who had carefully retained all his original 1912–13 correspondence and personal documents pertaining to the case, Leslie Harrison prepared a petition to the British Board of Trade to reopen the 1912 hearings to correct their findings regarding Lord.

Captain Lord, never in good health since retirement from the sea in 1927, died on 24 January 1962. He was never in any doubt that, even if he had known of *Titanic*'s sinking, he would have been unable to reach the disaster site in time to save any lives. In daylight it had taken from 6 am to 8.30 am to reach the spot where *Carpathia* was taking aboard the last survivors. Lord always maintained that if he had known of the disaster and tried to traverse the extensive ice-field at night, he would have joined *Titanic* on the bottom.

Captain Lord's death did not deter Leslie Harrison from pursuing his own wish – and duty – of trying to clear the captain's name. In February 1965 he presented to the Board of Trade a position paper setting forth the facts as he saw them, some of which were not offered in the 1912 inquiry, and requesting a reversal of the original board's findings.

Not included in the Petition was mention of a confidential report made by the first officer of the Norwegian sealing ship *Samson* to Norwegian authorities in April 1912. The report, not made public until 1962, described in some detail how *Samson* purported to have been close enough to the sinking *Titanic* to see the liner's lights and to view the distress rockets being fired.

Samson's master failed to intervene, the report claimed, because he feared his own vessel was in violation of territorial seal-hunting regulations and that the rockets represented official attempts at signalling other ships to intercept his own. *Samson* had no wireless, which might have ascertained the situation. After sighting the rockets, the vessel is alleged to have changed course and headed northwards, away from the activity. (Subsequent research indicates that *Samson* was in the Icelandic port of Isafjordhur on 6 April, and again on 20 April, and thus likely nowhere near the sinking site on the night of 14-15 April.)

Harrison's first petition concluded that the vessels seen by *Titanic* and *Californian* were different ships; that Lord Mersey failed to consider that relative times kept by *Titanic* and *Californian* differed by 12 minutes; that '... personal opinions expressed by *Californian*'s third officer and her assistant donkeyman, that the ship they saw must have been *Titanic*, were in fact invalidated by their own evidence and consequently did not justify the extreme importance attached to them by the Court'.

Particularly poignant is Harrison's conclusion that 'The British Court of Inquiry failed in their duty to warn Captain Lord that his position before them was not simply that of a witness; that in consequence he was not given proper opportunity to defend himself; and this failure also deprived him of what otherwise would have been a statutory right of appeal.'

In a letter dated 6 September 1965 the British Board of Trade rejected the petition. In their view, no new and important evidence had been presented. The Board also cited the time which had elapsed since the original hearing, and the deaths of a majority of those involved, including the petitioner.

Marshalling his facts and forces, Leslie Harrison presented yet another petition to the Board of Trade on 4 March 1968. In it, he included new evidence from Lawrence Beesley, a science teacher and author of the book *The Loss of the Titanic*, long accepted as the most reliable factual account of the disaster.

Beesley, a second class *Titanic* passenger, had not been called to testify at either the American or British inquiries. In February 1963 he made a sworn declaration regarding *Titanic*'s distress rockets, but requested that this evidence not be made public until after his death. When this occurred in 1967, Leslie Harrison was able to incorporate the affidavit in his second petition.

Beesley swore that he personally had observed 'about eight distress rockets fired'. He continued, 'I left the ship in No. 13 lifeboat and I am quite confident that the last of these rockets had been fired *before* [Beesley's italics] this lifeboat cleared *Titanic*'s side after being lowered into the water'.

Members of *Californian*'s crew had stated that they observed rockets being fired until 2 am. *Titanic*'s boat number 13 had left the sinking ship at about 1.30 am. Even allowing for the 12-minute difference in relative ships' times, the discrepancy between the two statements is evident – enough to give cause for a reconsideration of the official stand.

The Board of Trade rejected the second petition on Captain Lord's behalf, saying there had been no miscarriage of justice in the original hearings and that the majority of the people concerned had died. Beesley's evidence was rejected because it was 'not evidence that could not have been produced at the [original] inquiry and also because that evidence is not "important" within the meaning of the Section' of the Merchant Shipping Act of 1894 requiring reopening of a hearing if important new evidence is produced.

With the 1985 discovery of *Titanic*'s actual wreck co-ordinates, important new evidence did become available. And it was introduced…

CHAPTER TEN

Dateline: North Atlantic

Almost before the 'cold waters of the North Atlantic closed over her stern plates', efforts – or at least suggestions – were afoot to salvage *Titanic*. Soon after the disaster a consortium of wealthy families (Guggenheims, Astors and Wideners) contracted with the Merritt and Chapman Derrick and Wrecking Company to raise *Titanic*. Merritt and Chapman studied the proposal but concluded that their 1912 equipment was inadequate to attempt salvage at the great depth involved.

Legends concerning highly valuable cargo, diamonds and gems, vast amounts of gold ingots, large quantities of valuable registered mail, and a fabulous jewelled copy of *The Rubaiyat* were soon well established. Over the years the tales grew until, to many, *Titanic*'s remains represented an immense treasure trove of almost limitless potential.

The truth, though known, was ignored in favour of greed, romantic imagination and media hyperbole. *Titanic*'s cargo manifest had been published on 19 April 1912 in several New York newspapers. The cargo was mundane, typical of the commercial goods most express liners carried during the period. There was no gold listed on the manifest, nor did the company's official cargo stowage diagram show any in the ship's specie room. No insurance claims were filed for valuable diamonds or other gems, apart from a few claims for personal jewellery.

The copy of *The Rubaiyat*, undoubtedly of historic interest, had recently been sold at a 1912 London auction for £405 ($2,025). Assuming present-day monetary values to be ten times (or even 100 times) the 1912 rates, they would scarcely compensate for the estimated £9 or £10 million required to mount a salvage expedition, plus the many thousands necessary to sustain each day's operations.

Yet through the passing decades, *Titanic*'s retrieval has been the subject of many plans and schemes: compressed air polyurethane foam, electrolysis of seawater to create hydrogen and oxygen for lift, deep-sea submersibles with remote-controlled 'arms', bags filled with petroleum jelly, encasing the ship in ice formed by liquid nitrogen… these schemes and others, it was said, could raise the sunken liner once she was found.

Technical limitations had caused Merritt and Chapman's decision to decline a salvage attempt. Subsequent schemes, too, were limited by inadequate equipment, inexpert knowledge, funding problems or failure to consider basic physical laws. Even the wreck's exact location remained elusive.

During the summer of 1953 the Southampton (UK) salvage firm of Risdon Beazley Ltd attempted to locate *Titanic*. Using high explosives to obtain echo profiles, the firm spent seven days in the vicinity of 43.65 N, 52.04 W aboard their salvage vessel *Help*. Their effort was unsuccessful.

Between 1968 and 1978 individuals such as Douglas Woolley, Mark Bamford, Joe King and his partner Spencer Sokale spent countless hours planning expeditions to discover and retrieve *Titanic*'s remains – and working out how to finance the efforts.

In 1977 a group of West Berlin businessmen set up Titanic-Tresor as a backing for Douglas Woolley; subsequently they withdrew their support. Also during 1977 a company named Seaonics was formed to investigate the wreck's location and to plan for its exploration. This group involved several prominent scientists and explorers.

During 1978 Walt Disney Productions, in collaboration with *National Geographic* magazine, investigated the possibility of making a full-length film of the disaster. Feasibility studies involving deep underwater photography were conducted by the Alcoa Corporation, owners of the submersible *Aluminaut*. The project was dropped late the same year.

In 1979 the British company Seawise & Titanic Salvage was formed. Headed by Clive Ramsay and Philip Slade – with the expertise of Derek Berwin, underwater photographic expert, and Commander John Grattan, underwater diving consultant – the group was funded by industrialist/financier Sir James Goldsmith, who hoped to profit through exclusive coverage for his magazine, *Now*.

This was by far the best thought-out group to undertake actual exploration of the wreck. (The others, up to this point, had been involved principally in research.) The original 'base position' established was in the vicinity of 41.40 N, 50.03 W, a site whose co-ordinates were subsequently reassessed. The expedition was planned for the summer of 1980, but the group failed to obtain sponsorship and was forced to suspend operations.

By this time American scientists on both the west coast (California's Scripps Institute of Oceanography) and the east (Massachusetts' Woods Hole Oceanographic Institution) were showing interest in *Titanic*'s wreck. (The two research organisations would later share a June 1981 exploratory voyage, funded by the United States Office of Naval Research.)

In New York City, Columbia University's Lamont-Doherty Geological Observatory seemingly became the scientific arm of a group headed by Texas oil man Jack Grimm and his partner, Florida film-maker Mike Harris. In earlier undertakings, Grimm had led searches for such historical artefacts as Bigfoot (a sort of colonial 'Abominable Snowman' also known locally as 'Sasquatch'), the Loch Ness monster and Noah's Ark, whose 350-cubit (525-foot) gopher wood hull traditionally rests on top of Turkey's 16,946-foot high Mount Ararat. Grimm's group hoped to realise a profit from *Titanic*'s exploration through the sale of photographs, books and a film.

Their 1980 voyage aboard the research vessel *H.J.W Fay* carried them to the area of 41.40/41.50 N, 50.00/50.10 W. Hampered by almost continuous bad weather throughout their on-site stay (from 29 July to 17 August), the expedition's members were disappointed in their search. Their sonar soundings produced only some fine, detailed images of the search area's floor.

Competition from Fred Koehler, described by the press as an 'electronics wizard', threatened the exclusivity of Grimm's 1981 expedition. Koehler, of Coral Gables, Florida, sold his electronics repair shop to finance completion of his two-man, 7 by 14½-foot deep-sea submarine, the *Seacopter*. He planned to dive on *Titanic*'s wreck, enter the hull, and remove the legendary diamonds from the purser's safe. Unable to reach agreement with Grimm on *Seacopter*'s use, Koehler set up his own expedition to exploit the wreck. He attracted moderate press attention but no financial backing and his expedition never materialised.

'We have highly technical equipment, and unless we're looking in the wrong area, and I don't believe we are, we'll find her.' With these optimistic words to the press, Grimm left on his 1981 expedition aboard the research vessel *Gyre*. He and his band of intrepid scientists reached their search site three days after the joint Scripps/Woods Hole expedition left the same general area. On station between 9 July and 18 July at approximately 41.39/41.44 N, 50.02/50.08 W, Grimm's second try also was hampered by storms.

There was to be yet another Grimm attempt in 1983, aboard the *Robert D. Conrad*. While Grimm declared that a rounded object first photographed in 1980 was one of *Titanic*'s propeller blades, maritime experts and oceanographers remained convinced it was a rock outcropping.

Beset by technical difficulties, internal management conflicts, incomplete historical research and uncooperative weather, the three expeditions had produced meagre results for their multimillion-dollar costs. Rather than answer questions, they had posed more: was *Titanic*'s 'CQD position' of 41.46 N, 50.14 W – where the expeditions had searched – correct? Had she been buried by a 1929 undersea earthquake? The world's press and *Titanic* scholars speculated. It seemed the ship never would be found.

By 1984, the glare of *Titanic* publicity had subsided. Editors now treated *Titanic* search stories with scepticism and minimal display. In a more productive atmosphere, two respected scientific organisations, the *Institut Français de Recherche pour l'Exploitation de la Mer* (the French Institute for Research and Exploitation of the Seas) and the Woods Hole Oceanographic Institution continued quiet preparations for a joint underwater expedition. Jean Jarry of *IFREMER* and Robert D. Ballard of the Woods Hole Oceanographic Institution's Deep Submergence Laboratory headed the mission.

French taxpayers and the prestigious National Geographic Society picked up part of the cost. Officially, the mission was described as 'deep-water engineering tests' of innovative, remote-controlled underwater equipment, with *Titanic*'s discovery a hoped-for but secondary bonus.

The equipment was, in fact, the first components of an advanced system, called *Argo-Jason*, which in final form would permit scientists to photograph and work efficiently in the oceans' depths without leaving their surface vessels. Because of its national security implications, the United States Navy's Office of Naval Research funded *Argo-Jason*'s development with a $2.8 million (£1.87 million) grant to Woods Hole's Deep Submergence Laboratory in 1983.

On 1 July 1985 the expedition's first phase began as the French left for the disaster site aboard their research vessel *Le Suroît*. Armed with considerable historical research and co-ordinates of the areas unsuccessfully searched in the three Grimm expeditions, the French concentrated their efforts in a 150-square-mile area largely to the south and east of *Titanic*'s distress position. They arrived on 9 July.

The French brought their new side-scanning sonar system, capable of 3,000-feet-wide, highly detailed sweeps over the ocean floor. Upon their subsequent arrival, the Americans contributed two remote-controlled, sonar-guided camera packages, *Argo* and ANGUS, to photograph the liner, once found.

For ten days, *Le Suroît* criss-crossed the designated area in an operation known to the crew as 'mowing the lawn'. No sign of *Titanic* was found. With relentless monotony the vessel towed the side-scan sonar around the clock, as scientists poured over reams of printouts. Their vigil was interrupted by a 45-knot gale that lasted two full days.

On 19 July the French left for refuelling and supplies at St Pierre et Miquelon, near Newfoundland. Here, Ballard and some of his team joined *Le Suroît* for a second try, resuming on 26 July. By 7 August, the French and their American colleagues had scanned 80% of the search area without success. Time had run out – *Le Suroît* was required elsewhere. Shortly before *Le Suroît* returned home, the Americans and several French colleagues flew to the Azores where they joined the Woods Hole research vessel *Knorr*. On 15 August she left Ponta Delgada with 24 scientists and 25 crew aboard.

Before tackling *Titanic*, a "warm-up exercise" had been necessary under Ballard's funding agreement with the U S Navy. Thus the *Knorr* detoured after it departed the Azores, and under total secrecy, her crew located and explored the wrecks of the American nuclear submarines *Thresher*, lost in 1963, and *Scorpion*, lost in 1968, both with all hands. The ANGUS and *Argo* camera systems were deployed, and photographed the submarines' wreckage, providing clues about their losses. (It was not until after newspapers reported the secret *Scorpion* prelude to the *Titanic* mission that the US Navy released several photographs of that vessel's wreckage.)

With systems and procedures thoroughly tested, *Knorr* then set out for the *Titanic* search area, arriving there on 22 August. *Argo*, containing video cameras and a sonar system, was lowered some 2½ miles down, and round-the-clock searching resumed under watchful chief scientists Ballard and Jean-Louis Michel.

The 'anomalies' once thought by the Grimm expeditions to be parts of *Titanic* were quickly despatched; observation confirmed all, including the so-called 'propeller', to have been large boulders. The expedition then began searching for a debris field, concentrating on the area the French had not surveyed.

Day after day, for about a fortnight, the television screens revealed only the sandy undersea floor. The mission experienced extraordinary weather; the sea was quite flat, as it had been the night *Titanic* sank. The routine was numbing: hour after hour observers sat before the televisions, watching for some sign of *Titanic*'s presence.

Early on the morning of 1 September 1985, Ballard was relaxing in his quarters with a book. Jean-Louis Michel, in the control room, recalled:

On 1 September 1985, a US-French team aboard the US Navy research vessel Knorr *located the wreck of the* Titanic. (© 1985 Woods Hole Oceanographic Institution; Reprinted by permission)

> 'I was on watch at the time of the discovery… at 1 am with members of my team. The first indication came from the video where unnatural forms appeared. Our attention was captured by objects lying on the bottom, and within a few minutes more and more of these man-made objects appeared on our screen, until the apparition of a boiler clearly belonging to the *Titanic*.
>
> '[I acted] to prevent the vehicle from hitting any obstacle [below] by raising the altitude of the *Argo*, to send somebody to wake Bob [Ballard], Captain Bowen and my French colleagues… Within a few minutes the control room was much too crowded… My joy was tempered by the fact that I knew we were on the site of a tragedy; I shared this moment with my 40-man team of *Le Suroît*, who should have been there.'

The ship's cook roused Ballard, who rushed to the control room and abruptly took over command of the watch. In the crowded space someone remarked it was 1.40 am. Remembering that Titanic had sunk at 2.20, Ballard led everyone to the ship's stern, where they observed a brief silence for those lost in the disaster.

Since the site's geography was unknown, the expedition was greatly concerned about accidentally striking the wreck with the camera package. Ballard gave orders to haul *Argo* up until fathometer and sonar readings could pinpoint the area's arrangement. A near-catastrophe occurred as the ship's winch broke while hauling *Argo* aboard. It took 14 hours of jury-rigging a spare part before another look at *Titanic* could be obtained.

Meanwhile the expedition deployed a network of underwater transponders which, with the ship's equipment, gave instantaneous accurate information about the relative positions of *Titanic*, *Knorr* and *Argo*.

The weather began to deteriorate, and winds built to more than 40 knots, with 14-foot waves, yet her unique cycloidal propellers enabled *Knorr* to maintain position; underwater photography continued.

It was an exceptionally difficult task: the camera package trailed some 2½ miles downwards from aft of the *Knorr*, pitching in the heavy seas. Ballard and Michel surveyed around the ship, then 'flew' *Argo* over her. *Titanic* was sitting upright, and initially it appeared that her second and third funnels were still standing. The forward mast had fallen back against the superstructure's port side, but the bow was in remarkably good condition, covered only by light sediment. In a joyous announcement to shore, Ballard said the ship was in 'museum-like' condition. Expedition scientists then decided to approach from the stern, but it could not be found. What had become of it? Ballard could only speculate that somehow it had broken off.

The high-'altitude' black-and-white video images from *Argo* were an excellent beginning. But with one day remaining before *Knorr* had to return home, it was essential to obtain some close-up photographs of *Titanic*. ANGUS was thus deployed. At times gliding to within a dozen yards of the ship, it recorded a series of stunning views, eerily tinted in blue.

The world soon saw them. The giant hole where number one funnel had been. The anchor chains, frozen in position. The crow's nest and its telephone alcove, now hanging precariously over a forward hatch. Unbroken wine bottles, still corked, but probably now filled with seawater. Debris once part of the ship's structure. The starboard bridge wing, smashed flat by the falling forward funnel (was this how Captain Smith had died?). A piece of shell plating, torn from the hull. Cargo cranes, twisted in the wracking forces during and after the sinking.

ANGUS had to be 'flown blind', with no immediate video feedback to those controlling it. Ballard called searching near the wreck 'one of the most harrowing experiences of my life'. It was his concern for *Titanic*'s sanctity – and the multimillion dollar camera unit's welfare – that prompted the decision to attempt only high-altitude, downward-looking views.

There was time for no more. Transponders were retrieved, all equipment was stowed. The voyage home began, but not before an intruding aeroplane had repeatedly circled the ship. The expedition had tried to keep *Titanic*'s exact location a secret to prevent plunderers and armchair salvage experts from disturbing the wreck, possibly damaging it further. With the plane's arrival, it appeared the secret would eventually leak out; *Titanic*'s depth, public opinion, and individual conscience apparently would be all the protection she would have.

As *Knorr* sailed westwards scientists reviewed the mission's data and photographs. The stern – now in pieces – had been located after all, 1,900 feet behind the 'bow section' in the midst of a mile-long debris field.

Thousands of well-wishers, hundreds of reporters and more than a dozen film crews from around the world greeted the expedition at Woods Hole, Massachusetts, on 9 September. The quiet New England town was mobbed by those seeking to learn more about 'the people who found the *Titanic*'. Elsewhere, *Titanic* survivors were being bombarded with interview requests. Once again the White Star ship and her people were headline news.

At a Washington, DC, press conference, Ballard concluded his prepared statement saying:

> 'The *Titanic* itself lies in 13,000 feet of water on a gently sloping alpine-like countryside overlooking a small canyon below.
>
> 'Its bow faces north and the ship sits upright on the bottom. Its mighty stacks point upward.
>
> 'There is no light at this great depth and little light can be found.
>
> 'It is quiet and peaceful and a fitting place for the remains of this greatest of sea tragedies to rest.
>
> 'May it forever remain that way and may God bless these found souls.'

His noble idea did not last very long. Within two weeks of the discovery, a Welshman had proposed raising the ship (notwithstanding its fracture into at least two pieces). A British insurance company said it might own the wreck. Several new improbable schemes involving refloating or salvage were announced.

One proposed to raise the ship using giant underwater slings lowered from a 'semisubmersible platform [that] would rest on two watertight supertankers' (presumably drained of oil). The procedure, admitted promoters, would have to be performed twice, since *Titanic*'s stern had broken off. 'It could take more than five years to complete the salvage operation,' noted a breathless magazine reporter.

'It's like the Great Wall of China,' said a proponent. 'Given enough time and money and people, you can do anything.'

A Belgian entrepreneur promised 40 lucky passengers the opportunity to dive in a chartered submarine to the *Titanic*, recover artefacts, then return to the surface for a memorial service marking the sinking's anniversary and featuring several Hollywood celebrities – all for $25,000 (£17,241) a piece.

In an effort to protect the ship, North Carolina Congressman Walter B. Jones introduced the 'Titanic Maritime Memorial Act' in the United States House of Representatives. It called for establishment of strict scientific guidelines for the wreck's exploration and salvage, and asked the American Secretary of State to enter into discussions with Canada, the United Kingdom and France, urging them to pass similar legislation. By late 1986 the bill had overwhelmingly passed the House and Senate. On 21 October 1986 President Ronald Reagan signed the measure into law. It might well be a moot gesture: *Titanic* lies in international waters beyond any legal jurisdiction, some law experts said.

Two Englishmen felt otherwise. On 5 November 1985, just two months after *Titanic*'s discovery, Leslie Pink and Leonard Brown founded the Titanic Preservation Trust in Portsmouth. Declaring that 'delving in the innards of the *Titanic*, two-and-a-half miles down in the Atlantic, is like trespassing with intent to do damage in a graveyard,' the Trust hoped to 'encourage litigation to keep the ship and its contents together as a memorial, instead of fragments and contents being removed piecemeal to go to various bidders'. The group would support 'restrained archaeological and oceanographic research at the site of the foundered vessel'.

While answering some questions, an expedition had once again posed new ones. When and why had the ship broken up? In how many pieces had she broken? How large was the iceberg's gash, and where was it located? Was the ship really in 'museum-like' condition? The overhead views of *Titanic* provided mere hints about the night of 14–15 April. It was apparent that there was still more to learn. And apparent, too, was the need for a manned craft that could negotiate safely around *Titanic*'s broken hull to take pictures from additional angles and viewpoints.

Once again, underwater equipment tests provided the basis for another visit to the ship. *Jason Jr* (or '*JJ*'), a prototype of the Jason portion of Woods Hole's undersea exploration system, was ready for trials, funded by a $220,000 (£146,700) US Navy grant.

Jason Jr was a lawnmower-sized, self-propelled, high-tech camera unit, powered and controlled through a 250-foot-long umbilical cord. Its four thrusters allowed instantaneous

For the 1986 expedition, the Woods Hole team used the research vessel Atlantis II, *seen here launching the deep-diving submersible* Alvin *over the* Titanic's *final resting place.* (© 1986 Woods Hole Oceanographic Institution; Reprinted by permission)

manoeuvring even in tight quarters in depths up to 20,000 feet. It carried high-resolution colour video and still cameras and powerful light sources. *JJ*'s use would pinpoint modifications needed on *Jason* itself, the larger, more capable unit planned for 1989. Navy personnel joined the 1986 expedition for hands-on operating experience. Once again, Dr Robert Ballard headed the team.

Ultimately, Jason would be launched from *Argo*. But its predecessor *Jason Jr* required a ride to the ocean floor. The three-man deep-diving submersible *Alvin*, a veteran of more than 1,700 dives since its construction in 1964, was specially modified to increase its depth capabilities and to accept the hitch-hiking *JJ*, mounted in a basket-like 'garage' on *Alvin*'s forward end.

The Woods Hole research vessel *Atlantis II* sailed for the *Titanic* site on 9 July 1986, carrying 56 scientists and crew. Not on board were *IFREMER*'s representatives, who had had disagreements with the Americans over the release of photographs from the 1985 expedition.

A 3½-day voyage brought *Atlantis II* to the wreck site without difficulty. The sunken liner's exact co-ordinates, kept in a safe, had been fed into *Atlantis II*'s navigational computer, taking her directly to the spot.

The expedition first installed a series of transponders near *Titanic*'s location, allowing pinpoint positioning to within tens of metres, vitally important for *Alvin*'s safety.

Alvin's first dive, number 1,705 of her busy career, began on Sunday 13 July. Dr Ballard and two crewmen played classical music on one of *Alvin*'s tape recorders during their 2½-hour descent to the ship's final resting place, approximately 12,500 feet (3,800 metres) below.

As pressure on *Alvin*'s titanium hull mounted steadily, water temperature dropped. Sunlight quickly faded to gloom, and then to perpetual blackness. Ballard noticed rivulets of water forming on the submersible's inside walls. Outside pressure was now 6,500 pounds per square inch and he expressed concern to the two *Alvin* crewmen. They reassured him such water condensation was normal.

The downward journey ended. With guidance from *Atlantis II*, the submarine inched forward on its electric motors, its powerful electric lights piercing the abyssal darkness. Suddenly, the search was over. Before them lay 'a tremendous black wall of steel [that] seemed endless in all directions,' as Ballard described it. For the first time in 74 years, human beings were seeing *Titanic* first hand.

The reverie was brought to an abrupt end after just a few minutes. An alarm buzzer clamorously announced that, somehow, seawater was reaching *Alvin*'s batteries, upon which everything – including vital life support systems – depended. There was no more time for *Titanic* observations. It was necessary to get to the surface, and quickly. Chief pilot Ralph Hollis released ballast, manoeuvring slightly to ensure it would not fall on to *Titanic*, and the submarine rapidly ascended.

Safely on board *Atlantis II*, *Alvin* was put in technicians' care. Repair time would not be wasted. ANGUS, a 1985 expedition veteran, was towed over the wreck in a nightly ritual

Rust covers a double-bitt bollard located forward on the starboard side of the sunken vessel. (© 1986 Woods Hole Oceanographic Institution; Reprinted by permission)

An unbroken window marks a first class single berth cabin on Titanic's *starboard boat deck, aft of the officers' quarters.* (© 1986 Woods Hole Oceanographic Institution; Reprinted by permission)

An electric lifeboat winch on the starboard side of the boat deck lies under a heavy mantle of corrosion. (© 1986 Woods Hole Oceanographic Institution; Reprinted by permission)

The camera aboard ANGUS, the unmanned towed vehicle, peers directly into the collapsed remains of Titanic's *forward first class entrance. To the left of the hole is the roof over elevator machinery.* (© 1986 Woods Hole Oceanographic Institution; Reprinted by permission)

The portside aft corner of the ventilation shaft at the base of the second funnel (top) has had its louvred grating torn away. The large circular hole marks the former location of a cowl ventilator above the first class reading room. To the right the decking begins its steep downward plunge aft to the breaking point. (© 1986 Woods Hole Oceanographic Institution; Reprinted by permission)

The unbroken, inch-thick glass of a midships porthole resists the flows of iron-eating bacteria's 'rusticles' cascading down the vessel's side. (© 1986 Woods Hole Oceanographic Institution; Reprinted by permission)

The 1986 expedition located the 200-foot stern section, lying almost 2,000 feet from the bow and rotated 180 degrees from the bow section. A cargo crane juts out over the starboard side; the cowling for the crane's heavy-duty electric motors has been torn away, revealing white porcelain electric insulators. (© 1986 Woods Hole Oceanographic Institution; Reprinted by permission)

The chaotic appearance of Titanic's *stern section reflects the immense forces that wracked the area upon its impact with the seabed. Electrical cables, torn from their conduits, criss-cross the underside of a deck bent backwards over the rest of the stern (right).* (© 1986 Woods Hole Oceanographic Institution; Reprinted by permission)

providing photographic and video reconnaissance for the following day's manned search. Meanwhile, other technicians tested *Jason Jr* and connected it for the first time to *Alvin*.

Launch procedures were established quickly. Each morning, *Alvin* would be deposited on the ocean's surface with *JJ* in its 'garage'. After a five-minute check-out, the submarine would then descend in a free-fall to the *Titanic*. The deposit point was 'upstream' of *Titanic*'s position, with moderately strong undersea currents pushing the submarine closer to the ship. Eventually, the expedition could place *Alvin* in such a way as to arrive within 150 feet of *Titanic* after a 12,500-foot descent.

Working conditions inside *Alvin* were cramped and uncomfortable. Her pilot sat or kneeled at the front porthole. To the portside was *JJ*'s operator, while the dive's scientist was at the starboard viewing port. Ballard said the experience was 'like working inside a Swiss watch'.

Dive number two examined the forward first class entrance's collapsed dome, through which Ballard planned to send *JJ* on the next dive. The dive provided four hours for photographing the ship and ascertaining its condition and arrangement.

'We couldn't see the [*Titanic*'s] name,' Ballard radioed *Atlantis II*. 'There are rivers of rust pouring down the side of the ship and running down into the sediment.' Presumably, the indented, 18-inch high, gold-painted letters were well hidden by corrosion.

Alvin then headed for the wheelhouse. 'We landed where the wheelhouse was and saw the ship's wheel minus the wood,' he reported. The wheelhouse itself, also made of wood, had been eaten down to a six-inch-high nub. Ballard reported that all wood had been consumed by undersea worms, whose calcified skeletons now cover much of the ship. The submarine then headed for the opening for number one funnel, moving aft and out over the collapsed grand staircase dome.

Dive number three was to feature *JJ*'s debut. Upon arrival at the wreck, the explorers found strong ocean currents that hadn't been there before. Sweeping across *Titanic* from the starboard side aft to the port side forward, they repeatedly forced *Alvin* toward the *Titanic*'s towering hull. With the strong current rendering *JJ*'s deployment impossible, Ballard and the crew used the time to photograph the ship more fully, including her previously unseen port side.

The dive concluded, Ballard radioed its findings to shore. 'Today was a hard dive,' he said. 'The current was very strong and there was a lot of ticklish matter in the water, so it was a hard-working dive ... The objective today was still imagery. We saw the beautiful light on the [top of the forward] mast, a big brass fixture, and we could see a lot of door knobs [and] things like that.'

Next morning the current had quietened considerably. *Alvin* 'landed' next to the gaping hole that was once *Titanic*'s forward grand staircase. Using controls resembling those of a video game, *JJ*'s pilot Martin Bowen gingerly nudged the robot out of its 'garage' and into the ship. As one newspaper headline put it, 'After 74 years, *Titanic* has guests'.

Downwards the 'swimming eyeball' went, perhaps reaching as far as B deck. The ship's interior was an utter shambles. Only the steel columns that had supported the dome and staircase survived. All wood had disappeared here, too. The staircase's lower portion was filled with debris. Several crystal-and-brass light fixtures still hung from their overhead wires, accompanied by an unending succession of yellow, red, brown and orange stalactites.

On 16 July dive number five commenced. A landing near the bridge included a close-up examination of the metallic remnants of the ship's wheel. A tense moment arose when *JJ*'s control cable became badly snagged on a piece of jagged metal. Bowen's repeated back-and-forth manoeuvring eventually freed the craft without damage.

An attempt to go through A deck's large windows for another inside look was blocked; *JJ* was a bit too big to fit. 'He'll have to go on a diet,' Ballard quipped. The expedition instead peered through some of the many unbroken first class cabin portholes. Like the public rooms, *Titanic*'s staterooms are largely filled with dangling 'rusticles' and debris, though subsequent expeditions determined that wood panelling, metallic bed frames and marble fireplaces remain in some places. Coming up along the ship's side, the submarine bumped an overhanging lifeboat davit, sending a shower of rust fluttering down.

JJ was then sent to inspect the crow's nest and the foremast's navigation light. The submersible next moved aft along the boat deck, and again 'parked' near the grand staircase for a brief interior look.

'I'm very relieved not to find any human remains,' Dr Ballard reported at the conclusion of the dive. The sea and its creatures appear to have claimed *Titanic*'s people. Scientists said the water's low mineral content and steady bottom currents aided the dissolving process.

Exploration continued. The 18 July dive concentrated on the debris field near the ship's stern. Ballard reported sighting 'thousands and thousands of items laid all over the bottom,' the vast majority from second or third class areas of the ship. They included chamber pots, electric stateroom heaters, dishes, cups, pots and pans from the galley, thousands of lumps of coal, and several of the ship's four safes, emptied during the ship's evacuation, according to eye-witness reports.

Approaching the largest, probably from the second class purser's office, *Alvin*'s manipulator arm gave the handle a tug, but the Milner's safe remained secure. 'It had a big handle of bronze or gold, and we saw the dial.' The door bore a 'beautiful crest', and was 'polished and clean; it looked brand new,' Ballard said.

Only a handful of personal belongings were found. They included a shoe, the porcelain head of a child's doll, and a Romanesque statue.

After six ten-hour dives in six days, crew fatigue caused 19 July to be a day of rest. Technicians swarmed over *Alvin* and *JJ*, doing necessary maintenance. Meanwhile scientists examined photographs to plan future dives.

The seventh dive was a departure from previous ones: Ballard remained on *Atlantis II*, and three Navy personnel dived to *Titanic* to gain valuable experience in operating *Jason Jr* and *Alvin*.

Working some 1,900 feet behind the bow section, dive eight concentrated on the mangled and broken stern section. It was a sobering visit that left the explorers deeply moved with the realisation that hundreds of *Titanic*'s people had spent their last few terrifying moments here. 'It was the hardest place to work emotionally,' Ballard recalled.

Explorers were surprised to find the stern section in basically one piece, sitting upright and pointing in the same direction as the bow. The rudder's upper portion could be discerned. The two wing propellers were visible, bent upward in the stern's impact with the

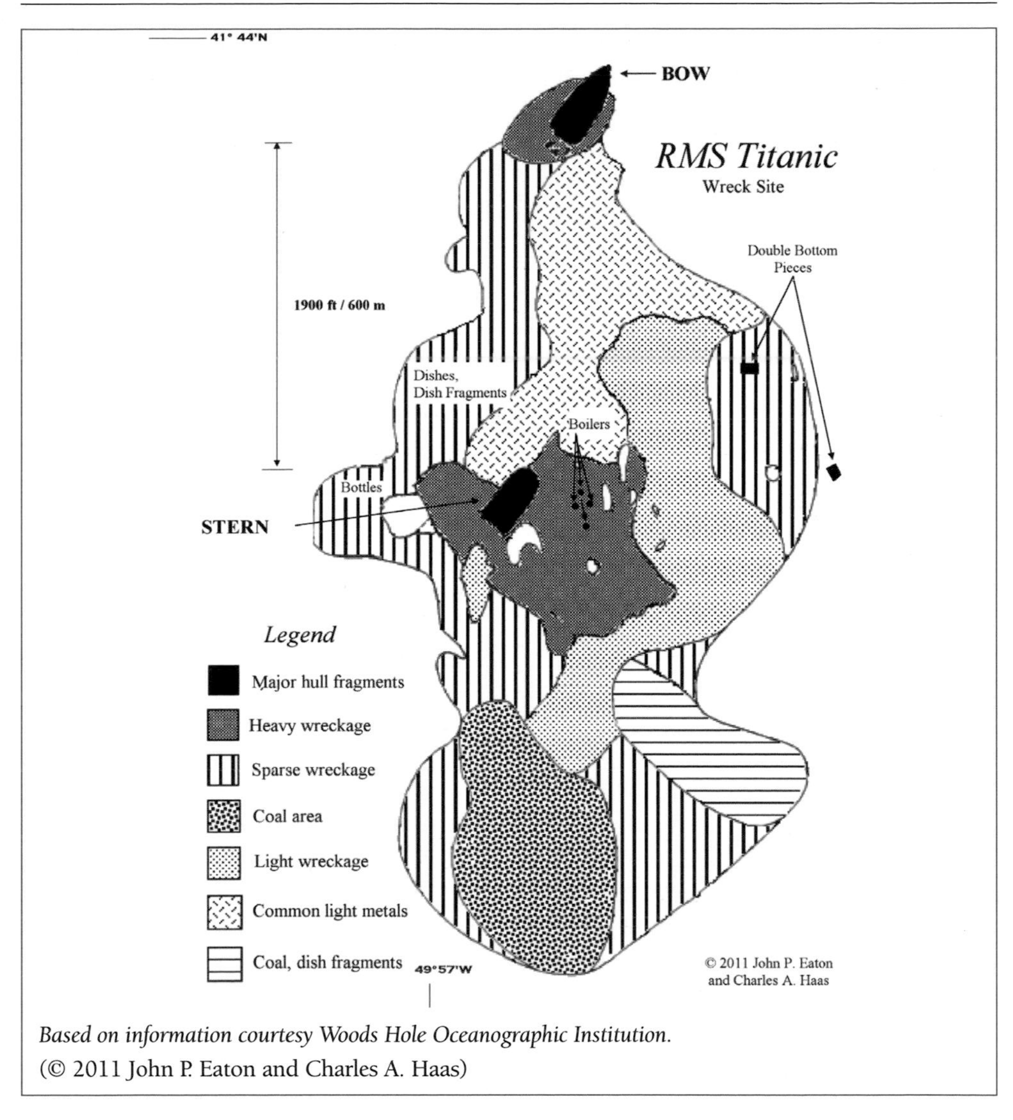

Based on information courtesy Woods Hole Oceanographic Institution.
(© 2011 John P. Eaton and Charles A. Haas)

bottom, but the centre propeller remained buried in the ocean floor's sediment. Other stern pieces were damaged almost beyond recognition. Ballard called the stern 'a carnage of debris. It looked violent and torn, fragmented and jumbled like a rat's nest.'

The poop deck was peeled up and flattened back on itself, exposing under-deck beams and electrical cables. A 2½-ton cargo crane was twisted outwards over the ship's side. The stern's unpredictable shapes made diving difficult and dangerous.

Apparently, *Titanic*'s hull had broken on or near the surface. The huge engines plummeted quickly to the ocean floor, while bow and stern sections pirouetted to points some distance away. As they spiralled downwards, their contents scattered, forming the debris field.

On one occasion, *JJ* provided some moments of high drama. As *Alvin* surfaced in heavy seas, the robot fell out of its 'garage' and dangled from its umbilical cable which chafed against a cutting tool on the submarine's bow. With each passing swell, damage became increasingly likely, and only prompt action prevented the cable's severing and loss of the multimillion-dollar robot. Later, two days of dives had to be cancelled because of other electrical problems with *JJ*.

A historical accident also occurred. As ANGUS was hauled aboard after a night of unmanned photography, it was found to have snagged a steel cable from *Titanic*. Throughout the mission, personnel had adhered scrupulously to a 'hands off' policy regarding *Titanic* artefacts. As Ballard later put it, 'We thought the artefacts looked better exactly where they were.' Reverence and respect were observed. The wayward cable was dropped overboard immediately, and crewmen executing the order were asked to wash their hands, lest *Titanic* rust remain behind.

Another dive examined the break between the second and third funnels. At the bow section's after end, the decks had collapsed together as though crushed from the top, pulling the ship's hull plating inwards. The decks lie flat, suggesting the rupture was more of a direct pull than a twisting motion.

The expedition attempted to ascertain the iceberg's damage. But *Titanic*'s bow section had struck the bottom at a 45-degree angle, ploughing up the seabed for perhaps a hundred feet. When it came to a stop, the bow was buried 50 feet deep in sediment with the ship's anchors, still in place, just a few feet above the ocean floor. Thus the iceberg's gash could not be inspected. 'I'm glad the bow and stern are buried so deeply,' Ballard said later, for this factor would make salvaging unfeasible. 'The *Titanic* will protect itself. It's very fragile and any attempt to raise it would break it up.'

Buckled plates and sprung seams were found below the superstructure's forward end. Ballard suggested these may have been iceberg-related, but subsequent evaluation indicates that impact with the bottom probably caused them.

Limitations imposed by existing lighting equipment made it impossible to obtain views of the entire wreck. *Titanic* was simply too large. Ballard likened the experience to 'walking in a redwood forest at night with only a flashlight. You could take great pictures of the bark but not of the tree.'

Extensive photographing of individual sites eventually allowed construction of a 'photomosaic' of the entire bow section as seen from overhead.

Alvin's 1,715th career dive was her last to *Titanic*. The mission was over. In 11 journeys to the great liner and through nightly unmanned examination, more than 50,000 still pictures and 100 hours of videotape footage were obtained. Scientists and support personnel felt a tired jubilation at the successes of their 'picture perfect' cruise.

The explorers were greeted by 500 friends, relatives, reporters and Woods Hole colleagues upon their 28 July arrival.

Within a week, Texas oil man Jack Grimm had announced his intention to retrieve artefacts from the ship. He entered into negotiations with *IFREMER* to mount a 1987 expedition to *Titanic*, with joint ownership of anything retrieved.

CHAPTER ELEVEN

Explorations and Exhibitions

But Jack Grimm was not to head a 1987 expedition to recover *Titanic*'s artefacts.

'Expedition Titanic 1987', a French-North American venture headed by Titanic Ventures, a Connecticut limited partnership, and Westgate Productions, contracted with the French Institute for Research and Exploitation of the Sea (*Institut Français de Recherche pour l'Exploitation de la Mer*, or *IFREMER*), through Taurus International, which also managed the expedition. *IFREMER* is a public agency of the French government, with scientific, industrial and commercial roles. It acts on behalf of the French government to direct, fund and promote French programmes in oceanic research and development.

IFREMER, with the Compagnie Generale Maritime, provided the 'mother ship' *Nadir*, the manned submersible *Nautile*, the remotely operated probe *Robin*, and all necessary scientific and technical support personnel and equipment.

The expedition was at the wreck site – 41°43' N, 49°56' W, and vicinity – from 22 July to 11 September 1987. Thirty-two dives to the wreck were completed and approximately 1,800 artefacts were recovered. Numerous still photographs and many feet of motion picture film and videotape were taken. Several projects of an investigative nature were undertaken.

Considerable controversy surrounded the objects' retrieval. Dr Robert Ballard, the wreck's initial explorer, expressed grave doubts concerning the looting of 'a burial site'. Sympathetic media stories and rumours of desperate pillage bombarded the public. Those who sought to recover and preserve *Titanic*'s objects were painted as blackguards and grave robbers, ignorant of history.

On 11 September 1985 a bill was introduced by Walter B. Jones, chairman of the Committee on Merchant Marine and Fisheries, United States House of Representatives, to 'designate the shipwreck of the *Titanic* as a maritime memorial and to provide for reasonable research, exploration and, if appropriate, salvage activities'. The bill was passed by the House on 3 December 1985 and introduced to the Senate on 27 January 1986 by Connecticut's Senator Lowell Weicker, Jr. After committee hearings and minor amendments, the bill was passed on 6 October 1986 and signed into law by President Ronald Reagan on 21 October 1986. Though well-intentioned, the legislation called mainly for an international study of the situation – it had no authority.

Fearful that the July expedition to salvage objects from the wreck might result in the sale of or trafficking in the objects, the United States Congress again attempted to intervene in a

IFREMER's *submersible* Nautile *is launched over* Titanic's *wreck from the support vessel* Nadir *during the 1993 Research and Recovery Expedition. Atop the* Nautile, *preparing to separate it from the launching crane, is 'cowboy' Frederic Biguet.* (Authors' collection, © 1993 RMS Titanic Inc)

venture of private enterprise; on 3 August 1987 Senator Lowell Weicker introduced a Senate bill 'to prohibit the importation of objects from the RMS *Titanic*'. After due consideration, the bill passed the Senate and was then tabled by the House, which took no further action.

With the telecast *Return to the Titanic... Live,* beamed throughout the United States on 28 October 1987, preservationists' concerns were apparently justified. Originating at the Museum of Science and Industry in Paris, the programme purported to display objects recovered from the wreck in a dignified atmosphere and with due respect for survivors' feelings.

Instead, the programme was characterised by loud music, ominous armed guards, and a host (the former star of a police-detective television series) who looked over the artefacts and inquired, 'What is this stuff?'

Injurious impressions left on many concerned historians and the general public were a long time in healing.

In October 1989 many of the artefacts were exhibited at the Musée de la Marine in Paris, where they were viewed by more than 37,000 persons.

Between the spring of 1991 and the spring of 1992, another exhibition of artefacts toured several Scandinavian museums, including the Sea Historical Museum in Stockholm, Sweden; sea museums at Malmö and Gothenburg, Sweden; and finally the Sea Museum of Oslo, Norway. Over 28 weeks, divided among the four museums, the exhibitions attracted more than 292,000 enthusiastic visitors. The artefacts then were carefully packed and returned to secure storage in France.

During the summer of 1991 *Titanic* was visited by a team of independent film-makers. They chartered Russian support and diving equipment and used the IMAX film process and the latest lighting equipment to produce the best footage to date of a deep-sea wreck. As originally released, the film's first part was characterised by a flippancy and frivolity that detracted from the spectacular underwater footage with which it concluded. A subsequent re-release eliminated many, but not all, of the distractions; the film *Titanica* nevertheless played worldwide to a steadily successful public attendance.

But as important as the discovering, recovery of artefacts and filming were, the establishment of the sunken liner's true co-ordinates enabled a long-standing error to be at least partially corrected after 80 years.

Until the 1985 discovery of *Titanic*'s wreck, the British Board of Trade's refusal to reconsider Captain Lord's alleged culpability ignored the facts: Stanley Lord was not given the opportunity to explain or defend himself at the 1912 formal investigation; allegations of questionable reliability were made against him long after he left the stand as a witness assisting the inquiry; introduction of significant testimony by a reliable witness at a subsequent inquiry, regarding the timings of distress rockets, was denied because it was 'not important'; and vessels which in strong likelihood were closer to *Titanic* than *Californian* were never more than superficially considered or investigated by the inquiry.

Titanic's wreck was found some 13 miles from the position accepted by the 1912 British inquiry. This 'new evidence' led to a reopening of the inquiry, although at first the Department of Transport (now having responsibility for shipping matters) had refused. In 1990 the then Secretary of State for Transport, the Right Honourable Cecil Parkinson MP, determined that the Department's Marine Accident Investigation Branch should re-evaluate the relevant evidence.

Though authorised in 1990, the report was not quickly forthcoming. Reappraisal of the evidence was assigned to Captain Thomas Barnett, former principal nautical surveyor for the Department of Transport. His report was delivered in 1991, and Captain Peter Marriott, head of the Investigation Branch, spent nearly a year studying it. To those inquiring about the delay, authorities explained that a large number of shipping accidents had created more urgent work for the understaffed Marine Accident Investigation Branch. In March 1992 the report was published.

Captain Marriott did not agree fully with all of Captain Barnett's findings. Captain James de Coverly, deputy chief inspector of marine accidents, was asked to carry out further examinations. His own conclusions on two key points differed from those of Captain Barnett.

Barnett, unnamed in the final report but referred to as 'the inspector', found *Titanic* and *Californian* to have been between 5 and 10 miles apart, as believed in 1912, and probably nearer the lesser figure. Captain de Coverly, the report's author, found the distance to have been between 17 and 20 miles, probably about 18 miles, with *Californian* north-west-by-west from *Titanic*.

Captain Barnett also found that *Titanic* had been seen and kept under observation by *Californian* from 11 pm until she sank 3½ hours later. Captain de Coverly, however, concluded that the ship seen was probably another, unidentified, vessel, citing the *Samson* as a possible suspect, but naming no other vessel.

Captain de Coverly reassessed the role of Herbert Stone, *Californian*'s middle watch officer, in charge of the ship between midnight and 4 am. Actions not taken by Stone included having the master called when he sighted what he thought were rockets and, if necessary, *reporting to him in person*; alerting the engine room for immediate readiness to get under way; and waking wireless operator Cyril Evans. Stone did none of these, save sending Gibson, the ship's apprentice, to notify the drowsing captain.

Stone had performed none of the actions expected – indeed, required – of an experienced, licensed officer. His inattention to his required duties, for which he was paid, resulted in the vilification of Captain Lord who, in a state of exhaustion, was confident that his vessel was in the charge of an attentive, competent officer.

However, Captain de Coverly did not, as hoped, fully exonerate Captain Lord. He stated in his report:

> 'I do not think that any reasonably probable action by Captain Lord could have led to a different outcome of the tragedy. This of course does not alter the fact that an attempt should have been made.'

This statement, forever casting the possibility of doubt on Stanley Lord's honour and integrity, appears just 14 lines after the conjecture, 'More practically, if proper action had been taken, *as set out in the above* [authors' italics], Captain Lord would have been on the bridge at perhaps 0055 hrs and begun heading toward the rockets ...'

'As set out in the above' refers to those actions, *supra*, that second officer Herbert Stone *should* have taken, *but did not*.

Nor is there any possible doubt as to how Captain Lord would have reacted or what actions he would have taken if he had been properly informed.

A final footnote to the story... Following Captain Stanley Lord's death in 1962, his son, Stanley Tutton Lord, had assisted the former secretary of the Mercantile Marine Service Association, Mr Leslie Harrison, with two unsuccessful efforts in 1965 and 1968 to petition the Board of Trade to reopen his father's case. The younger Lord was deeply disappointed in the 1992 MAIB report, for it had not exonerated his father completely.

Stanley Tutton Lord died at the age of 86 in December 1994 in Wirral, England. A lifelong bachelor, he had worked for a British bank and lived with his parents while they were alive. Upon his death he willed £270,000 (about $432,000) to Chester Cathedral, and made a similarly sized bequest to the Royal Society for the Prevention of Cruelty to Animals. He was buried next to his parents, Mabel and Stanley, in Earlston Cemetery in Wirral, across the Mersey from Liverpool.

As the 80th anniversary of the disaster came and went, attention returned briefly to the artefacts recovered in 1987. Because the 1,800 objects from the *Titanic* debris field had been retrieved by a French government-subsidised company, landed in France and preserved by the state-owned utility Electricité de France, French law required that ownership claims be invited before the objects could be returned to Titanic Ventures, the limited partnership that had originally financed the 1987 expedition. (Under its contract with *IFREMER*, Titanic Ventures – and later its successor company RMS Titanic Inc – agreed not to sell artefacts from the wreck. Other individual owners could, however, sell any items they could recover.)

Notices inviting claims were placed in *The New York Times*, *The Times* of London and three French newspapers on 15 December 1992. Potential claimants were given the opportunity to study artefact photographs at the French embassies in Washington and London, as well as at the Merchant Marine Secretariat in Paris. Potential owners were to provide incontestable proof of ownership, and, as provided under French law, to contribute to the cost of retrieving the object, calculated as a proportion of the expedition's $5.5 million (£3.44 million) total cost.

There was but one legitimate claimant, survivor Edith Brown Haisman, who recognised her father's watch from a photograph of the recovered artefacts. Upon learning of her identification, RMS Titanic Inc presented her with the watch, restored and mounted in a presentation box, for her to keep during her lifetime. Upon her passing in January 1997 at age 100, the watch was returned to RMS Titanic Inc's care.

Since its 1912 loss, *Titanic* and related matters have been the subject of many hearings, investigations and court actions. The 1990–92 MAIB inquiry, which partially relieved Captain Lord of his historic culpability, was not the last formal action taken in the lost liner's fascinating history.

NEW YORK, TUESDAY, DECEMBER 15, 1992

NOTICE

In 1987, items taken on the wreck of the TITANIC were landed on French territory in Lorient.

Pursuant to its laws, the French State is applying the procedure which allows assigns of the shipwrecked to secure the restitution of these items.

Interested persons may immediately contact:

— either **the French Embassy in the USA**
4101 Reservoir road
NW WASHINGTON DC 20007

— or **the Secretariat d'Etat a la Mer in Paris**
Direction de la Flotte de Commerce
3, Place de Fontenoy
75007 PARIS

They will find all the necessary information, at the abovementioned locations, regarding the procedure and the evidence required for proving the claims, as well as a list of the items and a form for the request for restitution.

A set of photographs may be inspected on location.

Potential requesting parties are reminded of the fact that they must:

— send in their request **within a period of 3 months from the date of publication of this notice**

— establish proof of ownership,

— participate in the costs of finding the items.

French law mandated a search for possible owners of the artefacts preserved in that country. This advertisement, appearing in New York, London and French newspapers, invited potential claimants to contact French authorities. (New York Times)

During the 1991 filming expedition, all participants – film crew, support staff and other project members – were prohibited from doing any salvage. Despite this restriction, a pill bottle and a metal hull fragment were surreptitiously retrieved by a member of the film crew.

In September 1992 the salvage company Marex-Titanic Inc, based in Memphis, Tennessee, mounted its own expedition to *Titanic*. Marex's chief executive officer, James Kollar, was joined by Texas oil man Jack Grimm, in assembling a team of 'investors, scientists, divers and adventurers' to salvage objects from the wreck. The expedition departed Lisbon, Portugal, aboard the chartered research vessel *Sea Mussel*, and soon arrived at its goal.

Just as *Sea Mussel* prepared to head for the wreck site, Titanic Ventures filed suit in United States District Court, Eastern District of Virginia, Norfolk Division, before Judge J. Calvitt Clarke, Jr, bringing the Marex venture to a halt in mid-Atlantic, 2½ vertical miles directly above the wreck. (The court's jurisdiction related to several of the wreck's salvaged artefacts stored in nearby Hampton Roads, Virginia, awaiting preservation. Lack of an agreement with a nearby university had precluded the completion of a marine archaeological laboratory there,

One of the most massive objects retrieved from Titanic's *debris field was a 2½-ton thrust bearing journal, seen here being manoeuvred on* Nadir's *fantail.* (© 1993 RMS Titanic Inc)

and in December 1993 a federal judge approved Titanic Ventures' application for transfer of the artefacts to a French laboratory.)

Marex-Titanic argued in court that Titanic Ventures had abandoned its claim by not having returned to the wreck site since 1987, buttressing its own claim with a pill bottle and hull fragment Jack Grimm said had been salvaged by his company. The objects' origins were disputed amid allegations that the pill bottle had come from the 1991 filming expedition, whose members had been barred from salvage.

After three days of arguments, Judge Clarke ruled that Marex-Titanic Inc had to leave *Titanic* alone, and that Titanic Ventures was 'salvor in possession'. The judgement covered artefacts in the hull sections, as well as those in the huge, surrounding debris fields.

(Grimm reportedly strolled across the courtroom to 'cut a deal' with his opponents. They refused. In talking later with reporters, Grimm shrugged and said that his quest for *Titanic* was 'just another dry hole'.)

But James Kollar was not yet finished with his quest. Out 'some $600,000 (£375,000)' according to Jack Grimm, Kollar changed law firms and in March 1993 appealed against Clarke's ruling. Marex-Titanic now claimed that it had filed a motion for voluntary dismissal of the case, but the motion had been denied by Judge Clarke, who at the same time had granted exclusive rights to Titanic Ventures.

In its decision of August 1993 the Fourth US Circuit Court of Appeals said that Clarke should have dismissed the case, since Marex had followed proper procedures in seeking the dismissal. Thus Judge Clarke's granting of salvage rights to the wreck was denied on a legal technicality.

The appeals judges, however, did state that Marex had misled the court, and in a footnote indicated that the district court could impose sanctions. Kollar and Marex-Titanic did not renew their claim and withdrew from the case.

Now reorganised as RMS Titanic Inc – successors in interest to Titanic Ventures – the new company moved for the sanctions. On 23 December 1993 the district court granted RMS Titanic sanctions of more than $62,000 (£41,000).

A later claim, filed in Judge Clarke's court by a British insurance company, the Liverpool and London Steamship Protective and Indemnity Association, a marine insurance group that had paid out hundreds of claims after the 1912 sinking, was dismissed by Judge Clarke in June 1994.

In September 1993 results of a study on metal used in *Titanic*'s hull were released. The report's contents threatened to rob *Titanic* of the excellence and integrity with which

The essence of Titanic's *story is encapsulated in the dramatic moment when one of her davits is winched aboard* Nadir. *Found in the debris field, the davit weighed 4 tons.* (© 1993 RMS Titanic Inc)

Practically intact after more than eight decades in the sea's depths, one of Titanic's *portholes gleams after extensive restoration.* (© 1995 RMS Titanic Inc)

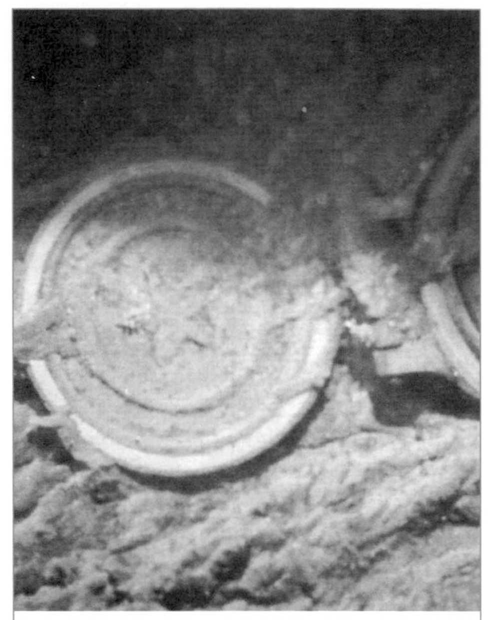

During their 1993 dives to the Titanic, *the authors discovered for themselves that the exterior faces of the portholes' deadlights had the White Star emblem cast into their metal surfaces.* (Photo by author, © *1993* RMS Titanic Inc)

These water taps/faucets, likely from a lavatory, appear almost as new after conservation. (© 1987 RMS Titanic Inc)

her construction had historically been associated. Its authors, headed by William Garzke, a senior naval architect for an Arlington, Virginia, firm, based the report on steel samples recovered from the wreck during the 1987 and 1991 expeditions, and analyses of the fragments done by Canada's Bedford Institute of Oceanography and France's *IFREMER*.

The tests indicated that the steel used in *Titanic* (and her sisters *Olympic* and *Britannic*) became brittle when exposed to low water temperature (which, at the time of *Titanic*'s collision with the iceberg, was about 31°F/-0.6°C), and became prone to 'brittle fracture', a reaction where low-grade steel breaks violently, rather than bends, when chilled, as was the case, the authors argued, with *Titanic*. The samples of *Titanic*'s steel did have a high sulphur content, making the metal more subject to fracture.

The delicacy of the metalwork in this bench end used on one of Titanic*'s upper decks recalls an era when artistry was apparent even in everyday objects.* (Courtesy National Maritime Museum, © 1994 RMS Titanic Inc)

'The real tragedy of *Titanic*,' the team concluded in its paper, was that better construction techniques and 'a better quality of steel plate might have averted her loss or resulted in an even slower rate of flooding that may have saved more crew and passengers'.

While the authors of the present book, as lay persons trained neither in metallurgy nor naval architecture, do not wish to dispute the august body of formidable experts who prepared the report, several points, in all fairness to *Titanic*'s builders, Harland and Wolff, might be raised.

Titanic and her sisters *Olympic* and *Britannic* were constructed on a cost-plus basis; that is, the builder was given carte blanche to produce the best possible ship using the finest available materials, and to bill the owner for all costs in excess of the original agreement.

While the three White Star liners were under construction, Harland and Wolff's order books were comfortably full; the economy was in generally good health, and the builder's finances were stable. There was no reason to stint on any part of the work.

For example, there was no reason for the builder to order – or even accept – low-grade steel for the hull plating, then bill the owner for 'top quality'. Though surely not the relatively ductile metal used in modern shipbuilding, *Titanic*'s steel was indeed top quality for the 1909–14 period.

Indeed, the authors have personally viewed *Titanic*'s bow section plating in the area above the impact with the iceberg and with the sea bottom, and conclude that there is no visible evidence of brittle fractures. A large opening exists in the bow's starboard side, directly below the bridge, but as far as can be seen there are no apparent signs of brittle fracture, displacement, cracking or crazing demonstrating frangibility. There are sprung rivets here, but their height on the hull argues forcefully for their cause being the bow's impact with the bottom.

Granted, the thickness of the shell plating (almost throughout the hull it was a mere one inch) may itself have been a source of fragility. Granted, the 'state-of-the-art' hull plating steel of 1909–14 did contain a high sulphur content that made it brittle. Why, then, did not the hull's entire plating – already presumably brittle from the 31°F seawater and 32°F air temperature – shatter like glass when it struck the bottom?

The steel's chemical composition can be questioned. In the light of present-day knowledge, even design techniques might be in doubt. But something that cannot be doubted or questioned is the appearance of *Titanic*'s wreck, calm and serene on the sea bottom, looking as though it struggles to sail again. That the hull – bow and stern alike – even resembles a ship after undergoing the most unimaginable stresses and contortions that a man-made object has likely ever undergone, that the hull even *begins* to resemble its former self, speaks volumes for her shipyard's materials and craftsmanship.

Now in full possession of the artefacts (supplemented by further recoveries in 1993 and 1994), RMS Titanic Inc wished to share its treasures with the world and affirm *Titanic*'s position in history's pantheon. An exhibition of a tiny portion of the wreck's most evocative and beautiful artefacts was planned with the full endorsement and co-operation of the world's most prestigious marine historical museum, the National Maritime Museum at Greenwich, just east of London.

The Museum announced the proposed exhibition on 2 August 1993. Museum officials and its Board of Trustees, chaired by Admiral of the Fleet The Lord Lewin, expressed their satisfaction that

> '... RMS Titanic Incorporated has undertaken its excavations with scrupulous regard to both archaeological good practice and the sensitiveness of *Titanic* survivors and their descendants. We fully support RMS Titanic Incorporated's decision in all of the following areas: they guarantee that all material is being fully documented and professionally conserved; they undertake that the material will never be sold or otherwise dispersed, and will be kept together in permanent display after the completion of the touring exhibition.'

The announcement also addressed professional and ethical issues relating to the wreck's excavation and the artefacts' display. The announcement, of hopeful intent rather than firm commitment, made no mention of a possible opening date.

In due time and after careful consideration, the Museum's Board of Trustees approved the exhibition, and on Tuesday 22 March 1994, at the Queen Elizabeth Conference Centre overlooking the Houses of Parliament in London, a press conference was held announcing the exhibition's preparation and its expected dates, 4 October 1994 to 2 April 1995.

Reactions to the announcement were swift and diverse. Indignation and apprehension were voiced, particularly by a small portion of the British press, ranging from gentle rebuke to downright outrage.

The primary concerns appeared to centre around the 'breaching of the sanctity of what is an international grave whilst the tragedy is still within living memory'; the fear that treasure hunters would be encouraged to interfere with other wrecks whose integrity it was important to preserve; and the fear that following the exhibition, *Titanic*'s artefacts would be dispersed and sold.

In a concise, dignified statement via a letter printed in the London *Times*, The Lord Lewin, Chairman of Trustees of the National Maritime Museum, wrote, in part:

On 22 March 1994 Britain's National Maritime Museum announced a forthcoming exhibition of almost 200 artefacts at Greenwich. At the press conference, The Lord Lewin, the Museum's Chairman of Trustees, and Titanic's *youngest survivor Miss Millvina Dean, admired the carefully preserved ship's telegraph from* Titanic's *after docking bridge.* (© 1994 National Maritime Museum)

> '... It is well understood that some people feel that a grave site is being exploited, while others regard the wreck as a memorial to the tragedy which took place on the surface, two and a half miles above the wreck. The exhibition will not shirk this controversy and will address the question whether it would be better if sites like this were left undisturbed.
>
> 'The wreck of the *Titanic* was discovered in 1985. When an expedition returned two years later to recover objects from the site (a perfectly legal and therefore inevitable consequence of the wreck's discovery) many maritime museums and archaeologists assumed the worst, that the site would be damaged and the artefacts sold off.
>
> 'Visitors to the exhibit at Greenwich will be able to see that these concerns prove to be unfounded. Conducted by *IFREMER*, the French national underwater exploration institute, the recovery work was undertaken with scrupulous care through continuous site plotting, photography and subsequent conservation.
>
> 'The exhibition will allow people to see for themselves artefacts from the *Titanic* and through them to be introduced to the story of the ship and the use of modern technology in maritime archaeology.

'The company which organised the recovery expeditions, RMS Titanic Inc, has already given an undertaking to keep all the artefacts together permanently as a memorial through public display. The National Maritime Museum is setting up an international advisory committee to determine how this might best be achieved and how to safeguard the future of the wreck on the seabed.

'The trustees of the museum have given their approval for this exhibition precisely because they are acutely aware of the cultural value and vulnerability of the underwater heritage.'

In his letter, Lord Lewin expressed the rationale for not only the Greenwich exhibition itself but also for the entire spectrum of *Titanic*-related activities: exploration, preservation of archaeological integrity, preservation, and public awareness of *Titanic* and her significant heritage.

After months of design, development and construction, the exhibition, 'The Wreck of the *Titanic*', opened to the public on 4 October 1994. Its introductory phase traced how the elusive wreck yielded its secrets to modem technology and depicted the difficulties salvors encountered in bringing artefacts to the surface. Period motion picture films (including

During the summer of 1994, the preparation of displays to be included in the artefact exhibition proceeded. In a London workshop, workers consult while completing a model depicting Titanic's *bow section as it now appears under the sea. The model would be a highlight of the artefacts' exhibition.* (Authors' collection)

some 1912 post-disaster footage), a 1:3 scale model of *Nautile*, and a superb model of the wreck's bow section as it now appears, 2½ miles beneath the Atlantic's surface, were among the exhibition's opening segments.

Among the Greenwich exhibition's most startling and popular displays were a typewritten letter from an ostrich feather dealer, lamenting that feather boas were out of fashion; a steward's jacket, found squeezed in a ball, weakened by bacterial action and saturated with iron corrosion products; delicate glass vases and carafes from the ship's own table settings; colourful china, scarcely aged, from *Titanic*'s first and second class dining saloons; a Southampton newspaper dated 9 April 1912, describing the liner's appearance as she lay at her departure dock; one of the mighty ship's telegraphs, probably from the stern docking bridge… all these and many more articles of beauty and significance, of utility and poignancy, each an integral part of the ship, her people and their tragic history.

An auspicious day for the National Maritime Museum and RMS Titanic Inc, the 4 October 1994 opening of the Titanic *artefact exhibition commences with a ceremonial ribbon cutting. Doing the honours are second class survivor Mrs Edith Brown Haisman; third class survivor Miss Millvina Dean; and Mr William MacQuitty, producer of the acclaimed* Titanic *film,* A Night to Remember. (Robert M. DiSogra)

Controversy concerning the recovery, potential destruction and exhibition of *Titanic*'s artefacts was not skirted by the National Maritime Museum, as Lord Lewin had promised. An entire page from the exhibition's catalogue was devoted to statements, pro and con, regarding these matters:

> 'All this vast tragedy makes me look upon it as a different sort of grave. The ship is its own memorial. Leave it there.' (Eva Hart, survivor who lost her father in the tragedy.)

> 'I am proposing that any future revisits to the *Titanic* which would involve deep diving submersibles, dedicate a portion of their diving time to carefully recording and recovering those delicate items lying outside the hull of the ship itself. The artefacts recovered should be used to create a museum.' (Dr Robert Ballard, co-discoverer of the wreck, to the United States Congress, October 1985.)

> 'For now the greatest threat to the *Titanic* clearly comes from man, particularly in the form of crude dredging operations.' (Dr Robert Ballard, in his book The *Discovery of the Titanic*, 1987.)

'As a Titanic survivor, I am personally pleased to see the *Titanic* story remembered by your fine efforts. Your presentation of the recovered objects from the ship will help to teach the present and future generations the timeless human lessons learned from this great marine tragedy.' (Beatrice Sandström, Swedish *Titanic* survivor.)

'I feel that if research and salvage of the *Titanic* will benefit all people, then such activities should be encouraged.' (Louise Kink Pope, American *Titanic* survivor, to the United States Congress.)

'The Wreck of the Titanic' proved to be the most popular exhibition ever presented by the National Maritime Museum. On 7 March 1995, three weeks before the scheduled closing, the museum announced that the exhibition would be extended for another six months, to October 1995. Record-breaking numbers of visitors entered the museum during the winter; admission between the 4 October opening and 7 March was nearly 250,000, double the normal winter range. Later, during the summer of 1995, museum officials estimated that by the time of the exhibition's closing it would have been seen by nearly 750,000 people.

Visitors to the *Titanic* exhibition were asked via interactive computers to answer several key questions relating to the artefacts' recovery from the wreck site, their future, and the future of the wreck itself. Early results (from within seven weeks of the opening) appear consistent with results tallied at a later date:

Which part of the exhibition interested you most? Some 48% said the ship's story.

When a permanent Titanic *museum is created, where should it be?* 'England' was the answer of 73%.

The remains of the hull may collapse before long. What should be done? Some 70% said that it should be explored further.

Should museums display, as in this exhibition, material recovered from wrecks by commercial companies? The vote was 68% 'Yes'.

Should additional Titanic *artefacts be recovered in the future?* An affirmative answer was voted by 72%.

Although these 'exit polls' have no direct bearing on future plans for *Titanic* and her artefacts, it is hoped that those who control the wreck and her beautiful objects will give due consideration to the public response to these questions.

On 15 April 1995, the 83rd anniversary of the disaster, *Titanic* survivors Edith Haisman and Eva Hart participated in the dedication of a memorial garden in the grounds of the National Maritime Museum – the first public *Titanic* memorial in London – to those lost. It consists of the plants of remembrance – 'Peace' roses, purple sage, rosemary and Irish golden yew – and is marked by a stone of carved Cornish granite similar to that once used in ships' ballasts. On the marker is an engraved bronze plaque, whose typeface duplicates that used for *Titanic*'s name on her hull.

TO
COMMEMORATE THE SINKING
OF
R.M.S. TITANIC
ON
15TH APRIL 1912
AND ALL THOSE WHO
WERE LOST WITH HER
15 April 1995

Even as dedication ceremonies were concluding, work was continuing in the high-tech French laboratory caring for *Titanic* artefacts recovered during the 1987, 1993 and 1994 expeditions. For

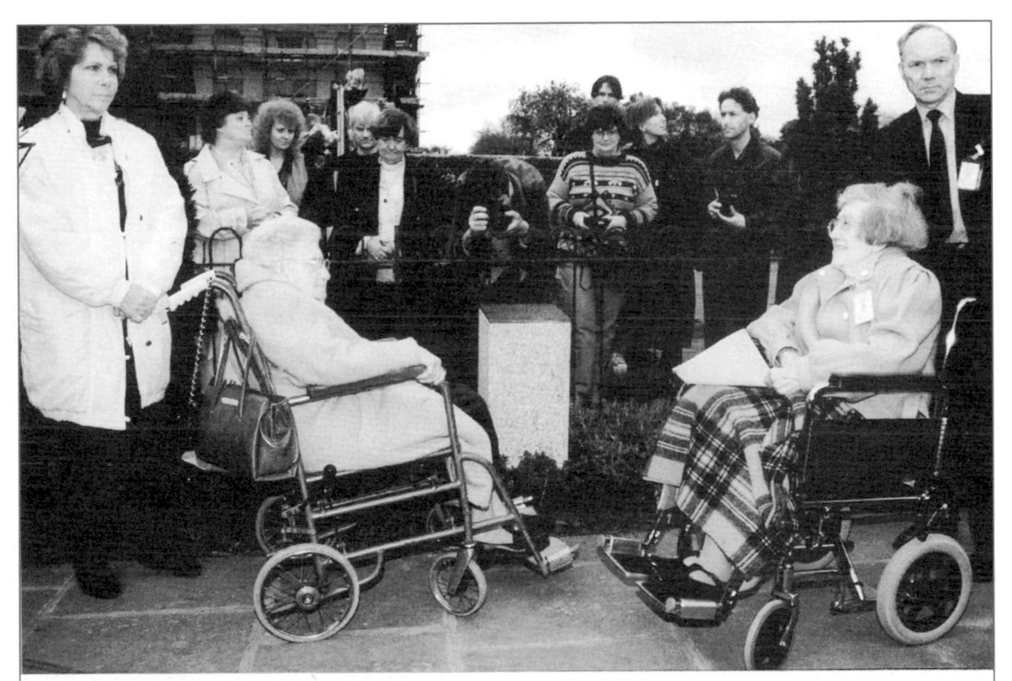

On 15 April 1995, the 83rd anniversary of the disaster, survivors Edith Brown Haisman and Eva Hart dedicate London's first public Titanic *memorial in the grounds of the National Maritime Museum.* (National Maritime Museum)

more than 73 years *Titanic* and her precious contents had lain in a harsh and hostile environment. Their recovery from 2½ miles beneath the ocean's surface, where there is no light, little oxygen, perpetual and progressive bacterial and chemical actions and pressure of more than three tons per square inch, represents an almost unbelievable scientific accomplishment.

Yet, without proper identification of pollutants, correct steps taken to remove them and proper procedures to stabilise and preserve them, *Titanic*'s artefacts could not withstand the rigours of exposure to surface pressure, atmosphere and light. They would deteriorate, disintegrate and, ultimately, be destroyed. How the artefacts are stabilised and restored to their original beauty and utility is one of the most fascinating aspects of their exhibition.

In 1987, when the first 1,800 recovered objects were brought to the surface, their conservation was begun by researchers at Electricité de France (EDF), the state-owned electricity company. An additional 800 artefacts were recovered in 1993 by a second expedition, of which the authors were privileged to be members; the story of their dives to *Titanic* in June 1993 is told in their companion volume *Titanic: Triumph and Tragedy* (Haynes Publishing, 2011). Dr Stéphane Pennec, who had worked on the objects at EDF, joined with partners to establish LP3, the company responsible for the restoration and preservation of artefacts recovered from 1987 through 1998. Subsequent preservation was performed at Eastern Michigan State University and, from 2001 on, at RMS Titanic Inc's own facility in Atlanta, Georgia.

Titanic's wreck contains an almost infinite variety of objects: large electroplated nickel-silver serving dishes from the ship's kitchens; metal flatware, delicate china, fragile glassware and beautiful crystal from the dining rooms; wrenches and metal ducting from the engine room; metal window frames, some almost like tracery in their delicacy; manufactured

Dramatically showing the effects of deep-sea acidic corrosion, this copper cooking pan would have been lost to time's ravages had it not been recovered and conserved. (© 1987 RMS Titanic Inc)

In contrast to the superior quality of the chambers comprising Titanic's *forward funnel whistles (see the colour photographs), this chamber from one of the after funnels, of a lesser quality metal, shows the effects of impact and submersion.* (Authors' collection, © 1993 RMS Titanic Inc)

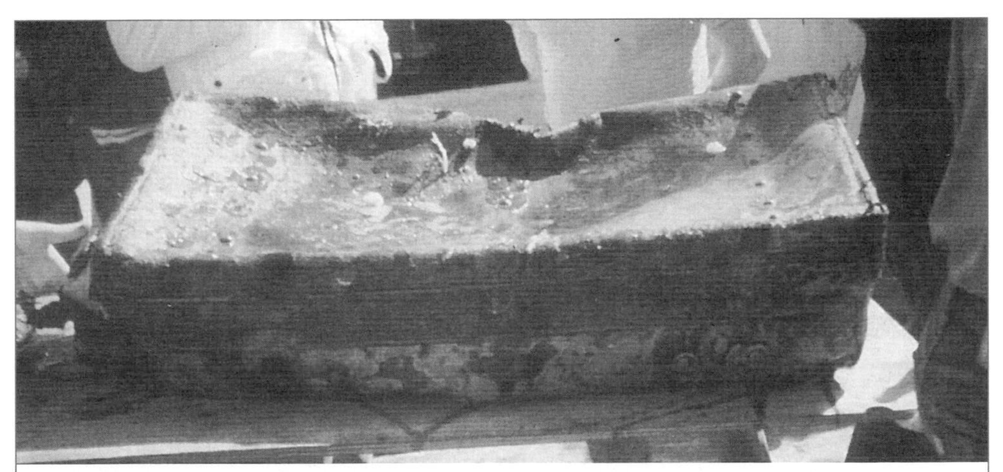

What historic insights into the daily lives of Titanic's *passengers are contained within this suitcase? Answers to the most intriguing questions – some of which otherwise might never be known – are being provided by the contents of luggage retrieved from the debris field.* (Authors' collection, © 1993 RMS Titanic Inc)

goods from production lines, including fabrics, a packet of cigarettes, pens and pencils, leather wallets and luggage; organic materials, such as a jar of olives, its contents intact; and a wide variety of paper, including books, postcards, correspondence, sheet music, and even a newspaper. Each type of object – frequently each piece – requires its own particular preservation method.

As the objects are brought into a laboratory on board the expeditions' research vessels, conservators wash off the acidic silt. The artefacts are then separated according to material type and packed with foam to minimise movement.

Objects from the wreck also absorb chlorides and sulphates from the seawater and become weakened, stained and encrusted. It is essential that, once on the surface, they are kept wet. Ceramic and glass items can lose surface layers if salts are permitted to crystallise. Leather can harden, crack and shrink as it dries out if salts in its pores are not removed before drying. Metallic objects undergo accelerated corrosion if exposed to oxygen.
According to one published account:

> 'When the [George] Rosenshine letter [regarding the feather boas] was found it was completely unreadable, part of an amorphous brown mass. Chemical analysis established that the paper was heavily contaminated with iron sulphides. "A metal wire

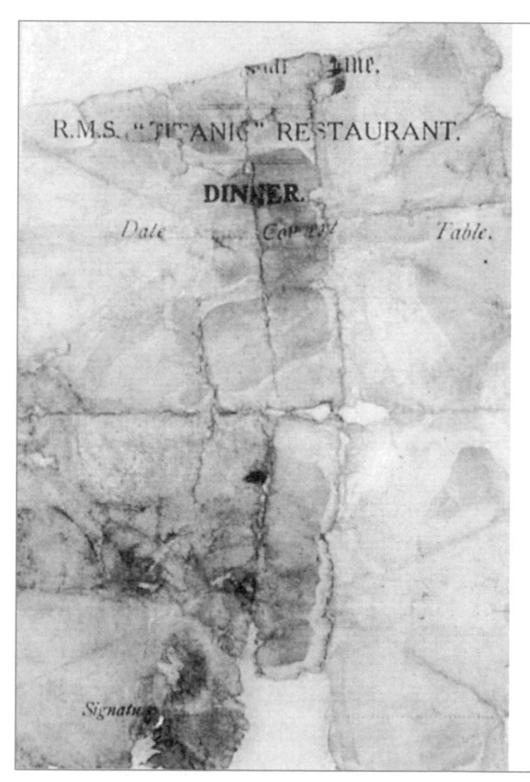
R.M.S. "TITANIC" RESTAURANT.

DINNER.

Date Table.

Almost as though awaiting the touch of the waiter's pencil, a paper receipt from Titanic's à la carte *restaurant has been restored from a blackened, unidentifiable mass through carefully controlled conservation.* (© 1987 RMS Titanic Inc)

Without an opportunity for historians to examine the contents of this Gladstone bag, its owner might well have faded into obscurity. Now, at least, the opportunity exists. (© 1987 RMS Titanic Inc)

A wallet and its contents belonging to first class passenger Major Arthur Peuchen, a Toronto businessman, clearly demonstrate the remarkable ability of organic materials such as leather and paper to endure submersion's rigours, with the conservators' help. (Electricité de France/RMS Titanic Inc)

Before being restored, a bundle of French postcards from a passenger's suitcase undergoes careful separation at the conservator's gentle touch. Paper's fragility is demonstrated by the unavoidable flaking, on the right, that occurs despite every precaution. (© 1995 LP3 Conservation/RMS Titanic Inc)

had been in contact with the paper and so you had iron and sulphur going into the paper," says [Stéphane] Pennec.

'The researchers used a two-step process to reveal its contents. The first was to oxidise the iron sulphides with a dilute (15 per cent) solution of hydrogen peroxide made alkaline with ammonia. The oxidation converted the sulphides into rust – a mixture of iron oxides and hydroxides.

'The second stage was to dissolve away the rust with oxalic acid in a solution with a sodium citrate buffer. The citrate buffer has the happy knack of not only controlling the pH of the solution but also helping to dissolve the rust.

'Pennec says it took two days to develop the letters to the point where they were legible. Finally the paper was freeze-dried. The developing process did not damage the text because the typewriting – carbon particles deposited from the typewriter's ribbon – was relatively inert. But inks are not always resistant to chemical treatment.'

It can be seen clearly that if such care, skill and complex technique is necessary for restoration and preservation of one piece of paper, handling *Titanic*'s myriad other objects – of paper, ceramic, metal, glass – entails a prodigious amount of knowledge and the ability to use it.

Wood and metal parts are common finds in shipwrecks, and techniques for conserving these materials are better established. Sodium compounds help to extract chloride ions from metal objects; some iron objects are treated with a dilute solution of sodium hydroxide (caustic soda), while copper is treated with sodium bicarbonate and sodium carbonate (baking soda and washing soda).

Wood is vulnerable to attack by bacteria that degrade its cellulose. Wooden parts may look deceptively sturdy when they surface, but drying them when their cellulose is gone causes them to shrink and even fall apart. Conservators replace the missing cellulose by impregnating the piece with a 5% solution of polyethylene glycol, which permeates the wood and restores much of its structural strength.

Even metal throughout the wreck is subject to bacterial action. Indeed, bacteria are the direct cause of the wreck's eventual total disintegration. When *Titanic* was discovered in 1985 and explored in 1986, Dr Robert Ballard specially commented about rivers of rust cascading down the sides of some areas of the wreck – he called them 'rusticles'.

In 1991 the Toronto-based Imax Corporation chartered the Russian research vessel *Akademik Mstislav Keldysh* to film the wreck. During one dive, the manned submersible *Mir-2* recovered nine metal fragments from *Titanic*. These were examined by research scientists with a power X-ray diffractometer and a scanning electronic microscope equipped with an energy-dispersive X-ray spectrometer. The study demonstrated conclusively that bacteria play a major role in promoting *Titanic*'s hull corrosion, and this results in fast-growing structures such as rust flows and 'rusticles'. The varieties of bacteria actually in the 'rusticles' are mainly sulphate-reducing species that multiply rapidly in environments with little or no oxygen. During decades of activity, their metabolism literally causes the wreck to dissolve as they feed on the metals' own microscopic structures.

Soon – in 10, 50, 100 years? – the wreck will collapse upon itself as bacterial action reduces metallic deck supports and other structures to rust. Soon only a ghostly outline of the wreck's form will remain, but even that will be consumed by the voracious bacteria and scoured away by sea-bottom currents.

In a short time, geologically speaking, no physical remnant of *Titanic* will remain. The sea – Nature – will have spoken.

CHAPTER TWELVE

Into the Second Century

For his testimony at the 1912 British Inquiry into the disaster, naval architect Edward Wilding had calculated the total area of the iceberg's punctures to Titanic's *hull to be approximately 12 square feet. During the 1996 Titanic Research and Recovery Expedition, special sonar equipment penetrated the sand concealing the area, and confirmed the amazing accuracy of Wilding's estimate of the damage's extent and location.* (Authors' collection)

The closing years of the 20th century saw extensive scientific exploration and evaluation of *Titanic*, leading to new understanding of the events of 1912 and the ship's current state; recovery of thousands of objects from the ocean floor; worldwide artefact exhibitions enthralling millions; courtroom hearings on the future of the ship and its artefacts; and a continuing presence in media reports and popular culture.

Under the leadership of George H. Tulloch and Paul-Henri Nargeolet, who had conducted the highly successful 1987 and 1993 expeditions to the ship, RMS Titanic Inc's 1996 '*Titanic* Research and Recovery Expedition' brought together scientists, naval architects and historians from five countries for the ship's first in-depth evaluation and continued artefact recovery. Over four weeks in August, employing four surface vessels and *IFREMER*'s submersible *Nautile*, the team documented *Titanic* and the wreck site in unprecedented detail, and retrieved samples of *Titanic*'s rivets and hull plating, the ocean floor and the bacterial colonies consuming the iron in the ship's hull. A specially designed sonar device penetrated 50 feet (15.2 metres) of sand around the ship's bow and confirmed naval architect Edward Wilding's 1912 testimony that the

This photomicrograph of Titanic's *steel reveals the impurities called 'slag' which, with the steel's tendency to become brittle in very cold water, may have contributed to the ship's fate.* (National Institute of Standards and Technology)

iceberg's penetrations of *Titanic*'s hull totalled 12 square feet (1.11 square metres) – six punctures no wider than a finger's diameter had opened six compartments to flooding at the average rate of 400 tons per minute. Extensive mapping of the wreck site was completed.

Metallurgical studies of several dozen recovered *Titanic* rivets revealed a high percentage of impurities called 'slag', weakening their structure and allowing rivet heads to pop off as the iceberg travelled down the ship's side, opening seams through which more water had poured.

Subsequent tests of two hull samples by the University of Missouri at Rolla and the Metallurgy Division of the National Institute of Standards and Technology, under the auspices of the Marine Forensics Panel of the Society of Naval Architects and Marine Engineers, showed 'The steel used to construct *Titanic*'s hull, though adequate in strength, possessed a very low fracture toughness at ice water temperatures,' though the 1997 report cautioned that only two sample plates had been tested. It added, 'It is possible that brittle steel contributed to the damage at the bow due to the impact with the iceberg, but much more likely that the brittle steel was a factor in the break-up of the ship at the surface.'

New species of bacteria were identified as causing the rust-laden stalactites covering decks, side plating, support columns, bulkheads and railings, and silently destroying the ship's structural integrity over time, consuming, the expedition's microbiologist estimated, between 200 and 600 pounds of iron from the ship's hull each day.

In 1985, Robert Ballard had stated that the wreck site was a 'peaceful place'. It may have looked peaceful, but ocean floor samples revealed that the sand in which *Titanic*'s artefacts lay was highly acidic in places, and together with galvanic action, time's passage and immersion in corrosive salt water, threatened artefacts' continued existence. Strong currents buried other artefacts and placed significant stresses on the ship's hull and superstructure.

During the 1996 expedition, massive high-intensity light towers illuminated the wreck as never before, revealing hitherto-unknown features that enabled the expedition's naval architects to revise significantly the ship's sinking scenario.

Members of the 1996 Titanic *Expedition Cruise line the starboard sun deck of the cruise ship* Island Breeze *expecting to witness the appearance of the 'Big Piece' after its journey from the ocean floor, but technical difficulties thwarted their hopes.* (Authors' photo)

Two cruise ships, *Island Breeze* and *Royal Majesty*, and a yacht, *Ballymena*, brought more than 1,600 members of the public to observe expedition activities first-hand. Among the honoured guests were *Titanic* survivors Michel Navratil, Edith Brown Haisman and Eleanor Johnson Schuman, and *A Night to Remember* producer William MacQuitty. Despite Dr Ballard's public pronouncement that the cruises were a 'carnival', participants learned from extensive onboard lectures by *Titanic* experts, viewed live television feeds from the ocean floor and participated in emotional memorial services.

The expedition's only disappointment came when Hurricane Edouard roared through the area, thwarting recovery of a 22-ton (19.5-metric-tonne) piece of the ship's hull dubbed 'the Big Piece' after it had been lifted to within just 260 feet (80 metres) of the surface.

The 22-ton 'Big Piece', the largest Titanic *artefact ever reclaimed from the ocean floor, is hoisted aboard the recovery vessel* Abeille Supporter *on 10 August 1998. Soon it would be placed gently on the* Abeille*'s after deck for transport to America.* (Authors' photo, © 1998 RMS Titanic Inc)

RMS Titanic Inc's August 1998 expedition continued many of these investigations, and discovered several new debris fields; one, to the west of the stern, contained many pieces of passenger luggage. Bow and stern sections were photographed in ultra-high resolution. Among the 70 artefacts recovered were a D-deck shell door, and 'the Big Piece', brought to the surface on 10 August 1998.

Using the latest in fibre-optic technology, the expedition sent the first-ever live television feeds from the wreck to hundreds of millions worldwide; the broadcast set a world's record for the deepest live underwater broadcast.

The expedition teams of what might be called the 'Tulloch Era' of *Titanic* exploration had discovered and disseminated through a series of acclaimed television documentaries a vast body of new information rewriting the story of the ship's demise, documenting its current condition and postulating its future. The work of the five expeditions, from 1987 through 1998, had been done with constant respect for the wreck, regard for historical accuracy, appropriate tone, and application of many traditional archaeological principles at unprecedented depths, including *in situ* documentation of artefacts' places of origin, cutting-edge conservation techniques, and thoughtful exhibitions that skilfully blended the elegance of beauty and science.

In late 1997, a firm called Deep Ocean Expeditions began planning and advertising 'tourist dives' to *Titanic*'s wreck. For $32,500 (£20,000), participants would be taken to the site aboard the Moscow-based P.P. Shirshov Institute of Oceanography's research vessel *Akademik Mstislav Keldysh*, then board one of its two submersibles, *Mir-1* and *Mir-2*, to dive to the wreck and photograph the ship. Upon learning of these plans in early May, RMS Titanic Inc's management sought a preliminary injunction barring the dives, and keeping Deep Ocean Expeditions and other parties at least ten nautical miles from the wreck. The company cited possible disruption to its upcoming summer expedition. It said its exclusive photographic rights to the wreck, already awarded by the court in lieu of possible revenue from selling artefacts – an action the court had explicitly prohibited – were essential in compensating the company for its expenditures in maintaining its salvor-in-possession status and recovering and conserving artefacts.

The Russian research vessel Akademik Mstislav Keldysh *and its twin* Mir *submersibles brought 'official' expeditions and tourists alike to the* Titanic's *wreck site from the late 1990s onward.* ('Digifruitella' via Wikimedia Commons)

Sitting in Norfolk, Virginia, United States District Court Judge J. Calvitt Clarke Jr supervised Titanic*'s wreck and artefacts for more than a decade.* (Authors' collection, courtesy of Judge Clarke)

On 23 June, US District Court Judge J. Calvitt Clarke, Jr, issued the injunction, declaring that the company had the right to exclude others from the site to prevent photographing the wreck. Deep Ocean Expeditions immediately appealed to the Fourth Circuit Court of Appeals in Richmond, Virginia. As word of Judge Clarke's injunction spread, many of the 60 people signed up for the expedition withdrew. But in apparent defiance of Judge Clarke's order, on Sunday 6 September 1998 *Keldysh* departed St John's, Newfoundland, with a dozen tourists; some had paid the full fee while others went as winners of various contests. On 9 September, two California undertakers and a history student and broadcaster from Germany became the first *Titanic* tourists.

On 24 March 1999, long after the tourists had returned home, the Fourth Circuit Court of Appeals reversed Judge Clarke's order. The company appealed to the Untied States Supreme Court, which declined to hear the case in October 1999, leaving the appeals court's decision in place. *Titanic* would be 'open to the public', although RMS Titanic Inc retained its exclusive salvage rights.

After a small number of RMS Titanic Inc shareholders intent on 'maximising shareholder value' engineered a hostile management takeover and the ousting of George H. Tulloch and Paul-Henri Nargeolet – leaders of the highly successful and historically sensitive 1987, 1993, 1994, 1996 and 1998 expeditions – and other company directors in November 1999, RMS Titanic Inc's new management announced a more aggressive approach to artefact recovery. Said one involved in the company's management hostile takeover, 'We all know there are billions of dollars down there under the water. It's like sitting on a gold mine.'

In a 29 June 2000 press release, the company said it would enter the ship through a cargo hold and retrieve 'valuable artefacts and historic items', including a supposed shipment of diamonds (not listed on the ship's cargo manifest or cargo stowage plan) valued at $300 million (£184,803,000) and William Carter's 1912 red Renault touring car (which, because of 'rusticle bacteria', likely had been reduced to its chassis, tyres and engine block). The company said it would sell diamonds, gold and currency 'of non-historical and archaeological significance that it hoped to recover'. It further hinted that, if necessary, it would cut into the ship's hull to retrieve items.

Angered by the company's announcement, and in response to concerns expressed by several parties, Judge Clarke issued an order on 28 July 2000 telling RMS Titanic Inc it was 'forbidden to in any way cut into the wreck or detach any part of the wreck', and reiterating his prohibition on selling artefacts. His order was faxed to the expedition vessels as they neared the wreck site. (RMS Titanic Inc subsequently appealed Judge Clarke's decision banning sale of the artefacts to the Fourth Circuit Court of Appeals in April 2002, then to the United States Supreme Court, which on 7 October 2002 refused to hear the case, effectively upholding Clarke's ruling.)

The 2000 expedition was beset by technical problems, bad weather and perhaps the practical inexperience of its leaders. Departing from Norfolk, Virginia, about two weeks late on 21 July, the expedition employed the *Keldysh*; its submersibles, *Mir-1* and *Mir-2*; recovery vessels *Ocean Intervention* and *SV Explorer*; and two remote-operated vehicles (ROVs), *Discovery* and *Magellan 725*.

The Magellan 725 *remote-operated vehicle (ROV) was deployed on several* Titanic *expeditions to take photographs and recover artefacts.* (Authors' collection, © 1998 RMS Titanic Inc)

The vessel SV Explorer *brought artefacts recovered during the 2000 expedition to Norfolk, Virginia.* (© 2000 RMS Titanic Inc)

The two ROVs, according to RMS Titanic Inc's website, 'did not function properly and an important part of the mission had to be abandoned'. The ROV crew were sent home on 31 July after one ROV's tethers reportedly became tangled in the support ship's propeller, and the other's camera failed.

The technical problems, together with Judge Clarke's order, had prevented penetration of or damage to the hull. The expedition did recover more than 800 artefacts, including two engine telegraphs, a portion of the ship's wheel, the base of the after grand staircase's cherub statue, and 65 still-fragrant perfume oil phials that first class passenger Adolphe Saalfeld had been bringing to his perfume business in the United States.

While this expedition was at sea, a previously recovered *Titanic* artefact was in jeopardy ashore. On 26 July 2000, a leather-covered address book exhibited at Chicago's Museum of Science and Industry was stolen, its display case jimmied open; an exhibition security guard subsequently was charged with theft and the book returned to the exhibition. On 28 June 2001 in Nashville, Tennessee's Opryland Hotel, ten coins and nine bank notes recovered from the wreck were stolen from a lobby display. That case remains unsolved.

In April 2001, the US government's National Oceanic and Atmospheric Administration issued its *Guidelines for Research, Exploration and Salvage of RMS Titanic* after consultation with the governments of the United Kingdom, France and Canada. Though lacking enforcement provisions, the guidelines provided a framework for future efforts at protecting the wreck.

On November 6 2003, the United Kingdom became the first – and at this writing the only – nation to formally put the agreement into effect. The United States indicated that it could not be bound under international law without 'implementing legislation'. Such legislation, modified slightly in 2009, has been sent to three different sessions of the United States Congress, from 2007 through 2011, for approval, but it has not proceeded to a vote. Neither Canada nor France has taken any action.

The agreement would not become effective until two of the four nations signed it. These guidelines would set standards for research, exploration and salvage activities at the wreck site, and would prohibit sale, ownership, possession or importation of individual artefacts recovered from the wreck by nationals or by means of vessels flagged in the four signatory countries and such other countries as might agree to the guidelines.

In August and September 2001, film producer James Cameron, whose 1997 film *Titanic* had smashed box office records, returned to the wreck with miniature robotic cameras 'Jake' and 'Elwood', and extensively explored the ship's interior. The resulting documentary, *Titanic: Ghosts of the Abyss*, was the Walt Disney Company's first 3-D film.

Thieves apparently were busy at *Titanic*'s wreck site in the late autumn of 2002. On 14 September 2002, RMS Titanic Inc's board of directors unanimously voted to surrender voluntarily its salvor-in-possession status and its exclusive right to recover artefacts from the wreck, and end its periodic expeditions. (The company cited several factors in its decision: recent financial setbacks, its inability to sell the artefacts; the district court's refusal to permit cutting into or detaching parts of the wreck; an April 2002 Fourth Circuit Court of Appeals ruling that RMS Titanic Inc had a salvor's lien on, but not title to, the objects, and

The Northern Horizon. *Documents filed with the US District Court for the Eastern District of Virginia included an allegation that an expedition which had chartered this vessel had recovered* Titanic *artefacts.* (Courtesy Marr Vessel Management)

thus could not sell what it did not own; and pending international legislation protecting the wreck.)

According to documents later filed with the Norfolk court, even as the company was making known its intentions to surrender its salvor-in-possession status, a chartered vessel, *Northern Horizon*, equipped with *Abyssub*, a deep-diving, remote-operated vehicle capable of recovering artefacts, allegedly was *en route* to a position above the wreck, preparing to recover artefacts. The ship's charterers were four former RMS Titanic Inc employees, including its former salvage master. According to *The Times* of London, once the company surrendered its salvor-in-possession status, 'The first company to retrieve artefacts would be able to stake a claim to the exclusive salvage rights, unhindered by the prohibition against selling [them]....'

Northern Horizon returned to Liverpool in December 2002. One crew member claimed that artefacts were, indeed, retrieved. 'We brought some good stuff up,' he was quoted as saying in court documents. (In 2006, both the BBC and ABC News in the US reported that a porthole from the ship was presented to its manufacturer, Utley's Engineering in St Helen's, Merseyside, for authentication; its serial number confirmed its origin. Its present whereabouts are unknown. Pieces of crockery allegedly from the wreck also apparently found their way into private hands.)

On 1 October 2002 Judge Rebecca Beach Smith, who had begun assuming jurisdiction over *Titanic*'s case before Judge Clarke's 30 July 1999 retirement, ordered a hearing on the company's intentions, and questioned whether the company could relinquish its salvor-in-possession status, one of its most valuable assets, without a shareholder vote. At a 25 November hearing the company's president testified he had no knowledge of his former colleagues' alleged illicit activities at the wreck site. The court reminded the company that

Judge Rebecca Beach Smith assumed jurisdiction over Titanic's *wreck and artefacts upon the retirement of Judge J. Calvitt Clarke Jr in 1999.* (Authors' collection, by courtesy of Hon Rebecca Beach Smith)

it was responsible for protecting the wreck from deep-sea pirates until released from that obligation by the court.

Spurred by the judge's admonition, RMS Titanic Inc's attorney conducted his own investigation into the so-called 'stealth expedition' and filed his findings with the court in March 2003. He reported that e-mails from an executive of the *Abyssub*'s owner corroborated the equipment's presence at the *Titanic* site from October to December, but did not confirm salvage had taken place. *Northern Horizon*'s movements had been traced through port calls in England, Canada and Bermuda. A US government satellite photograph showed a ship at *Titanic*'s position in the fall of 2002, but the National Oceanic and Atmospheric Administration (NOAA) could not tell whether the ship was transiting the area or stopped above the wreck.

The incident raised disturbing questions about the wreck's safety from unauthorised plunderers, and the capabilities of RMS Titanic Inc and interested governments to police and protect the wreck site.

On 5 April 2003, the company's board of directors rescinded the resolution calling for relinquishment of salvor-in-possession status, which RMS Titanic Inc retains to the present day.

The United States government itself decided to survey the wreck's condition, citing its 'vested interest in the appropriate treatment and preservation of the *Titanic* wreck site' under the authority granted it by the 1986 RMS Titanic Maritime Memorial Act. NOAA's Office of Ocean Exploration sponsored an 11-day expedition, from 22 June through 2 July 2003, aboard the *Keldysh*. Canadian and American scientists joined NOAA personnel in four dives in the *Mir* submersibles, assessing the wreck's condition, obtaining on-site video data, and further assessing the bacterial colonies' role in causing the ship's degradation.

The year 2004 saw two 'official' expeditions. On 15 April, the 92nd anniversary of the ship's loss, Robert Ballard announced plans to 'help the National Oceanic and Atmospheric Administration study the ship's rapid deterioration'. Although Ballard had not seen the wreck since 1986, he seemingly announced the expedition's findings before its departure, saying, 'I'm convinced that the deterioration is being accelerated by manmade impacts.'

Captain Edward J. Smith's bathtub on the boat deck's starboard side is nearly buried in rubble after his cabin's walls and ceilings collapsed. 'Rusticles' caused by bacterial colonies cover the inside and outside surfaces of the surviving walls. (Lori Johnston, RMS Titanic Expedition 2003, National Oceanic and Atmospheric Administration, Office of Exploration)

The 2004 NOAA expedition employed NOAA's research vessel Ronald H. Brown. (National Oceanic and Atmospheric Administration)

Before and during his first visit to the wreck in 18 years, Dr Robert Ballard alleged its deteriorated state was attributable to visiting submersibles. (Mass Communications Specialist First Class John Fields, United States Navy, via Wikimedia Commons)

The expedition, with objectives essentially identical to those of the previous year's effort, left Boston aboard NOAA's research vessel *Ronald H. Brown* on 27 May. On 3 June, during a telephone press conference at sea, Ballard confirmed, at least to his own satisfaction, his conclusion, saying, 'The mainmast [*sic*; presumably the foremast] of the ship has been bashed down and destroyed. Objects – the ship's bell, the ship's light [*sic*] have been torn off...You can clearly see, all over the ship, where the common [submersible] landing sites are knocking holes in the deck.'

The co-leader of RMS Titanic Inc's 1987, 1993, 1994, 1996 and 1998 expeditions, Cdr Paul-Henri Nargeolet, who had made more than 30 dives to the wreck over those 11 years, categorically rejected Ballard's allegations, noting the latter's 18-year absence from, and consequent unfamiliarity with the wreck.

Videotapes of each of the 119 RMS Titanic Inc/*IFREMER* dives over the years, he said, clearly demonstrated the ship's deterioration was gradual, and caused by the voracious iron-eating bacteria and strong undersea currents, not by submersible impacts. The tapes further proved that *IFREMER*'s submersible *Nautile* had never touched the foremast. Through proper ballasting, submersibles were made virtually weightless before landing on *Titanic*'s decks, Nargeolet said. He added, 'It is true we took the bronze mast light in 1987...The light was not bolted on to the mast, but was held in place by two inserted steel pins; the video shows we didn't even break the two pins, very fragile, when we removed the light....The bell was recovered from the debris field close to the stern, half-a-mile from the crow's nest; its surface is permanently scarred from lying in the acidic sand.'

RMS Titanic Inc, now a wholly owned subsidiary of Premier Exhibitions Inc, conducted its own expedition from 25 August to 8 September 2004, departing from Halifax aboard the vessel *Mariner Sea*. For the first time, the company conducted artefact retrieval using a remote-operated vehicle rather than a crewed submersible, permitting round-the-clock operations. More than 75 objects were recovered, including a gilded wall sconce from the *à la carte* restaurant and the 'surround' of a tile from the Turkish bath, its vibrant blue colour having survived more than nine decades in the ocean floor's acidic sand. Additionally, the expedition

RMS Titanic Inc employed the Mariner Sea *as its expedition vessel in late summer 2004.* (© 2004 RMS Titanic Inc)

located a previously unknown debris field, identified objects for future recovery and inspected the wreck for signs of alleged harm by previous visitors.

The *Keldysh* became little more than a '*Titanic* shuttle' in 2005, participating in four expeditions. Expanding upon his successful 2001 documentary expedition, James Cameron returned under the auspices of the Discovery Channel, and sent state-of-the-art ROVs deep into the ship. Phase One of his expedition departed St John's, Newfoundland, on 24 June and returned to port on July 7, as another charter of *Keldysh* was imminent.

The next day, Deep Ocean Expeditions' 'tourist dive' to the *Titanic* departed aboard *Keldysh*, with about a dozen passengers who had paid $36,650 (£20,899) to dive to the wreck. Five 'double dives' by the two *Mir* submersibles were made before *Keldysh* returned to St John's.

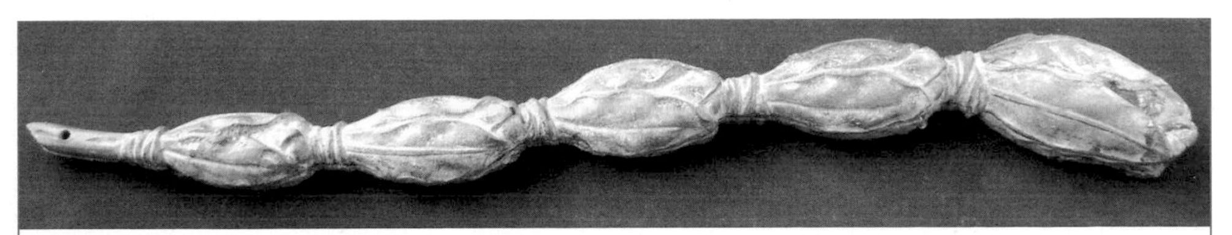

Among the artefacts recovered during RMS Titanic Inc's 2004 expedition was this delicate gilt piece, likely from the wrought ironwork beneath the railings surrounding the ship's after grand staircase. (© 2004 RMS Titanic Inc)

Cameron then resumed his interrupted expedition on 18 July. It culminated in a live two-hour broadcast from the wreck site on 24 July, providing stunning and often poignant views of the Turkish bath, passenger cabins, crew areas, the Marconi room and other previously unseen areas. Among its surprises was the presence of wood panelling in the ship's interior, possibly protected by its shellac coating.

Little is known of the activities of the '*Titanic* 20th Anniversary Dive', led by G. Michael Harris and employing the *Keldysh* and the *Mir* submersibles. It operated between 31 July and 9 August 2005, and reportedly recorded high-definition video of the wreck and debris field.

Keldysh would return yet again to the site, departing on 10 August. This time, American divers and television personalities John Chatterton and Richie Kohler planned to seek several reported additional large pieces of the wreck. Limited by finances and bad weather to just three days of diving on 12, 13 and 15 August, they finally located the pieces – portions of the ship's double bottom – on the last day, and photographed them extensively.

The resulting History Channel documentary, *Titanic's Last Secrets*, suggested the pieces were new finds. But they had been duly photographed during RMS Titanic Inc's expeditions in 1987 and 1996. Damage observed on the double-bottom pieces, the programme said, suggested the ship's bow and stern had fractured and broken apart at a relatively low angle, perhaps 11 degrees to 15 degrees, rather than the stern pointing upward, perpendicular to the ocean's surface, as depicted since 1912. But this scenario, too, already had been reported by the 1998 expedition's naval architects in 2002.

Robert Ballard again was in the news in December 2005, suggesting *Titanic*'s deterioration could be stopped through application of anti-fouling paint by remote-operated vehicles. His proposal apparently did not address pollution or funding considerations, nor the lack of accessibility for painting of much of the ship's interior structures due to collapsing decks.

Having purchased rights to another historic wreck in 2001, RMS Titanic Inc used remote-operated vehicles in August 2007 to retrieve approximately 100 artefacts from the wreck of *Carpathia*, in 500 feet of water off the south-western coast of Ireland. They included ship's telegraphs, portholes, china, wine bottles and floor tiles. The *Carpathia* artefacts made their public debut in April 2009 as part of the *Titanic* artefact exhibition at the Science Museum of Minnesota in St Paul.

After a six-year absence and another shareholder-initiated change in the company's management in January 2009, Premier Exhibitions/RMS Titanic Inc returned for the most extensive documentation of the wreck and associated debris fields yet, in late summer 2010, bringing a renewed commitment by the company's new management to historical and scientific exploration of the wreck site. Contributing their expertise to the expedition were the Woods Hole Oceanographic Institution, the Waitt Institute for Discovery, the Center for Maritime and Underwater Resource Management, Phoenix International, the NBC television network, the History Channel, NOAA, and Paul-Henri Nargeolet, who had returned to the company as its director of underwater research.

Departing from St John's aboard the expedition vessel *Jean Charcot* on 23 August 2010, the expedition arrived on site on 25 August. The team paused for a memorial service, placing

The Jean Charcot *was the floating headquarters for the 2010* Titanic *expedition, which performed extensive mapping and photographic documentation of the wreck's current condition and the entire wreck site.* (Paul-Henri Nargeolet)

The 2010 expedition drew upon the talents of many individuals and organisations to produce the most accurate maps of the wreck to date, enabling scientific assessment of the ship's present state and implications for its future. (© 2010 RMS Titanic Inc)

The remote-operated vehicle Remora *surveyed* Titanic's *bow, stern and debris fields in high resolution, two- and three dimensions.* (Paul-Henri Nargeolet)

flowers on the sea, before deploying a high-tech arsenal in learning more about the liner. It included an ROV, *Remora*, directed from the *Jean Charcot*, and two autonomous underwater vehicles (AUVs), *Ginger* and *Mary Ann*, which, once programmed, independently moved at three knots back and forth above the ocean floor with side-scan sonar and, depending on the specific mission, high-resolution digital still cameras, multi-beam sonars, or sub-bottom profilers that could penetrate the ocean floor's sand to seek buried objects.

For photography the AUV's automatically maintained a 'height' of 16 to 32 feet (5 to 10 metres); for sonar work or the sub-bottom profiler, a 98 to 196 feet (30 to 60 metre) altitude was programmed. Working continually up to 22 hours before surfacing for battery changes and downloading their recorded data, the AUVs provided data to create the most detailed maps of the wreck site yet.

Shown here on an earlier expedition, the autonomous underwater vehicle Mary Ann *is prepared for deployment. Together with its twin* Ginger, *it was programmed at the surface, then sent to hover 16–32ft (5–10m) above the ocean floor at* Titanic's *wreck site, moving back and forth and photographing with high resolution cameras before surfacing to download data to waiting technicians.* (Waitt Institute for Discovery)

On 26 August, to ensure that the wreck site's full extent would be determined, the expedition team surveyed an area measuring three by five nautical miles. Once this 'wide-angle view' was completed, it made high-resolution surveys covering two by three nautical miles, and one-and-a-half by one nautical miles.

Additionally, the expedition took 130,000 high-resolution digital photographs of the entire wreck site, permitting construction of a digital photo mosaic. The ROV *Remora* completed a 2-D and 3-D video survey of the bow and stern, and a portion of the debris field east of the stern. In addition, it took 3-D acoustic photos of the bow using three new high-frequency, sector-scanning sonars that provided resolution better than one centimetre (one-third of an inch). These images will help assess the hull's vertical and horizontal deformation.

Expedition members observed significant degradation: Decks were found to be collapsing throughout the bow section, aft of the grand staircase. The promenade deck in this area had sunk about three feet (one metre) away from the hull. Collapsing decks are causing some hull plates to let go, with undersea currents flexing other parts of the ship until they loosen. Large holes had opened in the Marconi's cabin roof, in other decks, and above the A-deck windows. The hull is sagging more and changing in shape. Significant collapsing and deterioration was also observed at the stern section.

Despite two approaching hurricanes that interrupted work for more than a week, teamwork and flawless operation of cutting-edge technology permitted the expedition to achieve all its objectives before leaving for St John's on 16 September.

The extensive data recovered during the expedition required considerable time for processing and interpretation; a television documentary revealing the expedition's findings was planned for *Titanic*'s centennial year, according to published reports.

While RMS Titanic Inc was preparing for its highly successful 2010 expedition, it received word of a positive ruling from the court that had supervised *Titanic*'s case for nearly two decades.

In October 1993 the French Office of Maritime Affairs in the Ministry of Equipment, Transportation and Tourism had granted the company outright title to the 1,800 artefacts recovered in 1987, which had been landed in France. When the US District Court declared the company *Titanic*'s salvor-in-possession in June 1994, it said that pursuant to international law of salvage, the company would hold a salvor's lien on artefacts recovered from 1993 onward, but would not have title to them. The ruling was upheld in 2002 by the Fourth Circuit Court of Appeals, in Richmond, Virginia, which returned the case to the District Court to provide RMST with 'an appropriate reward which may include awards *in specie* [*ie*, a monetary award from a court-supervised sale of artefacts], full or restricted ownership of the artefacts, limitations on use of artefacts, rights to income from display and shared research, and future rights to salvage.'

On 30 November 2007, the company filed a motion with the court seeking a salvage award 'for all of its efforts salvaging the *Titanic* wreck…'. The company's motion included an independent appraisal of the 1993–2004 artefacts' value as being approximately $110,859,200 (£69,188,002).

But before the court would act on the request, on 25 March 2008 it permitted the United

In 2002, Judge Paul V. Niemeyer wrote the decision for the Fourth Circuit Court of Appeals holding that RMS Titanic Inc had a salvor's lien on the artefacts, but did not own them outright. (Private collection)

States government's National Oceanic and Atmospheric Administration, which had closely monitored *Titanic*'s case from the start, to become a 'friend of the court', and at the court's direction, NOAA entered into lengthy negotiations with RMS Titanic Inc's management to draft a series of 'covenants' protecting the *Titanic* and its artefacts – 'an international treasure for posterity' – from sale or dispersal, requiring NOAA oversight of the artefacts' welfare, future artefact recoveries and expeditions to the wreck, and court approval of any sale of artefacts to other parties, in perpetuity. Once agreement had been reached on the 'covenants', the court proceeded to consider RMST's request for a salvage award.

On 12 August 2010, Judge Rebecca Beach Smith issued her 52-page decision, granting RMS Titanic Inc's motion for a salvage award 'in the amount of one hundred per cent (100%) the fair market value of the artefacts recovered in the 1993, 1994, 1996, 1998, 2000 and 2004 expeditions to the RMS *Titanic*', with the judge requiring an additional year, until August 2011, to determine how the award was to be paid.

The 'covenants' became part of the ruling. Among them:

- 'The *Titanic* Artifact Collection shall be kept together and intact forever… Individual objects or artifacts, or groups of artifacts, as well as all supporting documentation, shall not be dispersed through sale or other disposition except as through a process of deaccessioning as provided under these covenants…'
- 'The *Titanic* Collections shall be available to present and future generations for public display and exhibition, historical review, scientific and scholarly research and educational purposes.'
- 'The *Titanic* Collections shall be maintained in accordance with current internationally recognized museum standards and practices for collections management.'
- 'NOAA has the authority to gather information and to submit information and/or make reports and recommendations to the Court regarding the compliance of the Trustee [RMS Titanic, Inc.] with these covenants and conditions…'
- 'The subject *Titanic* Artifact Collection may not be sold, transferred, assigned, or

otherwise be the subject of a commercial transaction, except as approved by the Court. Such transfer or assignment will be subject to orders of the Court including the provisions of these covenants and conditions... These covenants and conditions...shall run in perpetuity and shall be applied to all subsequent Trustees...'

Survivor Edith Brown Haisman visited the site of her father's loss during the 1996 Titanic *Expedition Cruise, and participated in an onboard memorial service in his memory.* (David F. Hutchings)

Since the first artefacts' retrieval in 1987, RMS Titanic Inc's activities almost continually had been questioned – indeed, vilified – by those opposed to artefact recovery, who called it 'looting' or 'grave robbing'. Judge Smith's ruling repeatedly expressed the court's strong commendation of the company's activities at, and stewardship of, the wreck and its artefacts, which, the court said, faced 'serious danger' and 'peril' on the ocean floor before their recovery. Said Judge Smith, 'The salvage of *Titanic* has involved unprecedented feats of skill and dedication, both in the salvage of the artifacts and their conservation and exhibition.'

As the 20th century concluded, and the once-great ship and its contents decayed on the ocean floor, the personal links to history's most famous vessel also became more tenuous, with the passing of survivors and others who had brought the ship's story to millions around the world.

Fifteen-year-old Edith Eileen Brown and her parents had left South Africa so that Mr Brown could open a hotel in Seattle, Washington. They boarded *Titanic* at Southampton. Mrs Brown and her daughter left the ship in boat 14. Edith's final memory of her father was that he was dressed in a dinner jacket, smoking a cigar and sipping brandy on *Titanic*'s deck. Edith married Fred Haisman in 1917, and the couple had ten children. In 1993, RMS Titanic Inc's president George Tulloch presented Edith with her father's watch, recovered from the ocean floor, fully conserved and contained within a plaque that bore the inscription, 'What better use for scientific technology than to reunite a father with his child?' It remained in her possession until her passing, when it returned to RMST for continuing care and exhibition. Accompanied by her daughter Dorothy Kendle, Edith visited the wreck site aboard the cruise ship *Island Breeze* during the 1996 expedition cruise, and participated in poignant memorial services at the site and in Halifax, Nova Scotia. Among the last *Titanic* survivors

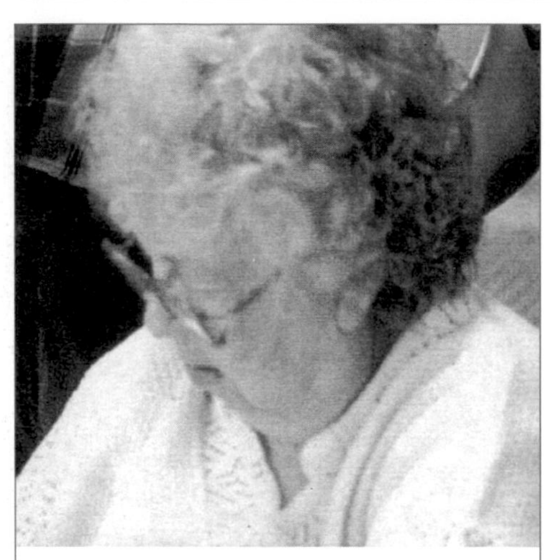

Eleanor Johnson Schuman signed many autographs and charmed members of the 1996 Expedition Cruise. She passed away on 7 March 1998. (Authors' collection)

Just four years old at the time of the disaster, survivor Michel Navratil Jr visited his father's grave for the first and only time when the 1996 Expedition Cruise ship Island Breeze *visited Halifax, Nova Scotia.* (© 1996 Charles A. Haas)

to have clear memories of the disaster, Edith Brown Haisman passed away in a Southampton nursing home on 20 January 1997 at age 100.

Louise LaRoche, aged 20 months, her parents and her older sister, the only known blacks among *Titanic*'s passengers, boarded at Cherbourg as second class passengers, intending to return to Mr LaRoche's native Haiti where he could find employment in keeping with his engineering degree. Louise, her mother and sister escaped, likely in boat 14, but Mr LaRoche was lost, and his devastated family returned to France in May 1912. Louise died on 28 January 1998 at the age of 87.

Eleanor Ileen Johnson was 18 months old when she, her mother and brother boarded *Titanic* to return home to Chicago, Illinois, following a visit to Sweden. They escaped in boat 15. As Eleanor Schuman, she charmed members of the 1996 expedition cruise to the wreck site on board the *Royal Majesty*. Eleanor died on 7 March 1998 at the age of 87.

Titanic's last male survivor, Michel Marcel Navratil, Jr, was nearly four at the time of the disaster. He and his brother Edmond, 2, had been spirited away from their Nice, France, home by their father Michel, Sr, who then planned to send for his wife and begin a new life in America. The boys were handed in to collapsible D, the last boat to be successfully launched, as their father stood back. Michel recalled his father's last words: 'My child, when your mother comes for you, as she surely will, tell her that I loved her dearly and still do.' He and Edmond were called 'the *Titanic* orphans', until their mother Marcelle came to New York to bring them home. During a stop at Halifax during the

Titanic Expedition Cruise in 1996, Michel visited his father's grave for the first and last time. He died in Montpellier, France, on 30 January 2001, at age 92.

Yet another loss came on 19 May 2002, when Walter Lord, whose bestselling books *A Night to Remember* (1955) and *The Night Lives On* (1986) introduced *Titanic*'s story to millions worldwide, passed away in New York City at age 84. The loss of his friendship, warm sense of humour and his deep knowledge of many historical subjects was mourned by many.

Author of more than a dozen books on a variety of topics, Walter Lord was best known for his bestsellers A Night to Remember *and* The Night Lives On. (Michael A. Findlay collection)

Winnifred Vera Quick, her mother and two-year-old sister boarded *Titanic* at Southampton, looking forward to reuniting with her father, a plasterer, who had gone on to Detroit, Michigan. Second class passengers, they evacuated the ship in boat 11, with Winnifred shoe- and sockless, her feet in freezing water until someone came to her assistance. With her husband Alois van Tongerloo, Winnifred visited every American state except Hawaii in 1966. She willingly spoke of her *Titanic* experiences. Winnifred passed away on 4 July 2002 in East Lansing, Michigan, at 98.

Winnifred Quick, eight years old at the time of the disaster, passed away in July 2002 as Winnifred Van Tongerloo. (Detroit Daily News)

On 31 January 2004, George Harmon Tulloch, who, with his best friend Cdr Paul-Henri Nargeolet, had led five extraordinarily successful expeditions to *Titanic*, died after a courageous battle with cancer. He was 59. Few people rewrite a major historical event; teach and emotionally touch and enthral millions worldwide; rescue priceless artefacts from destruction; become successful and respected in business; and maintain the highest ethical standards. Tulloch was one of those very few. Perhaps his own prescient words said it best: 'We know the rule of life is to have a great time living in such a way

George Harmon Tulloch led five successful expeditions to the Titanic *and helped to rewrite the story of the ship's final moments.* (Authors' photo)

Judge Joseph Calvitt Clarke Jr's supervision of Titanic's *wreck and recovery of her artefacts set significant precedents for future deep-sea salvage activities.* (The estate of Judge J. Calvitt Clarke Jr)

that all of us may leave this world with self-respect, and our descendants may enter it glad that we came before them. This is why we recovered *Titanic* as well as we could.'

Four days later, on 4 February 2004, Tulloch's close friend, film producer William MacQuitty, passed away in London, age 98. Many feel his classic 1958 film *A Night to Remember* remains the most accurate telling of *Titanic*'s story. As a boy, he had witnessed *Titanic*'s departure from Belfast. The 1996 *Titanic* Expedition Cruise had brought him full circle to *Titanic*'s final resting place, making him the only person to witness *Titanic*'s birth and visit the place of her death. Those privileged to know him mourned the loss of true 'Renaissance man' and gentleman.

Titanic lost another friend on 6 May 2004. Judge Joseph Calvitt Clarke, Jr, who had presided over *Titanic*'s case from the start, passed away in Norfolk at age 83. His rulings, based on law but shaped, too, by his keen awareness of history and consummate concern for *Titanic*'s wreck and artefacts, set significant new precedents governing dives to, and recoveries from deep-sea wrecks in international waters.

Many of *Titanic*'s survivors had lived to advanced old age, often into their 80s or 90s, and several living past age 100. Inexorably, as time passed, their numbers dwindled.

On 6 May 2006, Lillian Gertrud Asplund, 99, died in her home in Shrewsbury, Massachusetts. Five-year-old Lillian, her parents and four brothers had boarded *Titanic* at Southampton as third-class passengers; they were returning home to Massachusetts after a family visit to Sweden. In a rare published comment, Lillian recalled that *Titanic* 'was very big, and it had just been painted. I remember not liking the smell of fresh paint.'

Lillian's father and three brothers perished in the disaster. Never married, Lillian cared for her mother and surviving brother for much of her life. She steadfastly declined to speak of the family's experiences aboard *Titanic*.

Barbara Joan West was ten months and 18 days old when she, her parents and her sister boarded *Titanic* at Southampton as second class passengers. Her father, who had planned to become a fruit farmer in Gainesville, Florida, was lost. After being plucked from lifeboat 10 and being taken to New York, the family returned to England in May 1912. In later years, as Barbara West Dainton, she enjoyed a long career as a teacher and enjoyed being a volunteer guide at Truro Cathedral in Cornwall, where she resided. Too young to have first-hand memories, she nevertheless declined to speak publicly about her family's *Titanic* experiences, and asked that word of her passing, in a nursing home on 6 May 2006 at age 96, be kept confidential until after her funeral.

Lillian Asplund, the last American survivor, seen here in later life, steadfastly declined to discuss her family's tragic voyage aboard Titanic. (Authors' collection)

Barbara Joan West Dainton passed away in Cornwall on 6 May 2006 at age 96. She is seen here (right) with her mother and sister Constance, about the time of her Titanic *voyage.* (Authors' collection)

Of all the more than 1,300 passengers and 900 crew, it seemed somehow fitting that the youngest person of all on board *Titanic*, at age 2 months and 27 days, would become the last living *Titanic* survivor. Elizabeth Gladys Millvina Dean, her brother Bertram and her parents boarded *Titanic* at Southampton, travelling in third class. Her father, also named Bertram, hoped to open a tobacco shop in Wichita, Kansas. He saw his family safely away in lifeboat 10 and was lost. Georgette Dean returned to England with her two children in May 1912.

Millvina, as she was known, had no idea of her *Titanic* involvement until her mother told her when she was eight. After receiving an education, Millvina worked around her home, caring for the family's many animals.

Millvina Dean enjoyed seeing her many friends during her final public appearance on 15 April 2009 at the British Titanic Society convention, six weeks before her passing. (© 2009 Charles A. Haas. All rights reserved)

During the Second World War she worked for the British government as a mapmaker. Afterwards, she worked in a tobacco shop, and then in an engineering company's purchasing department. Millvina became publicly involved with *Titanic* in 1987, attending a 75th anniversary memorial service near Southampton's cenotaph. She attended *Titanic* conventions on both sides of the Atlantic, granted many television and radio interviews, graciously consented to thousands of autograph requests and made frequent public appearances at *Titanic* exhibitions. Her vibrant mind, sharp wit and warm smile endeared her to all.

Following a fall in November 2006 and a resulting hospitalisation, Millvina entered a nursing home, and in 2008 decided to auction off some of her *Titanic*-related possessions to help pay for her care. The sale realised £32,000 (about $51,000).

Touched by Millvina's plight, officers of the Belfast Titanic Society, British Titanic Society, and the US-based Titanic International Society established the 'Millvina Fund' to receive donations to assist her. Several celebrities involved with James Cameron's 1997 blockbuster film *Titanic* stepped forward to help. Actors Leonardo DiCaprio and Kate Winslet made a joint contribution of $20,000 (about £12,400). Writer/director James Cameron and singer Celine Dion donated $10,000 (about £6,200) each, these sums being supplemented by contributions from friends and strangers around the world.

Her last public appearance occurred on 5 April 2009 when Millvina visited the British Titanic Society Convention in Southampton. Crowds gathered round her to say 'hello', and Millvina was her usual gracious and effervescent self.

On the morning of 31 May 2009, the 98th anniversary of *Titanic*'s launch, Elizabeth Gladys Millvina Dean passed away from complications of pneumonia; she was 97 years old. The last personal link to RMS *Titanic* was gone. It truly was the end of an era.

At her family's request, her funeral was private, but on 24 October 2009 a poignant service of remembrance filled every pew at St Mary's Church in Copythorne, Hampshire. At the service's conclusion, Millvina's ashes were scattered in the waters of Southampton's Berth 44, where *Titanic*'s tragic voyage had begun so long ago.

With the express permission of its donors and Millvina's family, the administrators of the Millvina Fund decided to use the unexpended donations to provide an appropriate memorial to *Titanic*'s last survivor. In co-operation with the Southampton City Council and the city's design team, planning began for a new garden in her memory, to be located near the new Sea City Museum, adjacent to the Civic Centre, opening during *Titanic*'s 2012 centennial.

Despite the passage of a full century since the ship's construction and loss, and the passing of the last living link to the ship, *Titanic* remains in the news and embedded in popular culture. An Internet search for 'RMS Titanic' reveals more than 900,000 'hits'. A search for '*Titanic*' in an online bookselling service yields more than 2,700 results. A staff member at the Library of Congress in Washington, DC, once estimated the topic ranked in the 'top five' in numbers of public enquiries received.

In 1997, two major iterations of *Titanic*'s story encouraged a new awareness of the ship and her people.

On 23 April, the Broadway musical *Titanic*, with music and lyrics by Maury Yeston and book by Peter Stone, debuted at the Lunt-Fontanne Theatre in New York. Its technologically complex set caused trouble – *Titanic* sometimes would not sink – and, while eventually the problems were solved, the production opened to mostly negative reviews. The public felt otherwise, however, and the show became a surprise hit, especially after it won 1997 Tony Awards for best musical and four other categories. The production ran for 804 performances before touring the US for 100 weeks. Additional productions followed in Holland, Germany, Canada, Japan, Wales, Northern Ireland, Norway, Australia and England. The play has been translated into Japanese, French, Dutch, German, Finnish and Norwegian. Modified to a less-complex form technologically, it has been performed by many local and regional drama companies, and even by teenagers in American high schools.

Perhaps more than any other single event, the release of James Cameron's blockbuster film *Titanic* brought the ship back into worldwide public consciousness. Taking three years to produce, the film told a rather traditional, fictional love story, some suggesting it resembled '*Romeo and Juliet* on the *Titanic*'. Writer/director Cameron had begun work on the project in 1992, and in 1995 used his own new technology to photograph the ship during 12 dives launched from the *Keldysh* at the wreck site, though in the completed film, actual underwater footage was limited, with models and special effects substituted in many scenes.

Huge financial stresses, technological complexities, extensive use of digital special effects and Cameron's penchant for accuracy and perfection in every aspect of the production delayed the film's debut by some six months. Its sets were historically precise, though about 10% smaller than actual dimensions for economy's sake. *Titanic* became the most expensive film ever made, costing at least $200 million (£124,154,200).

Titanic debuted on 1 November 1997 at the Tokyo Film Festival, with the official Hollywood premiere on 14 December, and its public opening five days later. Reviews praised the film's technological achievements and generally accurate depiction of events relating to the ship itself, but faulted the screenplay and characterisations.

Word-of-mouth spread, however, and sold-out performances resulted and continued for nearly three months. The movie's three-hour-plus length permitted only three (rather than the usual four) showings per theatre per day, but it continued to smash performance records as early viewers came back for second or even third viewings. It was the top-grossing film for

Delegates from seven of the world's Titanic *societies visited the* Titanic *section of Halifax's Fairview Lawn Cemetery during the 2007 convention.* (Authors' photo)

16 consecutive weeks, and became the first movie to gross over $1 billion (£620.7 million) worldwide. To date, its total gross is estimated at $1.843 billion (£1.14 billion).

On 23 March 1998, *Titanic* won 11 Academy Awards, tying the record set by *Ben-Hur* in 1959; none were for acting.

The last previous *Titanic* film of any note, *A Night to Remember*, had premiered nearly 40 years earlier. With its attractive young actors delivering a poignant story of doomed love that appealed to every age, Cameron's production played a significant role in providing a new generation with its introduction to *Titanic*'s story.

Around the world, *Titanic*-related organisations grew, at least temporarily, as moviegoers sought to learn more. The United Kingdom, France, the Scandinavian countries, Germany, Switzerland, South Africa, Brazil, the United States, Australia, Canada, Ireland and New Zealand have *Titanic* organisations active to various degrees in researching and disseminating new research about the liner, its passengers and crew through journals, websites, weblogs, meetings and conventions.

In April 2007, members from seven of these *Titanic* groups came together for the first joint convention in Halifax, Nova Scotia, commemorating the 95th anniversary of *Titanic*'s loss; the weekend culminated in visits to three city cemeteries where *Titanic* victims lie, and a moving memorial service. It was at this convention that the re-identification of *Titanic*'s 'unknown child' as Sidney Leslie Goodwin was first announced.

In May 2011, delegates from *Titanic* organisations on both sides of the Atlantic journeyed to Belfast, Northern Ireland, to commemorate over a five-day period the 100th anniversary of *Titanic*'s launch. On 31 May, the actual anniversary date, participants marked the exact moment of launch from a boat moored near the remains of the slipways where *Titanic* and her two sister ships were built.

Yet another medium of disseminating the latest *Titanic* knowledge, the Internet, is perhaps best typified by *Encyclopedia Titanica* (www.encyclopedia-titanica.org) where one may find biographies of *Titanic*'s passengers and crew, research articles and member forums on almost every topic imaginable. The Internet has done much to break down barriers of language, distance and cost that once stood between researchers and essential information about the ship's onboard complement.

Seven months before her passing in February 1996, *Titanic* survivor Eva Hart, who had publicly criticised artefact recovery, expressed privately her understanding and acceptance that a time would come when all survivors would be gone, and that the recovered artefacts would offer the only direct, tangible link to the men, women and children of *Titanic*. To date, more than 22 million people have visited artefact exhibitions on five continents, and found themselves deeply moved – often unexpectedly – by the experience, as reflected in the written comments thousands have left as they departed.

Informative displays, beautifully designed and mounted, thoughtfully and respectfully tell the story of the ship and her people through everyday objects they used at home and on board, the contents of their luggage, and remnants of the ship herself. Among the most moving displays are the 'ice wall', inviting visitors to place and keep their hands on its frigid surface to suggest what *Titanic*'s people endured in the 28°F (–2°C) seawater that night, and the Memorial Wall, listing the names and fates of every passenger and crew member.

Other permanent *Titanic* attractions opened, including two in the American resort cities of Branson, Missouri, and Pigeon Forge, Tennessee. While lacking artefacts retrieved from the wreck,

Patrons of the Titanic *exhibit in Branson, Missouri, enter through an 'iceberg' at the building's starboard side. The building is shaped like the forward half of the liner.* (Paul Frederickson, CC-BY-2.5 via Wikimedia Commons)

they attracted thousands with recreations of rooms aboard the ship, actors interacting with visitors while portraying roles ranging from Captain Smith to a chambermaid, and objects loaned from private collections, all housed in buildings shaped to replicate the forward half of the liner.

Titanic's presence in the news continues without end. A small sampling of these events evokes the full range of emotions, from dismay to relief, from astonishment to pride, and demonstrates the ship's continuing relevance in the 21st century:

- On 28 July 2001, two young New Yorkers were married in one of the *Mir* submersibles while hovering over *Titanic*'s bridge during a tourist dive expedition, with the captain of the *Queen Elizabeth 2* relaying the service from the *Keldysh*. The wedding ceremony was denounced by some as lacking sensitivity to the tragedy that had occurred there.
- In January 2003, Harland and Wolff, *Titanic*'s builders, delivered its final ship, *Anvil Point*, to Britain's Ministry of Defence, going on to evolve from shipbuilders to a general engineering firm specialising in off-shore energy installations.
- In April 2003, preliminary plans were announced for 'Titanic Quarter' in Belfast, a £1 billion redevelopment of the former Harland and Wolff shipyard. In December 2006, the project having been revised considerably, applications were submitted. 'Titanic Quarter's' focal point is an exhibition centre, initially called the 'Titanic Signature Project', telling of the city's shipbuilding and industrial heritage, with special emphasis on *Titanic* and her sister ships. It is envisioned as a major tourist attraction. Hotels, shops, apartments

Scheduled for completion in Titanic's *centennial year, this striking building, called 'Titanic Belfast', is being built adjacent to the former slipways from which* Titanic *and her sister ships were launched. Designed to suggest ships' bows, it will become a* Titanic *museum and serve as the centrepiece for Titanic Quarter, an extensive redevelopment of the former Harland & Wolff shipyard.* (Sandra Gilpin, Belfast Titanic Society)

and restaurants will be built in areas once filled with the shipyard's engine works and other buildings. The slipways on which *Olympic*, *Titanic* and *Britannic* were built will be refurbished to help demonstrate the liners' huge size. Construction was expected to be completed some time in *Titanic*'s centennial year.

- In January 2006, the tender that had brought *Titanic*'s passengers to her side during her stop at Cherbourg, *Nomadic*, was purchased at a Paris auction by the Northern Ireland Department of Social Development, rescuing the craft from scrapping at virtually the last moment. Seven months later, this historic ship, the last White Star vessel in existence, was ferried by barge back to its Belfast birthplace, where it began a multimillion-pound restoration, funded by public donations, local and UK government funding, lottery proceeds and European Union subsidies. In 2008, *Nomadic* was named to the Core Collection of the National Register of Historic Vessels in the United Kingdom.
- Auction sales demonstrated *Titanic*'s enduring significance to collectors. In 2007 alone, keys from the ship's post office sold for a record £100,000 ($200,000 at then-current exchange rates); survivor Laura Francatelli's life jacket sold for £60,000 ($120,000); the deck log from the recovery vessel *Mackay-Bennett* fetched £51,000 ($102,000); a Chinese jeweller bought the key to the crows' nest telephone box for £78,000 ($157,930).
- In January 2008, the Belfast Titanic Society launched an intensive campaign to move 'the Big Wheel', a 200 ft (60m) Ferris wheel, which had been placed directly over the city's primary

The tender Nomadic, *the last floating White Star Line vessel, returns to its Belfast birthplace in July 2006 atop a barge.* (David Scott-Beddard, Nomadic Preservation Society)

For more than a year, the beautiful Titanic *Memorial near Belfast's City Hall was enveloped by and virtually hidden under the structure of the 'Belfast Wheel', a massive Ferris wheel. The structure was removed in January 2009.* ('Ardfern' CC-BY-SA-3.0, via Wikimedia Commons)

Titanic memorial in November 2007. After a protracted effort that included letters from concerned people on both sides of the Atlantic, the wheel ended its operation in January 2009 and was dismantled.

- In January 2009, an Australian behavioural economist published a report suggesting that Americans on board *Titanic* were 8.5% more likely to survive than other nationalities, while Britons were 7% less likely to do so. He explained, '...There would have been very few Americans in steerage or third class; and the British tend to be very polite and queue.' Within a day, other researchers responded that losses on the ship were based on wealth and the consequent location of the different classes' cabins, rather than any supposed stereotypical behaviour patterns.
- In April 2009, *Titanic*'s home port of Southampton announced plans to convert the Civic Centre's former police

An artist's impression of Southampton's splendid Sea City Museum, a new wing of its Civic Centre, planned for completion in 2012. A series of exhibits will recount stories of those who travelled through the port of Southampton over many years, and will highlight stories of Titanic's *crew, hundreds of whom called the city their home.* (© Southampton City Council)

department offices and magistrates' court into a *Titanic* museum, scheduled for completion by 2012. A controversy arose when it was proposed to sell off some of the city's art collection to help fund the project. The idea was soon dropped. Construction began in October 2010.

- On 30 April 2010, New York City's historic St Vincent's Hospital, which in 1912 had treated more than a hundred *Titanic* survivors upon their arrival aboard *Carpathia*, closed its doors, victim of severe financial difficulties. The future of a large bronze plaque near the hospital's emergency room, dedicated to the memory of *Titanic*'s surgeon, Dr William Francis Norman O'Loughlin, remained in jeopardy at this writing.
- On 22 May 2010, in West Roxbury, a suburb of Boston, Massachusetts, before an audience that included Ireland's consul-general in Boston, the chairperson of the Belfast Titanic Society, a Massachusetts state legislator, its own convention delegates, and a dozen of her descendants, the New Jersey-based Titanic International Society dedicated a memorial stone at the hitherto-unmarked grave in St Joseph's Cemetery of 22-year-old Catherine Buckley, from Ovens, County Cork, Ireland, who had hoped to join her half-sister in America and find work as a domestic servant. Catherine was the only third class *Titanic* victim to be recovered and buried on land.
- Scientists at Dalhousie University in Halifax, Nova Scotia, and the University of Seville in Spain announced in December 2010 the discovery of a new, fast-acting species of bacteria among those eating the ship's iron; in honour of its source, they named it *Halomonas titanicae*.

A large crowd that included her descendants witnessed the unveiling of this marker stone for third class Titanic *passenger Catherine Buckley in St Joseph's Cemetery in West Roxbury, Massachusetts, during the May 2010 convention of the New Jersey-based Titanic International Society.* (Authors' photo)

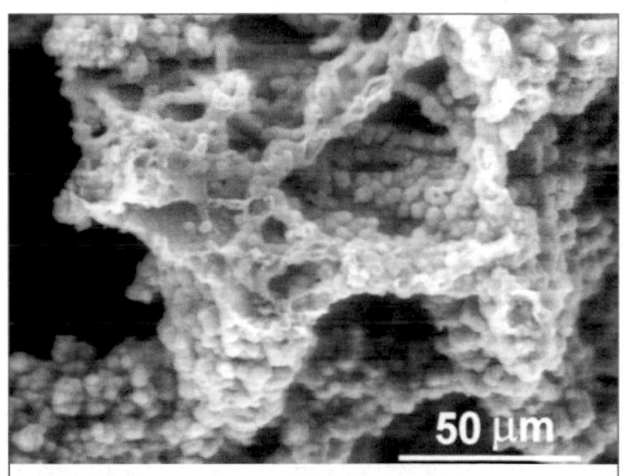

The bacteria causing the deterioration of Titanic's *hull forms a netlike structure in this environmental scanning electron micrograph. For comparison purposes, a single average human liver cell is about 50 micrometres long.* (Dr Henrietta Mann, Dalhousie University, Halifax, Nova Scotia)

As *Titanic*'s centennial approached, plans were well under way for commemorative observances in Belfast, Southampton, Queenstown, Liverpool, Halifax and many other cities. *Titanic*'s birthplace, Belfast, marked the centennial of the ship's launching with a series of events, culminating at 12.13 pm on 31 May 2011 with several hundred in the former Harland and Wolff shipyard grounds and aboard a flotilla of small craft cheering for 62 seconds as ships in the harbour saluted with their whistles, just as they had done as *Titanic* glided down the ways exactly one hundred years earlier.

Two memorial cruises to the wreck site were announced; the first quickly sold out with some 1,300 passengers booked. Another set of 'tourist dives', now priced at about $60,000 (£37,178), was offered. Dedications of new memorial plaques and stones; special services; cleaning and restorations of existing *Titanic* memorials; publication of dozens of books; a re-release (in 3-D) of James Cameron's *Titanic*; new television documentaries; a possible return to *Titanic* to retrieve additional artefacts; the openings of additional artefact exhibitions – the year 2012 promised to be a veritable smörgåsbord of *Titanic* activities, solemn and silly, gracious and greedy, commemorative and commercial.

But then what? Some suggested that once *Titanic*'s centennial passed, and the glut of 'everything *Titanic*' concluded, interest in history's most famous ship might fade or even disappear. Would the world reach a saturation point, saying 'Enough is enough. The ship sank. Get over it'? With all the survivors now gone, will *Titanic*'s story lose its personal impact, its human dimension?

Time, of course, will tell. Interest in other historic events has 'lived on' over many centuries, long after all participants had gone. Every April, media editors offer interviews with *Titanic* survivors' descendants, stories about local connections, and often 'new angles' to the story. Continuing digitisation of 1912-era newspapers offers even armchair researchers the opportunity to rediscover and share previously unknown details.

While, sadly, some use *Titanic* as a metaphor for failure ('rearranging deck chairs on the *Titanic*'), no other ship succeeds so well in generating high interest among all age groups. In particular, the continuing involvement of young people in *Titanic*'s saga, introduced to them through schools' curricula, research projects or visits to the artefact exhibitions, is a hopeful sign that future generations will not forget.

Today, in some respects, *Titanic* remains almost as controversial as she was during the days following the American and British enquiries into her loss. Some of the disaster's details and the wreck's mysteries may never be known. But each historic dive to the wreck (supported, it may be noted, not by government subsidy but by private enterprise) brings us a step closer to the answers to all our questions.

Through the 6,000 recovered artefacts, the Grace and Glory of a beautiful liner have been brought close, so that we may see for ourselves – and not through pictures, however authentic – the true shape and form of objects that gave life to this magnificent vessel.

When *Titanic* departed Southampton on 10 April 1912, her Destination was Disaster. Today, and hopefully for all time to come, *Titanic*'s destination is the Future, not only for herself, but for all those whose sense of History enables them to…Believe.

Appendix One

To help judge *Titanic*'s dimensions and capacities, the following comparisons may be made between the White Star ship *Mauretania* (potentially her chief rival of the period) and the *United States*, the most technically successful Atlantic liner.

	Titanic	***Mauretania***	***United States***
Laid down	31 March 1909	September 1904	8 February 1950
Launched	31 May 1911	20 September 1906	23 June 1951
Maiden voyage	10 April 1912	16 November 1907	3 July 1952
Length (overall)	882ft 9in	785ft	990ft
Beam	92ft 6in	88ft	102ft
Moulded depth	59ft 6in	57ft	72ft
Tonnage: gross	46,329	31,938	50,924
net	21,831	8,948	24,475
Decks	7	7	7
Engines	2 triple expansion and 1 turbine	4 turbines	4 turbines
Total horsepower	46,000	68,000	240,000
Service speed	21 knots	25 knots	33 knots
Top speed (est)	23–24 knots	'over 30 knots'	'over 38 knots'
Passengers 1st class	735	563	882
2nd class	674	464	685
3rd class	1,026	1,138	718
Officers and crew	885	812	1,068
Last voyage	10 April 1912	26 September 1934	1 November 1969
Length of service	4½ days	27 years	17 years

Appendix Two

Titanic's brief life can be measured in hours. The following are some significant dates and times in this short period:

1909		
31 March		Keel laid.
1911		
31 May		Launched.
1912		
20 March		Original scheduled date for maiden voyage departure; postponed due to construction delays caused by repairs to *Olympic* at Belfast following collision with HMS *Hawke*.
31 March		Outfitting completed (official number 131428).
1 April		Sea trials, scheduled for this date, postponed due to high winds.
2 April	6 am	Commencement of sea trials in Belfast Lough and the Irish Sea (to 6 pm).
	8 pm	Departs Belfast for Southampton, England. Fire in coal bunker number six.
	4 April	Arrives at Southampton shortly after midnight.
10 April	12.15pm	Departs White Star Dock, Southampton on maiden voyage. Aboard: first class 171; second class 250; third class 494; crew 909; local passengers for Cherbourg and Queenstown 29. Fire burning in coal bunker number six.
	6.35 pm	Arrives Cherbourg, France. Debarks 22 cross-Channel passengers. Takes aboard first class 150, second class 26, third class 102.
	8.10 pm	Departs Cherbourg for Queenstown (Cobh) Ireland.
11 April	11.30 am	Arrives Queenstown. Debarks seven local passengers. One crewman deserts. Takes aboard first class 3; second class 8; third class 113. Total aboard 1,317 passengers, 908 crew.
	1.30 pm	Departs Queenstown.
		Noon Thursday (11 April) to noon Friday (12 April) 386 miles logged.
12 April		Noon Friday (12 April) to noon Saturday (13 April) 519 miles logged.
13 April		Noon Saturday (13 April) to noon Sunday (14 April) 546 miles logged.
	1 pm	Chief engineer reports fire in coal bunker number six extinguished.

14 April	9 am	*Caronia* reports ice at 42° N, extending from Long 49° to 50°.
	1.42 pm	Ship's position 42°35' N, 45°50' W.
		Baltic reports ice 41°50' N, 49°52' W.
	1.45 pm	*Amerika* reports ice 41°27' N, 50°8' W.
	5.50 pm	Reaches 'The Corner' – 42° N, 47° W. Course changed from S 62° W to S 86° W.
	7 pm	Air temperature 43° (6.1°C).
	7.15 pm	Ice warning received from *Baltic* at 1.42 pm posted on bridge.
	7.30 pm	Air temperature 39° (3.9°C).
		Californian reports ice 42°3' N, 49°9' W.
	8.40 pm	Officer of the watch Lightoller orders ship's carpenter Maxwell to watch the fresh water supply as it may freeze.
	9 pm	Air temperature 33° (0.6°C).
	9.40 pm	*Mesaba* warns of ice 42° N to 41°25' N, 49° W to 50°30' W. Warning not delivered to bridge.
	10 pm	First officer Murdoch relieves second officer Lightoller on the bridge. Look-outs Lee and Fleet relieve Jewell and Symons in crow's nest. Air temperature 32° (0°C).
	10.30 pm	Sea temperature 32° (0°C).
	11 pm	*Californian* tries to warn of ice but is cut off by *Titanic*'s wireless operator.
	11.40 pm	Collision with iceberg.
15 April	midnight	Hogg and Evans relieve Lee and Fleet in crow's nest.
	12.05 am	Captain Smith orders lifeboats uncovered and crew mustered.
	12.10 am	Fourth officer Boxhall works out his estimate of ship's position: 41°46' N, 50°14' W.
	12.15 am	First wireless transmission of *Titanic*'s call for assistance – CQD.
	12.45 am	First distress rocket fired. First lifeboat, number 7, lowered. Wireless CQD transmission changed to SOS.
	1.40 am	Last rocket fired.
	2.05 am	Last lifeboat, Collapsible D, lowered.
	2.10 am	Last wireless signal transmitted.
	2.18 am	Lights fail.
	2.20 am	Ship founders, 1,512 lost.
	3.30 am	Rescue ship *Carpathia*'s rockets sighted by drifting lifeboats.
	4.10 am	First lifeboat, number 2, picked up by *Carpathia*.
	8.10 am	Last lifeboat, number 12, picked up.
	8.50 am	*Carpathia* heads for New York with 713 survivors.
18 April	9.25 pm	*Carpathia* docks at Pier 54, North River, New York, with *Titanic*'s survivors.

The preceding is only the barest outline of the events in *Titanic*'s life. Times are approximate and are expressed in local (ship's or city's) actual time.

Appendix Three

The courage and bravery of *Titanic*'s crew and passengers is not forgotten. Memorial statues, plaques and buildings are an ever-present reminder of the men and women who stood fast, of those who stood back. The International Ice Patrol, 24-hour manned wireless and sufficient lifeboat accommodation for all passengers now attest to the *Titanic*'s memory.

As long as men sail the seas, as long as the heart swells at hearing 'Nearer, My God, to Thee', the memory of the proud and beautiful *Titanic* and of her heroic crew and courageous passengers will not vanish from the hearts of men and women everywhere.

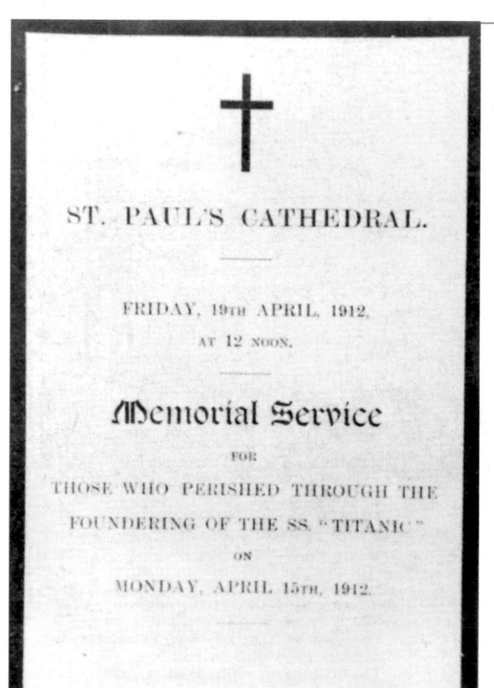

ST. PAUL'S CATHEDRAL.

FRIDAY, 19TH APRIL, 1912,
AT 12 NOON.

Memorial Service
FOR
THOSE WHO PERISHED THROUGH THE
FOUNDERING OF THE SS. "TITANIC"
ON
MONDAY, APRIL 15TH, 1912.

Among the earliest of Titanic *memorial services was the one at St Paul's Cathedral, London. Shown is the front page of the programme.* (Bob Forrest Collection)

DAILY SKETCH.

No. 997.—MONDAY, MAY 20, 1912. THE PREMIER PICTURE PAPER. [Registered as a Newspaper.] ONE HALFPENNY.

30,000 MOURNERS AT BURIAL OF TITANIC BANDMASTER.

In keeping with the heroism of the man who led the Titanic's band as they stood on the deck of the doomed liner calmly playing "Nearer, my God, to Thee" while the last of the lifeboats pulled away from the sinking ship were the striking scenes witnessed on Saturday when the remains of Mr. Wallace Hartley were laid to rest in the cemetery of his native town of Colne, Lancashire. From all parts of the country, and especially from Lancashire and Yorkshire, flocked crowds, estimated at 30,000, to pay their last tribute of respect to the memory of the central figure of one of the most touching incidents in the history of the sea.

(1) A close friend (X) of the deceased musician at the graveside. (2) Mr. Hartley's father (on right) and the principal mourners. (3) Mr. Hartley (X) and the chief mourners approaching the grave. (4 and 5) The Bethel Choir and the Colne Orchestral Society, who sang the hymn "Nearer, my God, to Thee" as the body was being interred. (6) Leaving the Bethel Chapel, where Mr. Hartley was originally a choirmaster and his father was choirmaster for twenty-five years. Inset: The heroic bandmaster.

Daily Sketch Photographs.

Bandmaster Wallace Hartley's funeral in his home town of Colne, Lancashire, attracted wide newspaper coverage. (Daily Sketch)

Hartley's fellow townspeople erected this memorial to the memory of Titanic's *brave bandmaster.* (Arnold Watson Collection)

The 'below decks' memorial was relocated to Southampton's Holy Rood Church in 1972. (Authors' collection)

The engineers' memorial in Southampton's Public gardens was dedicated in 1914. (Authors' collection)

A tribute to Titanic's *engineers graced a plot of city-donated land adjacent to the Liverpool Landing Stage.* (Authors' collection)

The Titanic *is remembered in the city of her birth. This memorial stands near Belfast City Hall.* (Authors' collection)

Mrs William Howard Taft, wife of the late American President, presided at the 1931 dedication of the Women's Titanic Memorial in Washington, DC. (Authors' collection)

The Titanic Memorial Lighthouse was a feature of the Seaman's Church Institute building at 25 South Street, New York. When the building was demolished in the 1960s, the lighthouse was moved to the South Street Seaport. (Authors' collection)

A stone tablet commemorates the heroism of chief wireless operator John George Phillips, as part of the memorial cloister in his home town of Godalming, Surrey. (Marconi Marine)

A reclining woman forms the central figure of a fountain dedicated to Isidor and Ida Straus. The memorial is located at Broadway and West 106th Street, New York. (Authors' collection)

Helen Melville Smith dedicated this life-sized bronze statue of her gallant father, Captain Edward J. Smith, at Lichfield, Staffordshire. (Arnold Watson Collection)

Appendix Four

Since 12.15 am on Monday 14 April 1912, when Marconi operator John Phillips' first transmission of *Titanic*'s position contained an error (quickly corrected), co-ordinates of the liner's wreck have, until recently, been mere conjecture.

The wreck's position eluded searchers for 73 years. Here are some of the co-ordinates associated with that search.

Fourth Officer Boxhall's calculated position	41°46' N, 50°14' W
Incorrect 12.15 am transmission	41°44' N, 50°24' W
Californian's position by dead reckoning, 14 April 1912, 10.21 pm	42°05' N, 50°07' W
Carpathia's position when picking up survivors,	
estimated by *Californian*	41°36' N, 50°00' W
estimated by *Birma*	41°36' N, 49°45' W
Woods Hole (Ballard), 1977	41°40' N, 50°01' W
Seawise & Titanic Salvage, 1979	41°40' N, 50°03' W
Grimm/Harris Expedition, 1980	41°40'–41°50' N, 50°00'–50°10' W
Grimm/Harris Expedition, 1981	41°39'–41°44' N, 50°02'–50°08' W
Grimm/Harris Expedition, 1983	vicinity of 41°08' N, 50°03' W
IFREMER, 1985	41°43'–41°51' N, 49°55'–50°12' W
Woods Hole, 1985	41°35'–41°46' N, 49°52'–50°10' W

Wreck position per Dr Robert Ballard's book, *The Discovery of the Titanic*:

Centre of bow section	41°43'57" N, 49°56'49" W
Centre of boiler field	41°43'32" N, 49°56'49" W
Stem section	41°43'35" N, 49°56'54" W

At latitude 41°43' N,	1° equals	1' equals
Nautical miles	59.86	0.99
Statute miles	68.88	1.14

Index

Page numbers in **bold** denote illustrations, although there is usually relevant text on the same page. Page numbers prefixed 'C' refer to the colour photograph section.

Abbott, Rhoda 24, 43
Abyssub 185–6
Adriatic (1907) 53–4, 76–7, **114**, 124, 126–7
Akademik Mstislav Keldysh 177, **181**, 182, 183, 186, 189, 190, 201, 204
Aks, Leah and Frank ('Filly') 26–7, 79
Almerian 44
Aluminaut 141
Alvin **147**, 148, 153–6
American Inquiry 106–11
Andrews, Thomas 22, 63, 66, 76–8
ANGUS 143, 145, 148, **150**, 156
Antillian 13, 19, 39
Argo 143–5, 148
Argo-Jason 142
Artefacts, *Titanic* 8, C135–6, 156–62, 166, **167–9**, 170–4, 178–9, **180**, 181–88, **189**, 190, 193–8, 203, 208
Asplund, Lillian Gertrud 198, **199**
Astor, John Jacob and Madeleine 22–3, **24**, 47, **63**, 80, 87, 91, 102
Astor, Vincent **102**
Athinai 12, 19
Atlantis II **147**, 148, 153–4
Autonomous underwater vehicles (AUVs) **192**
'Autumn' (hymn) 31–2
Ballard, Dr Robert 142–8, 153–7, 169, 177, 179–80, 186, **188**, 190
Baltic 12, 19, 53, 77, 126
Bandsmen 30–2, 71–2, 93, **213–14**
Becker, Ruth. *See* Blanchard, Ruth Becker
Beesley, Lawrence 16, **17**, 80, 139
Belfast 15, 19, 53, **55**, 58–61, 66, 68, 71, 86, 202, **205–6**, 208
Birma 46
Blair, David 72
Blanchard, Ruth Becker 34, 41, 45, 49
Board of Trade 65–6, 77, 111, 114–15, **119–20**
  inquiry into *Titanic* loss 123, 128, 138–9, 159–60
  lifeboat capacity requirements 18–19, 24, 116
Boat train, London–Southampton 78, 80, 85
  Paris–Cherbourg 85–6
  to Queenstown 88
Boxhall, Fourth Officer Joseph G. 12, 17–18, 20, 25, 37, 41, 65, 72, **90**, 124, **125**
Brice, Walter 16, 109
Bride, Harold S. 11–14, 31–2, **33**, 37, 46–7, 49, 71, **107**

Bright, Arthur 25, 37
Britannic (1914) 55, 72, 165, 205. *See also Gigantic*
'Brittle fracture' theory 165–6, **179**
Brown, Margaret Tobin ('Molly') 25, **52**, 87, 123
Burlingham, Charles C. **107**
Butt, Major Archibald W. 13, 47, 109–10

Californian 13, **14**, 19, **38**, 39–40, 43, **44**, 45, 111, 115–18, **119–20**, 128, **137**, 138–9
1992 reappraisal of evidence 159–60
Cameron, James 8, 184, 189–90, 200–2, 208
Cape Race, Newfoundland, wireless station **13**, 14–15, 20–1
Cardeza, Mrs Charlotte Drake 86–7, **122**, 123
Cargo, *Titanic*'s 94, **122**, 140
Carlisle, Rt Hon Alexander M. 19, **54**, 55, 76, 114, 123
Caronia 10, 12
Carpathia 20–1, 24, 26–7, 29, 34, 36, 41–3, **44–5**, 46–7, **48**, 49–51, 95, 97, 105, 108, 118, 138, 190, 207
Carruthers, Francis 66, 78
Cedric 53, 108, 126
Celtic 53–4, 74, 113, 125–6
Champion 50
Cherbourg 59, 67, 73, 80, 84, **85**, 86–8, 205
Claims against White Star Line 119–23
Clarke, Judge J. Calvitt 161–3, **182**, 183–6, **198**
Coffey, John 89
Cotter, John 91
Cottam, Harold T. 20–1, 46–7
Cunard Steamship Company (Cunard Line) 50, 54, 78, 124, 126, 128

Dean, Elizabeth Gladys Millvina **167**, **169**, 199, **200**
Dean, Horace J. 21
Devaney, Margaret 29
Dining saloons C130–2
Drew, Marshall 27, 33–4, 74, 79
Duff-Gordon, Sir Cosmo and Lady Lucile 16, 26, 87, **116**, 117, **118**

Electricité de France 160, 172
Empress of Ireland 72, 95
Encyclopedia Titanica 203
Enterprises, *Titanic* 140–1
Evans, Cyril F. 14, 22, **38**, 39–40, 43–4, 159
Expeditions, *Titanic*
Grimm-Harris 141–3, 156–7, 161–2
Scripps Institute 141–2
Titanic Ventures/RMS Titanic Inc–*IFREMER* (1993 and 1994) 163
Titanic Ventures–Westgate–*IFREMER* (1987) 157
Woods Hole Oceanographic Institution 141–3, 146–8

Fleet, Frederick 14–16, 22, 25, 113
Francatelli, Miss Laura 26, 87, 205
Frankfurt 43–4
Franklin, Philip A. S. **107**, 109

Gatti, Luigi 71, 93–4
Gibson, James 40, **120**, 159–60
Gigantic (1894) 55
Gigantic [*Britannic*] (1914) 54–5, 68, 77, 126
Gill, Ernest **38**, 39–40
Goodwin, Sidney Leslie 78, 104, 202
Gracie, Col Archibald **17**, 80
Grimm, Jack F. 141–3, 156, 161–2
Groves, Charles V. **38**, 39
Guggenheim, Benjamin **28**, 87

Haisman, Edith Brown 161, **169**, 170, **171**, 180, **195**, 196
Halifax, Nova Scotia 20, 77, **100**, **102–4**, 202
Harland and Wolff Ltd 18, 53, 56, 59–61, 67, 76–7, 79, 86, 123, 165, 204
draughting room **55**
Harrison, W. Leslie 137–9, 160
Hart, Benjamin and Esther 11, 80, 95
Hart, Eva 80, 169–70, **171**, 203
Hart, Thomas/James 72–3
Hartley, Wallace 30–2, 93, **213–14**
Hawke, HMS 19, 60, 72, 77, 210
Hays, Charles M. 25, 50, 100
Hichens, Robert 16, 25, 113
Hippach, Mrs Ida 80
'Hoffman', Mr. *See* Navratil, Michel
Horoscope, *Titanic* 18
Hume, John Law 30, **105**

Iceberg 15–22
Fenwick photo of **43**
Scarrott sketch of **15**
Ilford 105
Institut Français de Recherche pour l'Exploitation de la Mer (IFREMER) 142, 148, 156–7, **158**, 160, 167, 178, 188
International Mercantile Marine 58, 106, 109, 126–7
Ismay, Joseph Bruce 9, 12, 25, 29, 53, **54**, 55, 59–60, 63, 73, 78, **107**, 108–9, **114**, 116–17, **121**, 125, **126**, 127–8

Jarry, Jean 142
Jason Junior ('*JJ*') 147–8, 153–4, 156
Jean Charcot 190, **191**, 192
Jessop, Violet 72
Jewell, Archie 14, **118**

Kennels, *Titanic*'s 23, 96
Knorr 143, **144**, 145

Lapland 109, **111**
La Provence 20
Larnder, Captain Frederick H. 98–101, 104
LaRoche, Louise 196
Latimer, Andrew 29, 94
Laurentic 54
Lewin, Lord 166, **167**, 168–9
Lifeboat drill, *Titanic* 78, 111
Lifeboats, 1894 regulations concerning 24–5, 114–116
Lifeboats, *Titanic*: number 1, 26; number 2, 25; number 3, 25; number 4, 22–4; number 5, 25; number 6, 25; number 7, 25, 31; number 8, 25–6; number 9, 26; number 10, 26, 29; number 11, 26–7; number 12, 26–9; number 13, 26–7, **28**, 34–5; number 14, 29, **42**; number 15, **28**; Englehardt collapsibles 24, 115; collapsible A, 43; collapsible B, 31, 43; collapsible C, 29, 42; collapsible D, 29, **42**, 43, 196; at New York, **48–9**
Lightoller, Second Officer Charles H. 13–14, 22–3, 25, 29, 39, 43, 45, 72, 81, **90**, 94
Limitation of liability hearings, New York 119–20, **121–2**, 123
Liverpool 59, 78, 113
Lord, Captain Stanley **38**, 39–40, 43–4, 111, 115–16, **119–20**, 128, **137**, 138–9, 159–61
Lord, Stanley Tutton 160
Lord, Walter 124, 137
Lowe, Fifth Officer Harold G. 25, 29, 42–3, 72, 77, 83
LP3 Conservation 172
Lusitania 54, 72, 114, 126

Mackay-Bennett **97–8**, 99, **100–1**, 104, 205
MacQuitty, William **169**, 180, 198
Majestic (1895) 76, 95
Marconi, Guglielmo **107**, 115
Marconi wireless 11, 20, 37, 46, 71, 96

Marex-Titanic Inc 161–3
Marine Accident Investigation Branch (MAIB) 159–61
Mariner Sea 188, **189**
Mauretania 7, 9, 54, 73, 89, 114, 126
Maxwell, John 13
McElroy, Hugh W. 29, 94
Megantic 54
Memorials 30, **51**, 109, **113**, 146–7, 167–70, **171**, 180, 200–3, **206**, 207–8
Merritt and Chapman Derrick and Wrecking Company 50, 140
Mersey, Lord **115–21**, 127–8, 137–8
Mesaba 13, 19
Michel, Jean-Louis 143–5
Mir-1 and *Mir-2* 177, 181
Montmagny 100, 104–5, 183, 186, 189–90, 204
Moody, Sixth Officer James P. 15–16, 72, 77
Morgan, John Pierpont 58–9, 73, 106–108, 126–7
Mount Temple 20, 44
Mulligan, Henry L. 103
Mummy, alleged curse of 95
Murdoch, First Officer William M. 12, 14–18, 25–6, 29, 72, 81, 94

Nadir 157, **158**, **162–3**
Nargeolet, Paul-Henri 178, 182, 188, 190, 197
National Maritime Museum, Greenwich 166, **167**, 168–9
National Oceanic and Atmospheric Administration (NOAA) 184, 186, **187**, 188, 190, 194
Nautile C133–4, 157, **158**, 178, 188
Navratil, Michel and children **29**, 80, 103, 180, **196**
'Nearer, My God, to Thee' (hymn) 31–2
New York, near-collision with 19, **81–2**, 83
Niemeyer, Judge Paul V. **194**
Night to Remember, A 124, 137, 197–8, 202
Nomadic 59, 67, **86**, 87, **205**
Northern Horizon **185**, 186

Ocean Intervention 183
Oceanic (1899) 68, 72, **82**, 83–4, 105
Office of Naval Research, US 141
Olympic 12, 16, 19, 54, **56**, 57–60, **61**, 67, 72, 74, 77, 86, 94, 114, **117**, **121**, 126, 128, 165, 205
Ottawa 105

Pålsson, Alma and family 78, **104**
Panula, Eino Viljami 104
Pennec, Dr Stéphane 172, 176
Phillips, John G. 11–14, 20–1, **33**, 40, 71, **216**
Pirrie, Lord William J. 53, **54**, 55–6, 58–9, 63, 76
Pitman, Third Officer Herbert J. 37, 72, 83
Plymouth, crew's return to 111–13
Pope, Louise Kink 170
Postal clerks 18, 30, 77, 96
Premonitions of disaster 73–4, 94–5
Priest, John 72

Queenstown 9–10, 15, 84, 87–9, 114, 208
Quick, Winnifred Vera **197**

Reading and writing room C130
Remora **192**, 193
Remote-operated vehicles (ROVs) 183–4, 189
RMS Titanic Inc 160–1, 163, 166–8, 178, 181–8, **189**, 190, 193–5. *See also* Titanic Ventures
Robertson, Morgan 73
Robin C134, 157
Rockets 23, 25, 36–7, 40–1, 43, 138–9, 159–60

Ronald H. Brown **187**, 188
Rostron, Captain Arthur H. 21, 26–7, 41, 44–6, 111, 115, 118
Rowe, George 25, 37
Ryan v Oceanic Steam Navigation Co 121

Salvage proposals 140–1, 146, 157, 161–3
Samson 138, 159
Sanderson, Harold 63, 66, 125–7
Sandström, Beatrice 170
Sarnoff, David 47
Schuman, Eleanor Johnson 180, **196**
Senate, US, Investigation into *Titanic* loss 106–11
Smith, Captain Edward J. 10, 12–13, 17, 20–2, 25, 37, 65, 72, 76–8, 83, 92, 145, **217**
Smith, Judge Rebecca Beach 185, **186**, 194
Smith, Senator William Alden **106**, 107–11
'Songe d'Automne' 10, 31–2
Southampton 15, 19, **46**, 60–1, 66–80, **81–2**, 83–9, 101, 105, 112–13, 195–200, **214**
Speed, *Titanic*'s 66, 117, 209
St John's, Newfoundland 105, 182, 189, 190, 193
Stead, William T. 73, 94–5
Stewart, George F. 39, 43
Stone, Herbert 39–40, 159–60
Straus, Isidor and Ida 25, **26**, **63**, 80, **216**
SV Explorer **183**
Swimming bath C129

Thaxter, Celia 73
Thayer, John and family 13, 22–3, 50, 123
Titanic (films) 8, 32, 200–2
Titanic: Ghosts of the Abyss (film documentary) 184
Titanic Maritime Memorial Act 146, 186
Titanic Preservation Trust 147
Titanic Ventures 157, 160–3. *See also* RMS Titanic Inc
Titanica (film documentary) 158
Titanic's Last Secrets (documentary) 190
Tower, Frank 'Lucky' 72
Traffic 59, 67, **86**, 87
Trials, *Titanic*'s 62–6
Tulloch, George H. 178, 182, 195, 197, **198**
Turkish bath 93, C129

United States District Court 120–1, 161, 182, 193

Vanderbilt, George W. 73
Victims, recovery and burial of 99–105

Weicker, Senator Lowell 157–8
West, Barbara Joan **199**
White Star Dock 66–8, 83
White Star Line 9, 53–5, 58–9, 63, 67, 78, 88, 95, 97, 100–1, 106, 120–2, 125, 165
Widener, George D. and family 13, 22–3, 50, 140
Wilde, Chief Officer Henry T. 22, 29, 72, 81
Wilding, Edward 63, 123, **178**, 178–9
Woods Hole Oceanographic Institution 141–3, 146–8
'Wreck of the Titanic, The' (exhibition) 168–70
Wreck, *Titanic* 140 *et seq.*
site diagram 155